GREETINGS:
To *all whom God has called
to be captives of his word.*

Captives of the Word

BY LOUIS COCHRAN

Flood Tides
Black Earth
Son of Haman
Boss Man
Row's End
Hallelujah, Mississippi
The Fool of God
Raccoon John Smith
FBI Man, a Personal History

BY BESS WHITE COCHRAN

Without Halos

Captives of the Word

LOUIS COCHRAN

AND

BESS WHITE COCHRAN

GARDEN CITY, NEW YORK

DOUBLEDAY & COMPANY, INC.

1969

Library of Congress Catalog Card Number 73-84365
Copyright © 1969 by Louis Cochran
ALL RIGHTS RESERVED
Printed in the United States of America
First Edition

Contents

Prologue   ix

BOOK ONE

    I. "In the Beginning"   3
    II. The Dawn of Seventeen Uneasy Years   15
    III. Following the Finger of God   27
    IV. "Come Out of Babylon"   35
    V. "Without Tarrying for Any"   49
    VI. "Good-bye to the Baptists"   61

BOOK TWO

    VII. "To Your Tents, O Israel"   75
    VIII. "Captives of the Word of God"   89
    IX. The Starting Flag Is Down!   105
    X. The City of Confusion   117
    XI. War of Words and Guns   129

BOOK THREE

    XII. The Long, Dark Tunnel   151
    XIII. "The Saints Their Watch Were Keeping"   161
    XIV. "Into All the World"   177
    XV. Approaching the Eye of the Hurricane   195
    XVI. The Great Divide   203
    XVII. Running Up the Flag   213
    XVIII. "He Drew a Circle"   221
    XIX. The Church with Three Faces Emerges   231
    XX. "Onward, Christian Soldiers"   243

viii   *Contents*

Afterword   251
Note to the Uninitiated   253
Basic Sources   255
Index   265

Prologue

This is the story of the stoutest Protestant Reformation since the time of Martin Luther, known to its followers as "The Restoration Movement," or "The Second Reformation." Without any preconceived notion that it would become a church at all this body became within the space of fifty years the largest and most influential brotherhood of Christian believers indigenous to Americal soil.

These "peculiar people," as their opponents at first styled them and as they often called themselves, or "Campbellites," a name they rejected, had in their lifeblood the tradition of the Free Church. They began by patterning their local congregations after the manner and form of the New Testament church, and preached the unity of all Christians through the abolition of human religious creeds and the restoration of the "Ancient Order of Things," as recorded in the Gospels and maintained by the primitive church.

This became their "Plea," and unceasingly, in season and out of season, these followers of the Restoration Movement held to it so tenaciously that their voices became as locusts in the land, and their numbers multiplied to such an extent that it seemed to some of them, by the mid-nineteenth century that the millennium itself was near at hand.

They abhorred the title "denomination" or "sect," and vigorously denied the application of either to themselves. They laid no claim to being the only Christians, but they insisted upon being Christians only. They practiced only two ordinances as scriptural—believers' baptism by immersion, and the Lord's Supper, and accepted as their only guide the Bible, and as their only Confession of Faith the affirmation of Simon Peter to

Jesus as recorded in Matthew 16:16, "Thou art the Christ, the Son of the Living God."

From the first tiny congregation of thirty members at Brush Run, in Brooke County, Virginia, formed after their rejection by the Presbyterians, the Movement spread like a forest fire with the opening of the American frontier, until by 1968 its membership in all its fragmented divisions numbered over six and a half million communicants.

There were many gifted men and women who devoted their lives to the Restoration Movement, and many more of humble origin and of equal evangelical fervor of whom the outside world never heard. But during its first half-century, its history is primarily the story of that indomitable Scotch-Irish American, Alexander Campbell, and his scholarly father, Thomas Campbell, late of Rich Hill, County Antrim, North Ireland, whose Scotch ancestors had emigrated from Scotland to Erin a hundred years before. Now, in 1807–1809, the Campbells had completed what must have seemed to them their flight from Egypt and, without the slightest notion of the chain of events they were setting in motion, Thomas and his son Alexander began and nurtured during its formative years, what became the Restoration Movement.

In order to understand the Restoration Movement, or the Second Reformation, and the early enthusiasms it aroused among the discontented, and the animosities it created among the orthodox, we must be acquainted with its background and genesis, and know something of the famous father-and-son team who supplied its teachings and its principal leadership. Without these two leaders it would have died aborning, and those great Christian communions, the Christian Church (Disciples of Christ), the Christian Churches (Independent), and the Churches of Christ, which began as one, however divergent they may now appear, would have been unknown.

The stories of Thomas and Alexander Campbell, and of their associates, contemporaries and successors, are all parts of the whole, and an integral part of the history of America in whose free soil the seeds of their Movement found the nourishment they needed to take root and come to fruition. In other lands other Restorationists of one sort or another had sought to reform the church by restoring its ancient features and using the Scriptures as their only guide. But their American counterparts were distinctive in that they alone emphasized that the ultimate purpose of such reforms was not the unity of God's people as an end in itself but "that the world might believe." And they alone, with their peculiar plea, and their dedication, and their passion for evangelizing among the liberty-loving pioneers in a frontier land, were destined to become a Great People.

And now, in the beginning—

Captives of the Word

BOOK ONE

"The trouble with them is . . ."

CHAPTER I

"In the Beginning"

Thomas Campbell, the father, and Alexander Campbell, the son, were born Argyle Scots by lineage in North Ireland in 1763 and 1788 respectively, a century after their ancestors had emigrated to North Ireland to escape the rigidities of the National Church of Scotland. Archibald Campbell, Thomas's father, fought the French under General James Wolfe on the Plains of Abraham outside Quebec in 1759, and helped claim the fortress for Great Britain. He was a Catholic at the time, but when he died at the ripe age of eighty-eight he was a staunch member of the Church of England.

His son Thomas joined the Old Light Anti-Burgher faction of the Associate, or Seceder, branch of the National Presbyterian Church of Scotland, and became pastor of that branch of the Presbyterian church at Ahorey, County Antrim. Here he married Jane Corneigle, the daughter of a French Huguenot family, and here Alexander, his first son, was born.

The Associate, or Seceder, Presbyterians had separated from the established National Church in 1733 in protest against the loss of the right of each parish to select its own minister, a right given instead to the "patrons" who owned the land. But the Seceders considered themselves Calvinists; indeed, they became more strict than the Church of Scotland. Later they divided into "Burghers," who believed that a Holy Oath could be administered by any magistrate, and "Anti-Burghers," who denied that right.

As Alexander grew to manhood he joined the Anti-Burghers, although not without some misgivings. He had been influenced by views held by an independent Congregational Church at Rich

Hill, and the preaching of John Glas and Robert Sandeman; and the celebrated independent English evangelists Robert and James Alexander Haldane, wealthy industrialists. John Locke's writings, to which he was first introduced when his father gave him Locke's "Essay on Toleration" for his seventeenth birthday, also contributed to the unease he felt in the strict Seceder church.

His father shared his unease. Thomas Campbell was a more gentle personality than his son, and his tolerant nature shunned controversy. But his convictions ran deep, and he did not refuse to defend them when principles were involved. The bickering between the branches of the Seceder church lay heavy on his heart, and in a mood of despair at ever effecting a reconciliation he turned his face toward the more tolerant atmosphere of America.

He was in his early forties when he sailed from Londonderry in April, 1807, on the vessel *Brutus*, leaving his family, consisting of his wife and six children, in the care of nineteen-year-old Alexander until he could locate in the new country and send for them.

Landing in Philadelphia on May 13, he found the Associate Seceder Synod of North America in session in that city. He presented his credentials and was promptly assigned to the Presbytery of Chartiers in southwestern Pennsylvania as an itinerant pastor. The Presbytery of Chartiers accepted him, but did not send him out to perform his duties alone. Possibly because it was recognized that the fresh recruit from Ireland was unfamiliar with the terrain, but possibly also because it was felt he might need observing, a young Calvinist, William Wilson, was assigned to accompany him as an assistant. The two traveled together all summer, and by October, when the Presbytery again convened, the Reverend Wilson filed charges against the newcomer, Thomas Campbell. The newcomer did, indeed, bear watching. He had committed the heresy of offering the Holy Communion to Presbyterians who were not Seceders, although they were members in good standing of the National Church of Scotland.

A formal trial by his peers followed, lasting several days, and Thomas Campbell was pronounced guilty. He was suspended from all clerical duties. It was a severe sentence, and Thomas Campbell appealed it the next year to the General Synod. This higher body lightened the sentence to a "rebuke and admonition" and also censured the Presbytery for irregular conduct of the case. It returned Mr. Campbell to his preaching duties in the Presbytery of Chartiers.

Smarting under its censure, the Presbytery retaliated by ignoring the culprit. He was given no preaching appointments. As a church rule forbade any preacher making his own appointments, Thomas Campbell was left with little to do. By September, 1808, he was ready to renounce the authority of both the Presbytery and the Synod, and he did so by severing his connection with the Associate, or Seceder, Presbyterians of the Church of Scotland. The Chartiers Presbytery countered by formally deposing him from "the Holy Ministry and from the Sealing Ordinances."

Many Presbyterian families in the community, already restive under the strict terms of the orthodox church, had been watching the scrimmage, cheering on the rebellious Mr. Campbell. When he was left stranded, their homes were thrown open to him for preaching services, and as groups could be assembled he began ministering among them. His preaching was revolutionary. He held that no church has a divine warrant for holding to any man-written confession of faith as essential; that at best such confessions were mere opinions of mortal men. He announced himself as ready to commune with other Christians, even Lutherans, as terms of communion were not to be found in the Philadelphia Confession of Faith. But it was his pronouncement that Christ died for all men, and that any man could believe on him and be saved, which provoked the strongest reaction.

Although the Westminster Confession of Faith, compiled in 1646 in an effort to conduce uniformity in the Church of England, had never been accepted by that body, its stern Calvinist doctrine had permeated the Presbyterian followers of John Knox in Scotland and as they immigrated to America they had brought it with them. Here many of its essential features, especially its emphasis on predestination, influenced the religious community in the new land. Even the Baptists, strongly opposing its espousal of a supervisory form of control over local churches, incorporated the Westminster Confession's doctrine of the "elect" into their own Confession of Faith drawn up at Philadelphia in 1742. Thus, Thomas Campbell's pronouncement that Christ died not only for the "elect" but for all men, and that any man could believe on him and be saved, was flagrant heresy, and marked his definite departure from the Presbyterian form of Calvinism, from which there was no return.

By August of the following year, 1809, his friends and sympathizers began wanting to "give more definiteness to the movement in which they had thus far been cooperating without any formal arrangement or definite agreement." Consequently, they assembled at the home of Abraham Altars on a farm between Mount Pleasant and the town of Washington, Pennsylvania, and formed a society (not a church), which they called the Christian Association of Washington. It was agreed that their proper rule or guideline should be, "Where the Scriptures speak, we speak; where the Scriptures are silent, we are silent."

To express more fully the motives and purposes of this Christian Association, Thomas Campbell drew up a document he called "The Declaration and Address," and on September 7, 1809, the Association, composed of about thirty men and women, approved the document and ordered it printed and distributed to all ministers in the area, and to other interested parties.

In the "Declaration and Address," Thomas Campbell discussed the "awful and distressing effects" of divisions among Christians. In an impassioned "Plea for Christian Union," he enumerated thirteen propositions which are today regarded by the entire brotherhood of his followers, regardless of their divisions, as the foundation stones of the Restoration Movement. They are:

1. The church of Christ is essentially, intentionally and constitutionally one.

2. Congregations, locally separate, ought to be in fellowship with one another.

3. Nothing ought to be an article of faith, or a rule, for the constitution and management of the church except what is expressly taught by Christ and His apostles.

4. The New Testament is as perfect a constitution for the worship, discipline and government of the New Testament church and as perfect a rule for the duties of its members, as the Old Testament was . . . for . . . the Old Testament church.

5. The Association will support only such ministers as conform to "the original standard."

6. The church can give no new commandments where the Scriptures are silent.

7. Creeds may be useful for instruction, but must not be used as tests of fitness for membership in the church.

8. Full knowledge of all revealed truth is not necessary to entitle persons to membership; neither should they for this purpose be required to make a profession more extensive than their knowledge. Realization of their need of salvation, faith in Christ as Savior, and obedience to Him, are all that is necessary.

9. All who are thus qualified should love each other as brothers, and be united as one.

10. Division among Christians is a horrid evil.

11. Divisions have been caused in some cases by neglect of the expressly revealed Will of God; in others, by assuming authority to make human opinions the test of fellowship, or to introduce human inventions into the faith and practice of the church.

12. All that is needed for the purity and perfection of the church is that it receive those, and only those, who profess faith in Christ, and obey Him according to the Scriptures; that it retain them only so long as their conduct is in accord with their professions; that ministers teach only what is expressly revealed, and that all Divine Ordinances be observed as the New Testament observed them.

13. When the church adopts "necessary expedients" they should be recognized for what they are, and should not be confused with divine commands, so that they will give no occasion for dissension or division.

Although his break with the established Presbyterian church was complete and final, Thomas Campbell did not reveal that fact to his family back in Ireland. Instead, as the Christian Association got under way and he felt himself taking root in the community of western Pennsylvania, he sent word to them to proceed on to America. He had been in the land now about fifteen months and had lodgings in the growing village of Washington, Pennsylvania, where his eye was on a house on Strawberry Lane which he proposed to purchase from an old friend from Ireland, Thomas Achison, as soon as he was certain the family was on the way. But soon news reached him that the family was not on the way.

On October 1, 1808, his wife and six children, with his son Alexander, now nineteen years old, in charge, had embarked according to his instructions. Their sailing vessel *Hibernia* sailed out of Londonderry harbor for Philadelphia, but after two days at sea the vessel ran aground on one of the islands of the Hebrides. For a time the Campbell family feared for their lives. But a kindly providence was on guard and rough but kindly sailors rowed them through the crashing waves to a safe shore, and Alexander even succeeded in salvaging his father's books from the hold of the stricken ship. The fearful incident also helped him in salvaging a dream that had possessed him since childhood. He reached the firm conclusion, on the stormy night the vessel tore at its moorings and threatened to crash against the rocks, that he would follow in the footsteps of his father and devote his life to teaching and to the proclamation of the Gospel of Jesus Christ.

As passage on another sailing vessel could not be secured so late in the season, the Campbell family found itself in Glasgow, Scotland, for the winter. Here Alexander enrolled in the University of Glasgow, then at the zenith of its fame, and the alma mater of his father. For the rest of his days, Alexander Campbell was to consider this year in Glasgow as one of the most blessed periods of his life.

Alexander Campbell had secured a letter of introduction to the great independent preacher Greville Ewing, who was in charge of the Seminary at the University of Glasgow, and through Mr. Ewing's friendly assistance lodgings were found for the family, and his own enrollment in the University assured. Here he again encountered the thinking of John Glas and his son-in-law, Robert Sandeman, and Robert and Alexander Haldane, and soon their vision of restoring primitive Christianity became his vision. Not only did he embrace the general concept of a needed restoration of the early church, but he embraced specific details in connection with its restoration. These included the independence of each local congregation; the weekly observance of the Lord's Supper; the denial of clerical privileges; the rights and duties of laymen to participate in the edification and discipline of the church; and a concept of faith which appealed to reason rather than to emotion.

The difficulty of reconciling this fresh concept of the church with the orthodox Presbyterian body soon became apparent, and, although separated from his father by thousands of miles, and without any knowledge of his action, it was not long before Alexander made the same decision as to his future course. The practice and teachings of the Presbyterian church were not in harmony with the original church, and were not what he felt destined to proclaim. But it was not until near the end of his year in Glasgow that he made a formal renunciation of his allegiance to that body.

The occasion was the celebration of Holy Communion. The Elders of the Seceder church strode among the tables, examining the faithful as to their worthiness to partake. They found Alexander worthy and presented him with the leaden "token" which signified he had been examined and duly qualified. But when the emblems were passed to him, Alexander only stared at them. How could any man dare to presume to judge the conscience of another man? Only the Lord could invite, and only the Lord could exclude men from His own table. He laid down the leaden token and left the service.

His echoing steps as he left the assembly were a repudiation of and a definite break with the Seceder branch of the National Church of Scotland, steps which he never retraced; and never regretted.

As the summons came from Thomas Campbell once more to attempt to join him in America, Alexander secured passage for the family on the vessel *Latonia,* and on August 12, 1809, the little group sailed from Londonderry. They reached New York on September 29. By stagecoach and wagon they proceeded to Philadelphia, and thence turned their faces west.

Thomas Campbell had purchased the house on Strawberry Lane and had it in readiness, but he could not restrain his impatience to see his family. When he learned they were en route from Philadelphia, he mounted his horse and rode toward them. The meeting took place on a lonely stretch of road in the hills of western Pennsylvania, a joyful reunion in body and mind. Thomas Campbell had brought with him the recently published "Declaration and Address," and as Alexander read it by candlelight in a wayside tavern that night, he realized that he and his father, although separated by a great ocean and a span of time, had been led as if by divine providence to reach the same stage in their theological and religious views. For the rest of his life, Alexander Campbell regarded this document as the clearest and most scriptural and irrefutable religious pronouncement of the age.

Settled in the two-story house on Strawberry Lane in Washington, the family merged into the community. Alexander started on a strenuous course of study, destined to prepare him in furthering the views as set forth by his father in the "Declaration and Address." He renewed his scrutiny of the Bible, convinced it was the only guideline needed by any church; he traced its sources in the original Greek; he studied Hebrew, Latin and church history.

His first sermon was preached in Templeton's Grove on July 15, 1810. In the next twelve months, he later estimated, he preached one hundred sermons, although as yet he had no license to preach. Indeed, he was a member of no church since he had left his Presbyterianism in Scotland and the Christian Association of Washington (County) was not a church.

This fact bothered his father. In the depths of Thomas Campbell's kindly soul there was a yearning for visible evidence of fellowship with other Christian people. Against the better judgment of Alexander, his father applied for the admission of himself and his small group to the National Presbyterian Synod of nearby Pittsburg. As the more realistic Alexander had foreseen, the application was rejected unanimously. The reasons were plainly stated. "By providing free admission to any errors in doctrine, and to any corruptions in discipline, whilst a nominal approbation of the Scripture as the only standard of truth may be professed, the Synod are constrained to disapprove the plan of union, and its native effects; and for other reasons."

The last phrase, "for other reasons," angered Alexander. What other reasons? What implication was intended? The rejection of the application had not surprised him, nor had the reasons for the action, but he had no intention of allowing the pious Synod to imply reasons it did not state. At his urging Thomas Campbell requested a full explanation of the "other reasons."

"It is not for any immorality in practice," the Clerk droned in reading the Synod's statement. "But, in addition to the reasons before assigned, for expressing his belief that there are some opinions taught in our Westminster Confession of Faith which are not founded on the Bible, and avoiding to designate them; for declaring that the administration of baptism to infants is not authorized by scriptural precept or example and is a matter of indifference, yet administering that ordinance while holding such an opinion; for encouraging, or countenancing, his son to preach the Gospel without any regular authority; for opposing creeds and confessions as injurious to the interest of religion; and also because it is not consistent with the regulations of the Presbyterian church that the Synod should form a connection with any ministers, churches, or Associations, that the Synod deems it improper to grant his request."

The Christian Association of Washington constituted itself a church on May 4, 1811. Alexander Campbell was licensed to preach, and Thomas Campbell was consecrated an Elder. The thirty members of the Washington Association desired only to worship God according to the dictates of their conscience, and could not have realized that they were, in effect, constituting themselves as the first church in the Campbell lineage of the Disciples of Christ. Four deacons were elected, John Dawson, George Sharp, William Gilchrist and James Foster. They observed the Lord's Supper the following Sunday, and thereafter on every Lord's Day. A simple frame building was erected on Brush Run, which wound its languid way through the tangled undergrowth near the state line dividing Pennsylvania and Virginia, and the first service was held in it on June 16, 1811. Alexander Campbell was ordained formally on the first day of the following year, 1812. The church was nameless, and for want of a better designation, the term "Reformers" was applied by the watching countryside.

The members of the new Brush Run Church took seriously the matter of their reliance on the Bible as their only guide. With one accord they began a close scrutiny of it. As a result, within a short time questions were asked concerning the practice of infant baptism. Thomas Campbell was not disturbed. "Infant baptism is not a command of Jesus Christ," he pointed out, "and hence not a condition of membership in the church, but a matter of forbearance." But what of the mode of baptism? Was the mere sprinkling of an adult sufficient? Did not the Bible specify immersion?

When three members of the church soon thereafter refused to partake of the Lord's Supper because they had not been immersed, Thomas Campbell, perhaps reluctantly, immersed them in Buffalo Creek as soon as winter released its frozen grip on the icy water. Alexander observed the incident, puzzled. "As I am sure it is unscriptural to make this matter [baptism by immersion] a term of communion . . . I wish to think and let think on the matter."

He was forced to think on the matter sooner than he had anticipated. He had married Margaret Brown, the only offspring of a well-to-do farmer, John Brown, and after the birth of their first child his wife, a staunch Presbyterian, insisted the child be sprinkled lest it die and go to hell as an unsaved soul. Alexander demurred; he was searching the Scripture for the authority to baptize the infant. His search had some long-range consequences. It led him to the conviction that the sprinkling of infants was not believers' baptism within the meaning of the New Testament, and the further conviction that neither he nor any member of his family, all of whom had been sprinkled, had been correctly baptized according to the teachings of Christ and the apostles.

Margaret soon adopted the reasoning of her husband, as did Thomas Campbell and his wife, and the four of them, with three other members of the Brush Run Church, were baptized on June 12, 1812, by immersion in Buffalo Creek by a Baptist preacher, Matthius Luce, upon their simple confession of faith in Jesus Christ. Most of the other members of the Brush Run Church soon followed their example, and those who did not withdrew.

With believers' baptism by immersion now the only method acceptable to the new Reformers' church—a requirement which, prior to that time, had been held only by the Baptists—it is not surprising that members of the Brush Run Church soon began sensing a kinship with their Baptist neighbors. Friendships among individuals ripened as the common bond became known; Baptist preachers who had avoided contact with the new body began dropping in at the worship services of the Brush Run Church, and were made to feel at home. Overtures were made by the Redstone Baptist Association, a body which embraced the Baptist churches in the immediate area, and on November 5, 1813, the Brush Run Church formally applied for admission to its ranks.

Although the application was accompanied by a guarded statement concerning the new church's position on other matters, including its rejection of human creeds, the Redstone Association accepted the application with enthusiasm. The Baptists had struggled single-handed long enough against the arguments of the Presbyterians and the Methodists on the matter of baptism, and recruits to its point of view were welcome.

A few Baptist preachers, however, had read the fine print in the application and were cautious in their endorsement of the new recruits. They thought they detected in Alexander Campbell an original thinker and theologian who could and probably would cause trouble in the ranks of the orthodox. They were better prophets than they knew.

The Dawn of
Seventeen Uneasy Years

It is not clear at what stage it became apparent that the Brush Run Church, the youngest member of the Redstone Baptist Association, was not conforming to the family ideas and customs. No one overt act can be pinpointed. The similar stand of the two bodies on immersion provided such a welcome bond that for a time everybody held his peace. But as the honeymoon waned points of disagreement appeared with increasing frequency, and soon friction began smoldering and then discord became open.

It was triggered by the discovery that the similar views on immersion held by the two bodies were not so similar after all. The rite became an issue when the Reformers let it be known that, as for them, baptism could be administered upon a simple confession of belief and faith in Jesus Christ. Since such a notion was an affront to the Baptist Calvinistic belief and practice, it was rejected by the Baptists. More, much more, they claimed, was required. A converting experience, for one thing, was essential on the part of the candidate, an experience so pronounced it could stand the test of scrutiny by a committee for its validity, and a subsequent confirming vote by the congregation. The Reformers admitted to the converting power of the Holy Spirit, but they refused to give an inch in their conviction that the rational powers of the human mind based on knowledge played an equal part.

The conflicting viewpoints brought to the fore differences in the concepts held by the two groups of the purpose and meaning of baptism. And the gulf widened. The Baptists, well entrenched in the community and solidly backed by tradition, were not about to alter their position, and the Reformers stood firm. The suspicions of both deepened. Other issues on which they did not see eye to eye were mentioned: the frequency with which the Lord's Supper should be observed; the distinctions between laity and clergy; the nature of faith itself.

In the providence of God such differences eventually may have been resolved, and the slow burn they fomented as the years passed extinguished, if a relatively minor incident had not occurred.

Thomas Campbell moved his residence in 1815 to Pittsburgh, where he conducted a school in his modest home. He also formed a group about him for worship and the study of the principles he and his son were advocating. Following the example of the Christian Association, he led the group, once it congealed as a body, into becoming an organized church. But the thought that it was a church without visible connection with the Christian world, nameless, isolated, dangling, its separate state a repudiation of his cherished dream of uniting all God's people, distressed him. The church of Christ upon earth was essentially, intentionally, constitutionally one, he had proclaimed in his "Declaration and Address." Yet his church was seemingly without the fold.

He watched the Brush Run Church nestling in the bosom of the Redstone Baptist Association. He knew its problems, and he sensed its friction, but he was confident nevertheless of the wisdom of its alliance with others in the larger framework. Why should his small church not likewise come within its encircling arms?

Ten years before, the gentle nature of Thomas Campbell, with his pleas for toleration, had become the target for the rebuffs of the Presbyterians, setting in motion the transformation of the mild Christian Association into a militant church. It was ironic that, now, an innocent gesture on his part should ignite the smoldering embers of wrath in the Redstone Baptist Association. With all the good intentions of his visionary soul, he made application for membership. And with all the fury of its suppressed anger at his son, the Redstone Association refused to accept him and his small church.

The reasons: His church did not conform to accepted Baptist practices and beliefs; he opposed creeds; he would not affirm adherence to the Philadelphia Confession of Faith. Such differences had been overlooked when the Brush Run Church had been received, but the Baptists had learned their lesson. Their dismay at the stubborn attitude of the Brush Run Church had not increased in any measure their regard for more of its ilk; they had had enough.

Alexander bristled at the rebuff. His reaction was not long in coming.

For some time the young preacher had been aware of another doctrine on which he differed with the Baptists. They disregarded the distinction between the Old Covenant of the Old Testament and the New Covenant of Christ. They quoted freely from each, giving to each equal authority. With open sarcasm Alexander had frequently asked if they were disciples of Moses, or of Jesus Christ. Why did they have to run to Moses to prove forms of worship, ordinances, disciplines and government? Christ was the authority, not Moses.

Alexander had prepared a sermon on the subject shortly after his closer connection with the Baptists had revealed to him this difference. He had delivered the sermon on an inconsequential occasion and few had paid it any attention. At the time Alexander was thankful. He had no desire to further widen the gulf between them. But the affront to his father aroused his anger, and circumstances played into his hand. When the Redstone Association was preparing to assemble for its annual meeting at Cross Creek in August, 1816, one of its speakers was forced to cancel his appointment. Casting about for a quick replacement, the committee selected Alexander. At once Alexander saw the occasion as of the Lord's leading. It was the opportunity he wanted.

He entitled the sermon "The Law," and as he stood to deliver it he realized with no regrets that he was challenging a basic Baptist tenet, one which held the teachings of the Old Testament as on a par with those of the New Testament. Without mincing words he presented his views of the teachings of Christ as supplanting and superseding the Hebraic laws of Moses.

"There is no need," he said plainly, "for preaching the law of Moses in order to prepare men to receive the Gospel of Jesus Christ. Christ is the end of the Law for righteousness, and to everyone that believeth. 'Go into all the world,' said Jesus, 'and preach the Gospel, not the Law. Teach the disciples to observe all things that I, not Moses, have commanded you!' In the Acts of the Apostles we see the Apostles and the first preachers proclaiming the Gospel with not one word advocating the ancient Jewish law. We have the substance of eight or ten sermons delivered by Paul and Peter, and not one of them proclaimed the Law to their hearers, whether Jew or Gentile, for their reception of the Gospel. Christ and not the Law was the Alpha and the Omega of their sermons. It follows then," he continued, his voice increasing in vibrancy, "that there is an essential difference between the Law and the Gospel, between the Old and the New Testament. No two words are more distinct in their significance than 'Law' and 'Gospel.' The Law is denominated the 'letter'; the Gospel is denominated the 'spirit.' In respect of existence, or duration, the former is denominated, 'That which is done away'; the latter, 'That which endureth.'"

Records indicate that the packed assembly began to stir; little eddies and whorls of sudden movement; loud, whispered comments. Several preachers arose and made their way to the rear, consulting with each other; a few voices called upon Alexander to stop this heresy. But Alexander Campbell did not stop. He had waited long enough to expose this error in Baptist doctrine, to explain to the world that the Brush Run Church of Reformers, while nominally a member of the Redstone Baptist Association, nevertheless preached only the Gospel of Jesus Christ, nothing more and nothing less. The spectacle of the preachers in huddled conference at the rear of the building doubtless reminded him of a scene enacted on the Palestinian shores long ago. It was the clergy, the priests, not the people, who had opposed new truth from the beginning.

"Christians live not under the Law of Moses but under Christ," he continued. "Since Christ and his teachings replace and supplant and include all the arguments and motives drawn from these ancient Jewish laws, and taught us even by our modern teachers of religion—such as that the disciples of Jesus should baptize their infants; pay tithes to their teachers; observe holy days or religious feasts as preparatory to the observance of the Lord's Supper; sanctify the seventh day; enter into national covenants; establish any form of religion by civil law—all such resorts which would excite the disciples of Jesus Christ into compliance with, or imitation of Jewish customs, are inconclusive and ineffectual, and repugnant to Christianity, being neither enjoined nor countenanced by the authority of our Lord, Jesus Christ."

As a result of this blatant and public affront to a cherished belief, convictions were freely voiced among Baptist preachers that an heretical group, led by an arch-heretic, had been taken into the fold. The only remedy was his expulsion.

Alexander Campbell had been in the Baptist body now for three years; he knew his fellow ministers in the Redstone Association well, and in a way he disliked them. To sever his connection with them would bring him little grief.

Years later, one of his contemporaries and his chief biographer, Robert Richardson, said of his attitude at this time:

"He found them [the Baptists in the Redstone Association] deficient in congregational and family discipline, and observing an order of things far from being either scriptural or beneficial. The practice of having but one Elder or preacher for four churches; monthly meetings; sitting in judgment on Christian experiences; speculative and textuary preaching, and the introduction of doctrinal questions even into Psalms and Hymns; the great neglect of the study of the Scriptures, and various similar aberrations from the teachings of the Bible, were noticed and lamented."

But at the time Alexander Campbell sought only to hold his detractors at bay, fending for time. He was not sure he wanted his fledging church to be cast adrift, a single, lonely group of Christians such as Thomas Campbell had in charge in Pittsburg. More than that, the idea had occurred to him with increasing frequency that he could better pursue the goal of eliminating the sectarian spirit in the Christian world by reforming the church from within one of its bodies, such as the Baptists, than outside any established order.

The storm about him was growing more threatening, however, and, until he could determine his course he felt he must placate his critics. When a Seceder Presbyterian minister at Mount Pleasant, Ohio, John Walker, challenged the Baptists in 1820 to debate on their position on immersion, Alexander accepted the challenge, genuinely glad of the opportunity to return to the good graces of the Baptists by defending the church's position on immersion as the only scriptural form of baptism. But he was determined in no way to compromise his other views.

The debate met with mixed reactions from his Baptist brethren. All of them considered it strengthened their stand on immersion, but many of them were outraged at the emphasis Campbell had given to the rite as being under the New Covenant; at the manner in which he had pointedly emphasized the strong distinction between the Jewish and the Christian dispensations.

Shortly after the debate an incident occurred which solved for Alexander Campbell his dilemma regarding his unhappy connection with the Redstone Association, and yet left him still not adrift from the Baptist fold.

The conservative mind then prevalent in the Redstone Association can be explained in part by the seclusion of its churches in the sheltered mountain area they occupied. There they were in a measure not only isolated physically, but also insulated against new ideas, snug in the truth they possessed. But in the more vigorous atmosphere to the west of them, in what was called the Western Reserve, occupying what is now northeastern Ohio, the frontier spirit was shaping men's minds to fresh points of view. There, new biblical interpretations were not only tolerated; they were welcomed and studied. A number of freethinking Baptist churches in Turnbull, Portage, Columbian and Mahoning counties in that region had recently broken away from the conservative Redstone Association and constituted themselves as the Mahoning Association. As news filtered through to them of the Walker debate, the outspoken Alexander Campbell aroused their curiosity.

Within a few weeks two of the preachers in the Mahoning Association, Adamson Bentley and his brother-in-law Sidney Rigdon, found opportunity to visit Mr. Campbell.

It was a warm summer afternoon when the two men dismounted from their horses at the Campbell turnstile in Buffaloe, and they sat the remainder of the daylight hours on the front porch of the Campbell house, talking with their host. They had intended riding on that night but instead, captivated by their discussion with Campbell, they lingered, rightly dividing the word of Truth until midnight. A few hours' sleep, and the discussion was resumed at dawn. When they departed that afternoon they were convinced that Mr. Campbell's views, while unorthodox, put the Bible in a new and much clearer perspective. They left with him an invitation to meet with the new Mahoning Association at its next assembly.

When Mr. Campbell reported the incident to the Redstone Association, and announced his intention of accepting the invitation to visit the new Mahoning Association, he learned that the preachers in the Redstone Association had no intention of allowing him to visit that, or any other Baptist association, as a representative member of their body. If he insisted on disregarding their attitude, action would be taken against him. At the next meeting of the Redstone Association, he was told, he and his Brush Run Church would be voted out.

The prospect of leaving the group did not exactly fill Alexander Campbell with pangs of regret, but he nevertheless had no wish for the discredit such a public exclusion would cast upon him. A bit of maneuvering occurred to him which gave evidence of the political sagacity with which he was endowed.

A number of members from his Brush Run Church had moved to the town of Charlestown, now Wellsburg, West Virginia, a few miles from his residence on Buffaloe Creek. They were in the process of organizing a church after the free-wheeling pattern of the Brush Run Church, and were debating the feasibility of seeking admission to the Redstone Association. Quietly, without mentioning his plan to any preacher in the Redstone Association, Campbell united with the new Charlestown Church and at once persuaded the church to affiliate with the more tolerant Mahoning Association. For a time few people were aware that he had thus removed himself from the bailiwick of the Redstone group.

Alexander Campbell was encouraged in this bit of strategy by a remarkable friend he had recently made on one of his trips to the growing town of Pittsburg, a man destined to play a significant role in the developing Campbell Movement.

The young friend bore the distinguished name of Walter Scott, a distant relative of the famous author and recently from Edinburgh, Scotland, where his talented father taught music. Of the family of ten children, Walter was the one most richly endowed with his father's musical ability and his mother's lively fancy, a fancy which led to his increasing hostility toward the strict Presbyterian doctrine of his parents, and which probably played a part in their consent for his departure for America after a period of study at Edinburgh University.

He was a youth of twenty-six years at the time, possessing a brilliant mind torn by conflict. His lyrical, poetic nature was given to speculative thought and imaginative dreaming, but a logical bent to his mind made him distrust all emotion. He lived for a year in New York City, his untamed spirit beating like a caged bird at its confining ways. One day he started walking west. He walked for four weeks, covering the distance from New York to Pittsburg, reveling in America's dense forests as he rambled along, bathing in its rushing streams, marveling at its mountains and blue summits.

At Pittsburg, Walter Scott found a kindred mind in the person of a lay preacher, George Forrester, who had broken with orthodox religious thinking. Mr. Forrester rebaptized him by immersion into a kingdom which knew no church boundaries. Finding lodging in the home of a well-to-do merchant, Nathaniel Richardson, Scott consented to teach the son of his Scotch Presbyterian host, a boy named Robert, and those of his friends, only on condition he would not have to teach the Presbyterian Confession of Faith. There Alexander Campbell, a friend of the Richardson family, met him.

Alexander Campbell was at the time conducting a similar school in his own home in Buffaloe. Most of his students were rapscallion young boys little given to studious pursuits, and he immediately sensed in Walter Scott the same frustration he himself felt with the task. As the friendship ripened he discovered that Scott held also the same dissatisfaction with the established churches. He also possessed a zeal, bordering on fanaticism, for preaching the pure, unadulterated Gospel.

Walter Scott and Alexander Campbell soon discovered they had drunk at the same theological fountains. As a student Scott had studied Latin and Greek at the University of Edinburgh, and was now reading the New Testament in the original Greek, comparing it word for word with the English translations. He also had read and absorbed the works of Sandeman, Haldane and Locke. Both were as one in agreeing with Locke in his assumption that the New Testament is the only court of appeal; and that Reason is its only arbiter. They saw alike that creeds, canons and governing councils are superfluous in religious matters; and they agreed heartily that the bond of union and the way of Salvation rest in Jesus Christ and in him only; that his life is the only creed a Christian needs.

Frequent meetings cemented a growing bond between the two men. Walter Scott poured out to Alexander his compulsion to preach, free of doctrinal entanglements; his yearning for a closeness with God; the mystic brooding that had haunted him since a child. Alexander listened, stirred by Scott's lyrical language, and by the musical cadences of his voice as it rose and fell. Here was a man Campbell could use. Here was a man of soulsearing eloquence, of profound sincerity, of rare power. For hours Scott entertained him with music from his flute, its exquisite, thin cries piercing in their poignancy. Scott confided in Alexander his love for a beautiful girl he had met in Pittsburg, Sarah Witsitt, and Alexander was not surprised when they married in January, 1823.

In turn Alexander Campbell shared with Walter Scott his dream of uniting the Christian world. He told of his disappointment in the Redstone Association, and of his strategy in avoiding exclusion from it. As he described for Scott the freedom from orthodox bondage existing in the newly formed Mahoning Association, both agreed it seemed a haven. Together they pored over the "Declaration and Address," absorbing the vision promulgated by Thomas Campbell. They studied together a pamphlet on baptism written by a man named Henry Errett in New York, and were confirmed in their conviction that immersion was the only scriptural form of the rite.

If the impractical aspects of Scott's idealism at times bothered the more realistic Campbell, he attributed it to Scott's inexperience and to his youth. Scott was almost ten years his junior. His enthusiasm for restoring the ancient church in such of its customs as the holy kiss and footwashing would dissolve, Campbell thought, as he grew in wisdom and realized such practices did not convey the sense of love or of humility in the world today that the Apostles once ascribed to them. In their place Campbell enlisted his interest in a plan he had in mind. He intended to make a frontal attack on creedal systems, and other departures from the simple plan of the early church, through the publication of a monthly journal. In it he would expose such things as the pretensions of the clergy; the unauthorized societies within churches which were doing the work of the church itself; the use of creeds as tests of fellowship. He planned to discontinue his school at Buffaloe and devote the major portion of his time to the journal, pursuing down to a crack in the floor the false notions of the orthodox bodies, especially the Baptists.

Walter Scott shared his enthusiasm for the venture. Together the two men drafted a statement of the paper's purpose. It would "espouse the cause of no religious sect; its sole object being the espousal of truth and the exposure of error in doctrine and in practice." An appropriate name for the paper seemed to Campbell to be the *Christian*. But some buried shrewd Scotch voice in Scott cautioned otherwise. Few men went by the simple name Christian; few would read it. Wider circulation and acceptance of the paper could be had by identifying it with a broader audience. Why not call it the *Christian Baptist?* The name would convey an identity with the Baptists while hinting at only qualified acceptance of their views.

His line of reasoning appealed to Alexander Campbell. The paper became the *Christian Baptist.*

The first issue of the *Christian Baptist* appeared in July, 1823, its name and its contents further inflaming the orthodox Baptists, and sealing any faint hope Alexander Campbell might have of remaining in their good graces. So he was not surprised when a month later, in August, 1823, as the Redstone messengers assembled at Cross Creek, they now presented a solid front of antagonism, a hard rock of determination to dissociate themselves from any connection with the heretic Campbell and his iconoclastic paper.

But Alexander was prepared for them. He seated himself on a rear bench in the small meetinghouse, his manner innocent of any wrongdoing. Not until his opponents began voicing their objections to his presence among them, putting in motion the wheels of procedure to exclude him, did he reveal the march he had stolen on them.

"Exclude me?" he said in effect. "How can you? I have left you. I have joined a new church in Charleston with thirty-three kindred souls, and we are embraced in the folds of the Mahoning Association."

"Never," he said later in telling of the incident, "did hunters on seeing the game unexpectedly escape from their toils at the moment when its capture was sure, glare upon each other a more mortifying disappointment than that indicated by my pursuers at that instant. . . . A solemn stillness ensued, and for a time all parties seemed to have nothing to do."

CHAPTER III

Following the Finger of God

Bolstered by the new relationship with the more friendly Mahoning Association, invigorated by contacts with the vibrant Walter Scott, and encouraged by the reception accorded the first issues of his paper, Alexander Campbell realized he was caught up inextricably in his mission. He was now thirty-five years old, his nearly six-foot frame sturdy, his demeanor stern but kindly. Thin lines were beginning to crisscross his high cheekbones, and his deeply set gray eyes held a brooding gaze, staring from over a strong nose which pointed slightly to the right, and from under a high forehead crowned by a shock of brown hair. He felt a new depth of maturity; he knew he was tapping the sources of strength which gave sustenance to his essential self.

He had sent the first issues of the paper to selected places and people over the country, and the response was gratifying. From Kentucky, where discontent with restrictive Baptist practices had infiltrated many Baptist churches, especially came words of rejoicing. He was putting into words what a host of preachers in that state were feeling. An invitation came to visit the area; the Baptists wanted to know more of his views. His position on baptism by immersion delighted them, and they suggested he debate with a Presbyterian preacher, W. L. McCalla, of Augusta, Kentucky, on the subject.

The debate took place in October in Washington, Kentucky, and spread the fame of Alexander Campbell both as a defender of the Baptist position on immersion and as an original and vigorous religious thinker. Scores of Baptist preachers in the Bluegrass State, who came out of curiosity to hear him, found his plea for a rejection of creeds and a return to the Bible as a

Christian's only guide, a heartening tonic, and they left more avowedly rebellious against the rigid Philadelphia Confession of Faith to which they were obliged to subscribe. He toured the state for a month, speaking everywhere to crowded houses. In erudite Lexington, calling itself the Athens of the West, he spoke for two hours on the first chapter of Hebrews, inspiring a young physician, Dr. Theodore Bell, to write of him years later: "I never heard anything that approached the power of that discourse, nor have I heard it equalled since. It lifted me into a world of thought of which I had previously known nothing."

A year later, in 1825, Alexander Campbell again visited Kentucky, and again drew great audiences. But as he was repeatedly acclaimed a great Baptist, he found himself embarrassed. He had been in the fold now for thirteen years, but his position was uneasy. "I have as much against you Baptists as I have against the Presbyterians," he protested time and again. Much of the doctrine he was frank to repudiate, making no secret of his views. But because he had found some release from its restrictions in the liberal climate of the Mahoning Association, there he determined for the time to stay, clinging to the hope he might eventually reform the whole body from within its organized framework.

"I do intend to continue in connection with this people so long as they permit me to say what I believe," he wrote in the *Christian Baptist*, endeavoring to make his position plain. "I have no idea of adding to the catalogue of sects. I labor to see sectarianism abolished, and all Christians of every name united upon the one foundation."

For a time Alexander Campbell was diverted from the dilemma of his position with the Baptists by two significant events.

In the summer following his second visit to Kentucky, his beloved wife Margaret died, the victim of consumption. Her going left a vacuum in his heart and in his life which was never filled. It also left him with five small motherless children. Less than a year later he remarried. His new wife was Selina Bakewell, a close friend of Margaret's and her nominee for the post.

Selina brought to the union the same devotion Margaret had

held for the handsome, brilliant Alexander. And she brought an even greater confidence that he was headed toward a wider destiny.

The wider destiny was not foreseen that summer day in 1828 when Alexander Campbell and Walter Scott rode together toward the little town of New Lisbon in the Western Reserve. The annual meeting of the Mahoning Association was in progress.

Walter Scott had hesitated about coming, and his hesitancy puzzled Campbell. They had attended a similar meeting of the group the year before, and Scott had preached for it, a magnificent display of oratorical brilliance such as few men possessed. It had evoked an enthusiastic response. But he was not a Baptist, he told Campbell, and had no intention of becoming one. He was determined to remain free of any of the existing churches.

Campbell had argued with him, emphasizing the value of a framework from which attacks on the orthodox bodies could be launched. How could Scott, a solitary voice, hope to make effective his assault to the entrenched churches?

Scott's reply evidently came as a complete surprise to his friend. He revealed a plan he had had in mind of publishing a paper of his own, just as Campbell was doing. He would call it the *Millennial Herald*; it would espouse his views and he would devote to it his pronounced literary talents and his flair for the dramatic. It was after this bit of news had filtered through Alexander Campbell's mind that he had insisted, and eventually persuaded Walter Scott to attend the Mahoning Association annual meeting.

As they rode along no records indicate that Alexander Campbell was disturbed at the prospect of having a rival paper to his own *Christian Baptist*. But if he was he had good reason.

Walter Scott's help in editing the *Christian Baptist* had proved inestimable. He was a facile writer with a penetrating insight into matters of the spirit, and a gift for expressing that insight vividly. Since he had moved his family, consisting now of his wife Sarah and three children, to Steubenville, Ohio, closer to Campbell's home in what was now designated by the United States Post Office Department as Bethany, his proximity had enabled Campbell to depend on him increasingly. The prospect of losing his services was not as alarming, however, as the prospect of having his brilliant abilities channeled into a rival publication, a prospect which may have suggested to Mr. Campbell a solution which could also mitigate another uneasy apprehension.

The additional apprehension had to do with the inroads being made in the area of the Western Reserve by a religious group whose views were remarkably similar to his own. If allowed to spread, they could supplant his own. The groups called themselves "Christians," or "New Lights," and some people called them "Stoneites" because they followed Barton Warren Stone of Kentucky.

Alexander Campbell had met Barton Stone briefly on his last visit to Kentucky. He was a former Presbyterian minister who had been expelled from the Synod of Kentucky for heretical views. While still a Presbyterian, preaching for the Cane Ridge and Concord churches in central Kentucky, Stone had attended the great Red River revival in Logan County. Deeply impressed, he had returned to his part of the state to instigate, in 1803, a similar revival. It attracted to Cane Ridge over ten thousand enthusiastic people, their zeal unrestrained in seeking salvation through wrestling bouts with the devil. Stone's participation in such religious fervor outraged his staid Presbyterian brethren, not only because of his seeming reluctance to condemn such bodily agitations as jerking, barking, dancing, jumping, as religious manifestations, but because he gave evidence that the revival had changed his way of looking at traditional Presbyterian doctrine.

And it was true. Barton Stone's association with preachers of every ilk during the revival had planted within him a new awareness of the tremendous power for righteousness that could be unleashed on the world if God's people would only pull together. At the conclusion of the Cane Ridge revival he resigned from the pulpits of his churches, convinced he could no longer conscientiously preach only Presbyterian doctrine.

The Synod of Kentucky suspended him, along with four other revivalist preachers—Richard McNemar, Robert Marshall, John Dunlavy and John Thompson—and the five dissenters formed their own independent branch, calling it the Springfield Presbytery.

But the Springfield Presbytery expired within a year. Its demise was accompanied by a document entitled "The Last Will and Testament of the Springfield Presbytery," which Mr. Campbell had read with sympathy and interest. In it, the Presbytery willed its own death in order "to sink into union with the Body of Christ at large," trusting that the spirit of life in Christ would rule all Christians instead of church dogma; that ministers would study not books of theology but the Holy Scriptures for instruction and for guidance. The Bible, the document stated, was the only sure guide to heaven, and was to have no competition. "It is better to enter life having only that one Book," the document stated in conclusion, "than having many, to be cast into hell."

After relinquishing all contact with the Presbyterian body, Barton Stone turned to farming for a livelihood. He had need for a reliable source of income, for his family was increasing, and eventually numbered nineteen children. But he continued to preach to independent groups of men and women seeking a more simple path to salvation than that offered by the established churches, and slowly, inevitably, the groups congealed into churches, nameless for the most part, devoid of any ties even with each other. And now they were appearing in northern Ohio.

The situation evoked mixed emotions in Alexander Campbell. He welcomed all efforts to break the encrusting mold which held the simple Gospel in its inhibiting grip, and he knew the groups of New Lights had that for their purpose. But their success in planting their doctrine also made clear to him the fact that the fields were ripe for his own similar doctrine. He had found an acceptance of his views in the Mahoning Association, but the Association was new and feeling its way. While thirsting for new waters as no other Baptist body he had encountered, it was lacking in a means of offering the new waters to others. In all the expanding territory, with throngs of new people entering the land each month, only thirty-eight converts to Campbell's doctrine had been made last year.

Yet religious unrest with the established churches was widespread in the Western Reserve. The insistence of the orthodox bodies on traditional forms of worship was not congenial to the new sense of liberty abroad in the land; people were yearning for a new freedom in expressing their faith. Whatever the merit of Barton Stone's views, Alexander Campbell was also spearheading a movement designed to give them that freedom. He, too, felt himself to be an instrument of God's will, and he needed to be about his Father's business. Who could imbue the Mahoning Association with a sense of urgency in spreading his doctrine? Who could proclaim his new plan for restoring the ancient church and uniting all God's children within its fold?

Walter Scott clearly had the makings of such an evangelist. He alone of all the preachers Alexander Campbell knew had the imagination, the fire, the zeal, the closeness to God, and the powers of persuasion and oratory which could penetrate the forests and fields in the new lands opening in the great Ohio country, and capture the hordes of its people who were seeking a new spiritual freedom.

No hint of this was conveyed by Alexander Campbell as the two men rode along. But when they reached New Lisbon and found the Mahoning Association annual meeting shrouded in apathy, its members discouraged, its program aimless, Alexander Campbell must have found occasion to mention to somebody the remedy he had in mind for the sad situation. At any rate, as the group assembled that evening, a delegate from the Braceville Church proposed that an evangelist be employed. Within minutes a committee was appointed to select a nominee, and the next morning it reported that Walter Scott be that evangelist.

The action was significant, and probably more far-reaching than even Mr. Campbell realized at the time. In employing a man to give his full time to evangelizing, it stamped his followers for the first time as constituting a pure New Testament body. This in itself indicated a clean break with the current practices of the orthodox churches. Their delegated bodies, including the Baptist associations, considered as their chief duties such things as the hearing of disciplinary cases, supervision of their preachers and general oversight of the churches. But the Mahoning Association refused to allocate to itself such functions; it recognized the autonomy of each church to solve its own problems and supervise its own work. It concentrated instead on dramatizing Alexander Campbell's basic doctrine that the primary task of any church body was to preach the Gospel. And it chose a man to carry out that task solely because he was aflame with the passion to do it, a man who was not a Baptist, not a resident of the area, not even an ordained minister of any church.

The freedom that characterized Walter Scott's selection extended to his task. He was bound with no creedal statement, with no specific doctrine, no articles of faith. He was given free rein to seek the salvation of men on their simple confession of faith in Jesus Christ. He could invade any part of the four counties covered by the Mahoning Association; he could plan his own schedule; engage his own helpers, go where the finger of God directed, unharnessed and free of any limiting, inhibiting control.

To the freedom-loving spirit of Walter Scott, the novelty, the power, the purpose and the glory of the opportunity sounded like the voice of God. It was the chorus of heavenly hosts; it was the song of angels. He was transported, and he accepted the appointment with joy.

CHAPTER IV

"Come Out of Babylon"

For three remarkable, unprecedented years Walter Scott strode across the Western Reserve, penetrating its forests, fording its streams, roaming its valleys and entering its settlements, his resonant, throbbing voice proclaiming the simple New Testament pathway to salvation.

The land he invaded was frontier territory with a background which made it receptive, and symbolically suitable for his work. The Western Reserve was a portion of the original generous grant to the Connecticut Colony which extended from ocean to ocean, about seventy-five miles in width. At the time the grant was made, around 1630, nobody knew what lands lay beyond the narrow stretch along the Atlantic coast, and the terms of their conveyance by the English Crown were of necessity vague. The indefinite western boundary ran "from the western ocean to the South Seas." Late in the eighteenth century Connecticut matched this gift of the Crown by deeding much of the fantastic holding back to the Congress of the new nation, reserving only the portion along the shore of Lake Erie. The section became known as the Western Reserve of Connecticut. After the danger of Indian attacks was lessened with the signing of the Treaty of Greenville by "Mad Anthony" Wayne in 1795, settlers were encouraged. The land was unsurveyed and undefined, but nevertheless parcels were sold for around 33 cents an acre, and Moses Cleaveland led a company of surveyors to map out townships of five miles square. The settlers ventured forth in the high hope of softening the raw edges of the frontier by transplanting to it something of the atmosphere and culture of New England. A youthful member of the first party, eighteen-year-old

John Holley, who kept a journal, reports a trading venture with the Six Nations Indians which showed the need of transplanting not only culture but a little Christianity.

In reluctantly accepting the terms of the white man, the leader of the tribe, Red Jacket, is reported by Holley to have said:

"You white people make a great parade about religion; you say you have a book of laws and rules which was given by the Great Spirit, but is this true? Was it written by his own hand and given to you? No, says he, it was written by your own people. They do it to deceive you. Their whole wishes center here (pointing to his pocket), all they want is money. He says white people tell them, they wish to come and live among them as brothers, and learn them agriculture. So they bring on implements and presents, and tells them good stories, and all appears honest. But when they are gone all appears as a dream. Our land is taken from us, and still we don't know how to farm."

For most of his sojourn in the region, Walter Scott confined his efforts to the four counties comprising the Mahoning Association in the eastern section of the Reserve, only occasionally extending his trips into the swampy, flat Firelands to the west, a region settled by a group from Connecticut known as the "Sufferers" because of their excessive losses during the Revolutionary War. Other Easterners, driven by the relentless cold of the year 1816, had harkened to the rumor that Ohio was a land of perpetual sunshine and easy living, and had settled in the Mahoning Association counties to the east, a steady tide of migrating Connecticut people to whom the land belonged. They came by every conceivable type of conveyance, bringing only the family household necessities. But invariably that included a Bible and Watts's *Psalms and Hymns*.

The first missionary to reach the territory was sent by the Connecticut Missionary Society in cooperation with the Congregational and Presbyterian boards. He was Joseph Badger, a fearless, dedicated man who had served as chaplain at Fort Meigs before settling near the village of Austinburg twenty years before Walter Scott arrived on the scene. There Mr. Badger committed his wife and six children to the care of the Heavenly Father, and began itinerating among the settlements. He found the situation deplorable. "They seem to glory in their infidelity," he wrote to his sponsors. "They bid fair to grow into a hardened, corrupt society."

His influence for decency and order, however, was soon felt, and he planted a hunger in the hearts of the settlers for a better life and saw to it that they dusted off their Bibles and dug their Watts's *Psalms and Hymns* from beneath the debris in their hastily constructed barns and put them to use. But in Mr. Badger's train had come a host of preachers of every known variety of moral and intellectual stature. A man named Dr. Zerah Hawley who practiced medicine in the Reserve, recorded at this time his impressions of the representatives of the zeal-filled early Methodists. "Methodist preachers," he wrote, "are uninformed and fanatical. . . . The sermons are without plan or system, beginning in ignorance and ending in nonsense, interlarded with something nearly approaching blasphemy in many cases."

When Walter Scott entered the territory, its harsh frontier lines were beginning to adjust to New England ways. Roads were appearing through the tangled wilderness, and crops were finding their way to market by the wonderous route of the Ohio-Erie Canal, a daring venture undertaken in 1826 and put into operation in 1828. Only a few of the villages, however, that Scott entered bore a resemblance to the New England communities their settlers had tried to transplant. Tallmadge was such a community, dominated by relatively educated men, and the Congregational Church they erected resembled the white-spired Colonial edifices which characterized the New England greens. But other settlements had been invaded by the Irish who had come to build the canal, and were bustling, rowdy communities, brash and argumentative. The New Englanders among whom the Irish settled were not only outnumbered but dispirited by the disillusioning experience of their trek west, and seemed resigned to allow the rowdy influence to prevail.

This raucous element paid the preachers little mind, except to ridicule them, but as schools were still scarce and "book learning" held in high esteem, the "common people heard them gladly." They accepted them as spokesmen for God and their sermons as revelations of his will. Meeting day became a happy break in their workaday routine, and hundreds of spiritually hungry people sat for hours on backless benches, shuddering in vicarious agony as any preacher who came their way pictured deathbed scenes and wrestling matches with the devil. But they failed to comprehend the high language and vague terms which many of the preachers felt called to give utterance, and some of them did not like the idea that God's wrath had doomed them, free men in a free world, to a destiny determined before the foundations of the world were laid.

In the light of such a situation it is not surprising that conditions were ripe for Walter Scott's offer of a Gospel which any man could understand, and of a salvation which any man could obtain merely by accepting it. To the people his sermons were fresh waters flowing over arid, parched land, relieving their thirst for comfort and consolation. They were hardy frontiersmen who had conquered the land, and they were tired of hearing they were helpless in conquering the devil. They were impatient with preachers who told them they were lost in a world of sin until, through the grace of God and at his pleasure, they might be rescued. They were free people, eager to stretch the wings of their freedom in the realm of the spirit as well as of the flesh, free moral agents entitled to make a choice regarding their salvation. They had listened long enough to preaching which denied them this freedom, preaching which damned them to hell unless they were of the Elect. And here was a man, a vivid, flaming evangelist named Walter Scott, who brought them a Gospel totally at variance with the Calvinistic, the Lutheran and the Augustinian doctrines which had entrenched themselves in the area. It was essentially a rational doctrine, appealing to the intellect, but as it filtered through Scott's peculiarly buoyant personality it became emotionally charged, and as intoxicating as heady wine. He became God's avenging angel. As he brought the welcome news that salvation comes not by way of an "experience" for which they must be resigned to wait, but by the simple process of hearing the word of God and believing it, Walter Scott gave his temperamental nature full play. Here in his extended hand was the Bible; it furnished all they needed to bring them a joyous life, here and now and for eternity. They could read it for themselves, and interpret its passages according to the measure of their knowledge and understanding.

This was news; welcome news to those despairing of finding a "sanctifying experience"; shocking news to the self-appointed preachers whose "call to preach" had specified it be the Calvinistic doctrine.

Shortly after Walter Scott accepted his work with the Mahoning Association he moved Sarah and their three children—John, aged five, Emily, three, and William, two—to Canfield, a beautiful Ohio village where Lombardy poplars lined the winding streets, shading sturdy frontier cabins and a few brick structures. He secured a four-room clapboard house on the outskirts of the village, and there another daughter, Sarah Jane, named for her mother, was born in December, 1828. She was an especially winsome baby, and became the object of an unusual devotion on the part of her erratic father, the symbol of his joy in his new work. A weedy garden and a belligerent cow provided the family with sustenance. There is no record that Walter Scott received a regular salary, and voluntary gifts from the churches he visited were uncertain.

But Walter Scott was of the temperament which made him oblivious to money; personal finances were nonexistent; the Lord would provide. When money found its way into his pocket, he looked at it incredulously. He gave to any in need he happened to encounter, and only when a good friend he made on the Reserve, Daniel Hayden, took it upon himself to salvage the contributions from the churches, and turn them over to Sarah, was the family ever solvent.

For three years in the Western Reserve, Walter Scott lived in the ethereal heights of the mountaintops, and he took thousands of people with him. His detractors stayed below—way below. In the first year of his preaching the churches in the Mahoning Association doubled in membership; the second year their numbers increased by over five hundred; in the third year more than one thousand new members were added. He preached wherever and whenever he could gather people about him—in open fields, in barns, in town squares, in meetinghouses, assuring every man of his right to be called a Christian.

An observer of the period, William Hayden, writes of one such meeting: "He straightened himself to his full height, his great chocolate eyes glistening, his whole face full of animation and earnestness. He brought his siege guns into position, and for an hour and a half the house rang with his eloquence. No man could do justice to that sermon. He was powerful, lofty and sublime. Until the next Thursday an incessant fire was kept up day and night. The Ancient Gospel was poured into their ears. They were astonished, amazed. They dusted off their Bibles and went searching for the truth. It was the simple Gospel of Christ in its facts and commands and promises."

Baptisms were dramatic occasions. Often Scott led a whole church at night to the banks of the Mahoning River, the members singing in the midnight air as they went. The enthusiasm engendered by such happenings spread like a fire on a prairie, kindling conflagrations in neighboring communities as it raced.

His message rang with the conviction that he had discovered the one clear plan of salvation. It would correct and reconcile all divergent practices of Christendom, destroying forever the mystery of conversion which was no mystery at all. The plan followed an orderly, logical, natural sequence of five simple steps he had worked out: faith, repentance, baptism, remission of sins and the gift of the Holy Spirit.

Walter Scott counted these steps to salvation on his fingers in rotation before entranced audiences. He invaded schoolhouses and playfields, fascinating the children with his snapping fingers. At home the children repeated the chant to their parents; and the parents occupied another bench at preaching that night to hear an elaboration of the theme. It embodied the belief that Faith is to destroy the love of sin, Repentance to destroy the practice of it, Baptism the power of it, Remission the guilt of it, and the Gift of the Holy Spirit to destroy the punishment of it. So the last enemy, Death, can and will be destroyed by those who accept and believe.

It should be noted that Walter Scott's foray into the Western Reserve occurred not only in a wilderness territory, unorganized and feeling its way, but at a moment in history when conditions fostered bitter competition among religious bodies. Aware that the surging tide of political liberty brought with it the tendency to break with all old restraints, the guardians of orthodoxy were on the alert. Strictures all the more rigid because of the circumstances were imposed. No crack in established dogma could be tolerated; no leaks allowed to become full streams. Suspicious of every innovation, the sects fought for every jot and tittle of their creeds. When new interpretations of the Scriptures threatened, the bells of alarm sounded. With one accord preachers of every ilk diverted their efforts from fighting the devil to resisting the inroads of any heretics.

It is no wonder the avowed purpose of what was now recognized as a new "Movement" led by Walter Scott, soon became suspect. His innocent-sounding plea for all Christians to unite on his simple plan of salvation, had within it the seeds of heresy. He was out to expose the errors of the denominations, to eliminate their creeds, to make an onslaught on every established church. A skeptical observer of the period writes:

"A shrewd follower of Campbell comes to a certain village where these errors are unknown. He at first calls himself a Baptist, and no one suspects the contrary. He professes great liberality of sentiment toward other denominations, preaches to please all, and appears full of zest. After a while he announces that on such a day he will preach a sermon on Christian Union. At the appointed time he portrays in glaring colors the evils of sectarianism, and traces it all to creeds and confessions. He then proposes a plan in which all can unite."

Walter Scott did nothing to allay the fears of such skeptics. Instead, in his first report to the Mahoning Association, he confirmed their apprehensions. He sounded a clear tocsin to rid the world of the existence of all other churches. "The Ancient Gospel and ancient order of the church must prevail," he shouted for all to hear, "to the certain abolition of all these contumacious sects which now so woefully afflict mankind!"

The orthodox churches, especially the Baptists, picked up their ears. The man and his followers were abiding in the Baptist household, nestling in the respectable Mahoning Association, where the tenets of the Baptist faith were exposed to them, and therefore were especially vulnerable to their attacks. Soon apprehension spread among the Baptists; were they marked as the first of the sects to be destroyed?

Many thoughtful Baptist preachers had enlisted at Scott's side as converts from strict Calvinism. But they still cherished affection for their former household of faith. Now they attempted to pacify the orthodox who were alarmed at Scott's inflammatory pronouncements by explaining that the purpose of the Campbell Movement was not the demolition of their church, nor of any existing church, except as it would occur as a consequence of establishing One Great Church. These men were to lay a solid, valid foundation upon which strong churches of the Movement would later be built. But less able men who had entered the fray confused their task of restoring the One Great Church with the more immediate and joyful job of destroying the present ones. Their battle cry became, Come out of Babylon! Their mandate for action became, not the Bible but Alexander Campbell's bristling paper the *Christian Baptist*. This they read and quoted and flaunted in the faces of the Baptists. Its rabid denunciation of creeds and confessions of faith and of the pompous trappings of the clergy became their marching orders. Reverberating across the expanding territory, their cries were heard beyond the confines of the Western Reserve. Into Illinois, down into Indiana, into southern Ohio, the Movement raced, gaining momentum as it spread.

And out of Babylon the people came.

In southern Indiana the call "Come out of Babylon" penetrated the log meetinghouse of the Blue River Baptist Church. Two lanky brothers, John and Peter Wright, heard it. They had planted the church near the village of Edinburgh fifteen years before, aligning it, not without some misgivings, with the Baptist faith. The influence of their father Amos was still strong upon them. Amos had been a Quaker back in North Carolina, content with its simplicities. But in migrating to Virginia, then on to Kentucky, and then across the great flowing Ohio River into southern Indiana, he had joined with others in the party and worshiped as a Baptist. But always he had wondered—the creed, the emphasis on the wrath of God bothered him.

Five sons had come to bless his home, and to help in turn with the farming: Peter, Levi, Joshua, Amos and John. Peter was the sturdy one, forthright, determined, a spiritual descendant of Peter the Apostle. And John was made in the likeness of the gentle Apostle John. About him was a strange reverence. The boy, Amos always said, would make a good preacher. But a Baptist preacher?

In time, Peter and John, separated by fifteen years in age and dissimilar in temperament yet strangely drawn together, established their own neighboring homes in the village of Edinburgh, engaging in business together, preaching on Sundays, finally "gathering" and preaching for what they called the Blue River Baptist Church.

When a group of migrating Kentuckians settled nearby and formed a church they called simply "Christian," Peter and John learned the group had emerged from a Presbyterian background and had brought with them from Kentucky a new liberty of interpretation of the Bible as propounded by Barton Stone. Their courage in making the break from the Presbyterians intrigued Peter and John Wright, already chafing under Baptist restrictions, especially the necessity to conform to the Philadelphia Confession of Faith. Why was any other book but the Bible necessary to a full understanding of God? What else did a man need to find God?

For a time they hesitated, attending prayer meetings and worship services of their new friends, the Christians. Would any Baptist dare emulate them? It would take daring, for the Baptists, alert to the heresy abroad in the land, were giving rigid oversight to such small churches as their Blue River group. But when itinerating preachers from the Mahoning Baptist Association up in the Western Reserve came into the neighborhood shouting, "Come out of Babylon," they listened. Gladly Peter and John Wright came out. They not only discarded their Baptist name, turning their church into the Church of Christ at Blue River, but constituted a formal union with the Christians in the community as led by Barton Stone.

They did not know it at the time, but the union the Wright brothers effected was only one of many such small voluntary mergers of groups of Christians and groups of Alexander Campbell's followers, widely known now as Reformed Baptists, taking place in all parts of Ohio, Indiana, Illinois and Kentucky. Neither group joined the other; they simply came together, uniting to form a new and distinctly different body. Only a few men were concerned that the new body had no connections, no name, no organized framework. It was a fellowship of kindred minds and hearts bound in Christian love by common faith in Jesus Christ and most of the people thought that was all they needed.

The year was 1829. Walter Scott was still roaming the Western Reserve, creating a high pitch of excitement, converting Baptists, Methodists, Presbyterians and plain sinners; riding herd on his refugees from Babylon. Thousands had "come out." Where they were now to go, how they were to be nurtured and instructed in the new doctrine, what structure their churches would assume, what degree of prudence, if any, was to be taken in cultivating the sprouting, rapid, shallow-rooted groups of Reformed Baptists that sprang up in the wake of his visits, were matters that may have occasionally crossed Scott's mind, but the hard, earthy thinking required to deal with such things was not to his liking.

At the close of the second year of Walter Scott's march through the territory, more than one thousand Reformed Baptists assembled in triumph for the annual meeting of the Mahoning Association at Warren, Ohio. They were a people possessing one spirit and rejoicing in one hope. And that was still all they seemed to need. The glorious, happy, contented meeting at Warren echoed across the land.

But by the end of the next year, the third year of Scott's charge, it was becoming apparent that after all perhaps something more was needed.

Hundreds of Reformed Baptists, for want of an organized body of their own, were still holding nominal membership in their original churches, most of them some branch of the Baptist faith. Were they still Baptists? They were uneasy about it. Some left and assembled themselves as separate groups, but the alignments they formed were nebulous. Conflicting interpretations arose of the doctrine held by Alexander Campbell and his persuasive evangelist Walter Scott. In attempting to clarify their beliefs when arguments arose with their orthodox friends, they found their footing insecure. But their faith in their new freedom held firm, and their persistence in seeking to further it continued.

"Mark my words, you boys! It won't be long until you will kick over the traces of the Baptist church as well, and then where will you be? All alone with that blind guide, Alexander Campbell! You'll have no church, nothing to hold you steady, nothing but a floundering group of bewildered, wild-eyed religious zealots, wondering what to do. Mark my word, you are headed for trouble!"

The stern-faced Presbyterian Elder must have stared at his two sons as he spoke his warning. Young Absolem Littell, not yet twenty years old, stared back. He had just announced that he and his brother John were renouncing the Presbyterian faith to join a new church at nearby Silver Creek in southern Indiana, a group nervously feeling its way into views held by some unorthodox Baptists. They had been reading the *Christian Baptist*, published by Alexander Campbell in Virginia. John probably extended a copy of it now, hoping his father would read it and relent in his judgment.

But the Presbyterian blood ran strong in the older man, and he brushed the wretched paper aside. "You're headed for trouble, mark my word!"

Headed for trouble or not, John and Absolem Littell not only joined the Silver Creek Baptist Church but started preaching for it the doctrine promulgated by the *Christian Baptist*. And eventually, as was happening at the same time in scores of other communities, they led the church to erase as superfluous the Philadelphia Confession of Faith to which it had tentatively subscribed, and to accept the Bible alone as its only infallible rule of faith and obedience, separating the little congregation irrevocably from the Baptists.

Without doubt Walter Scott still shared Alexander Cambell's hope of effecting a reformation of the existing orthodox Baptist body from within its sheltering wing. But his exuberant nature could not resist responding to the joyful mood of the moment. He was tasting the sweetness of success and he found it good. He was on the road toward the dream of his life, that of ridding the world of the evils of sectarianism. If the Baptist church was demolished in the process, that was a price that must be paid. When he invaded the town of Salem, Ohio, during the third year of his onslaught, he could not restrain his exuberance.

The Baptist church in Salem had fallen upon dull times. Although the village had been settled by the gentle Quakers, a raucous element in the town was now in charge. Indifference to religion had penetrated the ranks of the faithful. Thus it was that when Walter Scott, a man known now over all of the area as a flaming evangelist, announced he would visit the town, revive religion and restore prosperity to Zion, many devout men and women, including the Baptists, were ready to welcome him. If they had heard rumors that he was as intent on routing the Baptists as he was the devil, they gave no sign of apprehension. They knew only that his persuasive powers would lure back the wandering ones and kindle new sparks of life in their languishing congregation.

Their hopes were realized. Crowds of eager men and women thronged the Baptist meetinghouse, listening enraptured to the persuasive eloquence of Walter Scott at his best, proclaiming the Gospel of redemptive love. That he was also proclaiming a new pathway to that Gospel was lost upon them. Night after night he preached to overflowing crowds, leading them step by un-suspecting step from their Calvinistic doctrine into an acceptance of the simple plan of salvation as found in the Bible.

It had happened before in scores of places. Baptist churches had been won to his point of view before they knew what was happening, some of the members dimly suspecting, others not caring, all rejoicing in the newfound freedom to seek and find salvation unhampered by the requirements set forth in the Phil-adelphia Confession of Faith. This humanly devised standard of doctrine had grown out of a Confession of Faith issued by English Baptists in 1677. Although Baptists generally rejected all binding articles of faith, their adherence to the doctrine of the "elect" was so strong the Federation of American Baptists felt the need to reiterate it in a similar Confession of Faith drawn up in Philadelphia in 1792. Many Baptists felt free to accept it or reject it as they saw fit, but not so the Calvinists among them. They considered it as binding, and their numbers abounded in the Western Reserve. Thus in most instances a few hardy souls resisted his appeal and remained loyal to the Baptist doctrine, resigning themselves to rebuilding their shattered churches with what grace they could muster. But in this instance an indiscreet remark of Walter Scott's, as he left the town of Salem the final day of his revival, startled the remnant of remaining loyal Calvinists in the town's Baptist church, and stirred them to action.

"Who will now say there is a Baptist church in Salem?" Scott is reported to have said, riding away in triumph.

The words had an electrifying effect. The truth was out at last. The intention of the Reformers was clear. They were bent on the destruction of the Baptist church.

From that time on, lines were drawn, no quarter given. Opposition to the Reformers was in the open. Any wavering Baptist who was discovered lending a receptive ear to their preaching was refused fellowship with the orthodox. Any one of them observed partaking of the Holy Communion with the heretics was listed as not in good standing, and any Baptist church not making open warfare on them was placed under suspicious scrutiny. Every Baptist member had to take his stand and be counted.

One by one the count was taken. The staid orthodox body was confident the old beliefs would hold steady. But they had not taken into account the seeds of liberty that had taken root in the frontier country. Nor were they aware of the power of the deep and profound germs of truth in the new doctrine promulgated by Alexander Campbell. This truth had often seemed to be crushed to earth by its unlettered, often confused, sometimes irrational advocates, but it was there, and the people had heard it, and responded to it, and now they clung to it. Increasingly, alarmingly, Baptist churches in one community after another lined up with the Reformers.

The process was simple and undramatic. An entry which appears in the church record at Canfield, Ohio, where Scott made his home, is typical of those which appeared during the turbulent period in scores of other Baptist records, and not a few in Methodist and Presbyterian accounts: "The Baptist Church, constituted in 1822, so continued until 1829. During this time the brethren in attending to the word of God in search of truth, began to doubt the propriety of having creeds of Articles of Faith as bonds of Christian fellowship. The result was throwing them away as useless, believing the Scriptures sufficient to make us wise unto Salvation. We adopt them as our rule of faith and practice."

CHAPTER V

"Without Tarrying for Any"

Back in Buffaloe, Virginia, Alexander Campbell felt a sense of unease. He had meant it when he said he had no desire to add to the catalogue of sects. Yet, as a spiritual descendant of the early reformers in the sixteenth and seventeenth centuries, had he unconsciously no desire to remain within an established church? Whether he wondered if he also was possessed of the compulsion to act "without tarrying for any," as they had done, he was finding himself in that position.

Daily his forces were leading more and more people out of Babylon, and for that he rejoiced. But if a formal break came with the Baptists, he would be forced to give some thought to the future of his followers. Could they remain a fluid movement in the community of religious groups? If not, how could he structure a new church so it would not add to the catalogue of sects?

He scanned the latest potshot to come from the Baptist stronghold. It was the most virulent of many he had seen. It originated in Pennsylvania among a group of Baptist churches comprising the Beaver Association, long known as a stronghold of Baptist tradition. A handful of more liberal-minded preachers had left the body to join the Mahoning Association when it was formed, and, as if still feeling the sting of their departure, the Beaver Association labeled its pronouncement "An Anathema," glad to denounce the Mahoning group for taking into its bosom the heretic Alexander Campbell. In it the angered Baptists said:

"They [the Mahoning group of churches] now disbelieve and deny many of the doctrines of Holy Scripture on which they were constituted. They contend there is no promise of salvation without baptism; that it should be administered to all that say they believe, without examinaion on any other point; that there is no direct operation of the Holy Spirit on the mind prior to baptism; that baptism procures the remission of sins and the gift of the Holy Ghost; that the Scriptures are the only evidence of interest in Christ; that obedience places it in God's power to elect to salvation; that no creed is necessary for the church but the Scriptures as they stand; and that all baptized persons have a right to administer the ordinance. All of which sentiments have been publicly taught by the messengers of that Association. . . . We feel constrained to warn our brethren in other parts against them."

In addition to such attacks from the Baptists, rumors of Walter Scott's increasingly erratic behavior added to Mr. Campbell's unease. The furor the evangelist was arousing in the Western Reserve was growing. Some people considered him obsessed, even mad. He would follow no agreed plan of itinerating; he would make no financial accounting worthy of the name; he was the dismay of those who attempted to work with him. The denominational leaders in the area were loud in their criticism of him. A Methodist preacher, whose church Scott had invaded, claimed that several Methodists Scott had immersed had been strangled, and that a few had actually been drowned during the rite. Not only rowdy sinners but groups of Methodists and Presbyterians frequently lined the banks of the Mahoning River as he raised converts from the water, in order to greet the drenched participants with derision. Scott's horse was often set loose while he preached, and once when he located the horse he discovered its tail had been cut off.

The stories bothered Alexander Campbell. Scott was loved by thousands, he knew; he was a mighty spokesman for God, a veritable Son of Thunder. But what was he preaching? To learn the truth he persuaded his father Thomas to visit the Western Reserve and observe.

It was March, and the roads were quagmires of mud. The aging Thomas Campbell rode the distance on horseback. He lingered in the territory for six months, inspiring all he met, his gentle nature responding only to the good he heard and found. His report was generous in praise of Walter Scott. He recognized in the bold drive of the restless evangelist no element to cause concern; instead he rejoiced in an ingredient that had been added to the Movement.

"We have spoken and published many things correctly concerning the Ancient Gospel," he wrote Alexander, "but I must confess that I am at present for the first time upon the ground where the thing is practically exhibited."

They were reassuring words, but by the time they reached Alexander other events were demanding his attention.

In Kentucky the flame of interest in the new doctrine, which had been ignited by Alexander Campbell's visits to the state, had been fanned into a spreading fire by the circulation of the *Christian Baptist*. The paper was provoking cries of outrage from orthodox Baptists as intense as in the Western Reserve. And a counterpart of Walter Scott in the person of a freethinking Baptist preacher bearing the queer name of "Raccoon" John Smith, was leading a similar revolt in that state against cherished Baptist dogma.

The violence of the opposition surprised Alexander. The culture of the Bluegrass State stemmed from the Tidewater area of Virginia, and had supplanted the raw methods of the frontier; an air of gentle aloofness to conflict prevailed. But beneath it, he realized now, the spirit of the men who had made Kentucky a bloody battleground in their fight against the Indians still smoldered; no equivocation was in their blood.

The Baptist denomination was deeply entrenched in the state. Now it seemed to Mr. Campbell it was girding itself for battle as the attacks by "Raccoon" John Smith on its Calvinistic doctrine split asunder its district associations, setting afire the spirit of the new Movement.

But "Raccoon" John Smth, Alexander Campbell knew, possessed a more stable nature than Walter Scott. He was a firebrand, but he was not mercurial; his zeal burned with a steadier flame. The groups he was leading out of the Baptist fold were forming more solid frameworks for an eventual church.

Alexander had met this firebrand of a man called "Raccoon" John Smith on his first trip to the state, and instantly loved him. Smith was unschooled, brought up in the backwoods of southern Kentucky, but he possessed a native intelligence coupled with a scathing wit and a facility in speaking that set him apart as a leader. He was the only man he knew, Alexander had told him, who would have been ruined by a college education.

One evidence of Smith's leadership stature was the type of men who had enlisted to the cause at his side. One of them was a politician-turned-preacher named John T. Johnson.

The background of John T. Johnson differed from that of "Raccoon" John Smith as far as do the poles. Johnson's parents were of the Tidewater Virginia heritage, people of wealth who had migrated to Kentucky during the stormy period of the Revolution. His father, Colonel Robert Johnson, was conspicuous in organizing the territory and readying it for statehood, and had imparted to his eleven children a sense of civic responsibility which was to distinguish all of them. Several entered the political arena, and one of John's brothers, Richard Mentor Johnson, was to become Vice-President of the United States under President Martin Van Buren. The family settled in the center of the bluegrass region, acquiring extensive land holdings in that productive area, and John was reared in an atmosphere of luxury and culture.

He was barely thireen years old when he attended the Great Revival of 1803 at nearby Cane Ridge, Kentucky. The family connections were Baptist, and he had been taught that only if it was the Lord's will would he be saved. But at the revival he witnessed aghast the strange gyrations of those whom the Lord had seemingly chosen, and a suspicion regarding the validity of the Calvinistic doctrine took root in his youthful mind. As he entered manhood a compulsion grew in him to seek and find a better way to salvation.

He attended Transylvania University in nearby Lexington, and studied law with his brother Richard. Before he was twenty-one years old, he began practicing at Great Crossings, a small settlement near Georgetown, the center of his own extensive land holdings acquired after his marriage in 1811 to Sophia Lewis. In the war of 1812 he served as an aide to General William Henry Harrison at Fort Meigs, returning home to enter the state legislature in 1815. In the financial panic of the next few years he endorsed note after note for his friends, only to discover when the tension eased that he was in debt for over fifty thousand dollars, almost his entire fortune. He struggled to pay off the debt, and in 1820 his reputation for integrity and devotion to duty, as well as his ability to think straight and clearly, elected him to Congress. Here he further distinguished himself as one of the four men in the House of Representatives in 1825 who cast the deciding votes for General Andrew Jackson for President, when that election was thrown into the House.

But now he was concluding what he said was to be his last term in the Congress. He was through with politics, determined to devote the remaining years of his life to proclaiming the glorious discovery of what he had been seeking—a simple, direct pathway to the Throne of Grace. He had made the discovery through the pages of the *Christian Baptist* and through personal encounters with Alexander Campbell on his visits to the state. Joyfully he was joining "Raccoon" John Smith in spearheading a mighty battle in the Bluegrass State for the principles of what he called the "current reformation." Together the erudite, cultured Johnson and the more earthy, outspoken man from the hills, "Raccoon" John Smith, made a remarkable team.

Alexander Campbell rejoiced in the reports from Kentucky that indicated thousands were joining the new Movement. But the close ties the groups of former Baptists led by John T. Johnson and "Raccoon" John Smith were forming with the groups of "Christians," as led by their neighbor Barton W. Stone, gave him cause to ponder the implications.

He had watched with mild misgivings the union of the two bodies here and there in Ohio, where Walter Scott's groups had encountered them, and in southern Indiana and in parts of Illinois. But a general consolidation?

He was of two minds regarding it. There were striking points of similarity in the two groups, but there were also many points of difference. Most of the differences, it was true, were in the realm of opinion where men had the right to differ, but a few other points, some of them never openly mentioned, needed clarification.

Barton Stone had indicated several times that he had proclaimed the truths the two bodies held in common many years before Alexander Campbell came upon the stage to aid the good cause. This "squinted," Campbell frankly felt, toward a claim of priority in introducing the Movement. And he did not like it. Scores of similar movements, it was true, had arisen across the land, but he had virtually ignored all of them. Why should he now recognize Mr. Stone's as on a par with his own? He had never acknowledged the priority of the efforts of James O'Kelly in his break with the Methodist hierarchy over the matter of ecclesiastical control. He had never even applauded the work of Elias Smith in New England, in his plea to be considered a "Christian only," believing him tainted with the Unitarian doctrine. He had brushed aside as of little consequence the "Separate Baptist" Movement in the South, which had demanded freedom to constitute its churches on the Bible alone.

In fairness to Mr. Campbell, it must be stated that his reluctance to grant to Barton Stone a priority in promulgating their common doctrine did not emanate from vanity alone. If the Movement became accepted as originating with Mr. Stone, it might shift its emphasis in directions Mr. Campbell was not yet willing to go. Another thing, it would give Mr. Stone preference in the choice of a name for the Movement, and a name must soon be found.

Alexander Campbell thought of his own followers as still nominally Baptists, but with the rift widening between them and the orthodox body, he knew the term was increasingly a misnomer. The terms Reformers and Reformed Baptists were widely used, but he rejected them as firmly as he did the term Campbellites. In a way it appalled him that his name should be given to the Movement. To give the name of any man to a religious movement violated the express law of Christ; it was done by those who could not conceive of Christianity in any other light than as an "ism." But the name Christian, which Barton Stone preferred, smacked of an arrogance he deplored. It implied an exclusive claim to a state of grace, a denial of that state to other bodies, and he did not want such a charge fastened to his Movement. He preferred the term Disciples, or Disciples of Christ. It seemed to him descriptive and identifying, and he was happy that groups here and there were adopting it. He wished a congregation of his followers in southern Indiana, once known as the Hope Baptist Church, had assumed it. Instead they were awkwardly designating themselves the Church of God in Christ in New Hope. Yes, a common name must soon be found.

And there were other things. Barton Stone's attitude toward the office of minister seemed to him equivocal. While both men rejected all ecclesiastical authority, and Stone repudiated the trappings of the professional clergy as vehemently as Campbell, nevertheless Stone was edging toward the view that the doctrine of the priesthood of all believers was unrealistic in its practical aspects. He was indicating, both in his correspondence with Campbell and through the pages of his magazine the *Christian Messenger*, that some specific qualifications for holding the office of minister should be met by men who sought to preach. Could Barton Stone be right? Hundreds of men were now calling themselves preachers in both groups, most of them sincere, dedicated men. But their lack of training, and in many cases their obvious unfitness for the task, was becoming embarrassing. Yet who could say they should not be spokesmen for God?

And there was the matter of a difference in attitude toward immersion as the only scriptural mode of baptism. Barton Stone, once an Anabaptist, had now accepted immersion as the one scriptural method, a view Campbell had held since his early break with the Presbyterians. But Stone was also giving indication that he felt too great an emphasis upon immersion as the only accepted practice might prove a stumbling block toward the unity of Christ's followers, a goal to which they were both committed. Was he right? In making immersion a test of fellowship, would the Movement find it impossible to repel the imputation of being sectarian? Mr. Stone thought it might even be considered a creed. "A short creed," he had once said, "but such a short creed might exclude more Christians from uniting with each other than the more lengthy creeds of the denominations."

Such differences bothered Alexander Campbell, not because he feared they could not eventually be resolved but because they indicated Barton Stone had tendencies more liberal than he allowed himself to possess. Did the fact he did not reject Mr. Stone's views in toto indicate his own convictions were undergoing a subtle change? Once he had been so straight that, like the Indian's tree, he had leaned the other way. Once he would neither pray nor sing praises with anyone who was not as perfect as he supposed himself to be. "In this most unpopular course," he now wrote in the *Christian Baptist* in a moment of rugged honesty, "I persisted until I discovered that on the principle embraced in my conduct there never could be a congregation, or church, upon earth. This plan of making our own nest and fluttering over our own brood; of building our own tent and of confining all goodness and grace to our noble selves and the elect few like us, is the quintessence of sublimated pharisaism."

Was he now beginning to wonder if his stand on other doctrinal points was too rigid? Already the literal interpretation of the New Testament as voiced by many of his followers was creating apprehension among other thoughtful preachers, and confusion among scores of the men and women in the pews. The Movement was Bible-based but did that mean the Scriptures must be followed to the letter? Was the Bible, or was Christ, the final authority? Barton Stone's followers did not seem troubled by such matters; they seemed to possess a freer spirit, a more tolerant nature. Would a closer alignment with them introduce a freshening in the stream of the Campbell Movement?

If such thoughts occurred to Mr. Campbell he held his peace. The two groups were on the same foundation, in the same spirit, preached the same Gospel, and that was good. The final goal of each was "to sink into union with the Body of Christ at large," as Barton Stone had stated in the "Last Will and Testament of the Springfield Presbytery." And someday, somehow, in God's good time, the goal would be reached. Certainly Mr. Campbell did not foresee that the more liberal, freshened waters which were to be introduced by a union with Stone's movement, would eventually divide the mainstream.

"The great secret of church government is the indwelling of the Holy Spirit," Barton Stone had said. And Alexander Campbell believed it.

As the excitement in the Western Reserve occasioned by Walter Scott's preaching intensified, and as the situation in Kentucky, as spearheaded by "Raccoon" John Smith and John T. Johnson approached a climax, Alexander Campbell was diverted from giving either situation his full attention by two experiences which had far-reaching effects.

Robert Owen, a wealthy British manufacturer, had established a colony at New Harmony, Indiana, in cooperation with his father-in-law, Robert Dale, as an experiment in communal living. An advocate of infidelity, he felt he had found the solution to all the ills to which mankind is heir and hurled a challenge at the clergymen of the country to debate his system of moral and religious philosophy. Mr. Owen was such an articulate and able spokesman for infidelity that his challenge went unanswered. Alexander Campbell was dismayed. His convictions ran deep and his sense of responsibility for upholding them even deeper. He was as yet a relatively unknown religious leader in the mountain fastness of western Virginia, his head and heart occupied with mounting problems of his own. But he could not allow any man to proclaim, as Mr. Owen was doing, that all religions of the world were founded on the ignorance of mankind, that they were the source of vice, disunion and misery; that they were a bar to the formation of a society of virtue. When it became apparent that more prominent churchmen were ignoring the challenge to debate the infidel, he stepped forward. "Now, be it known to Mr. Owen and to all whom it may concern, that I, relying on the Author, and the reasonableness of the excellence of the Christian religion, will engage to meet Mr. Owen at any time within one year from this day at any place . . . in a public debate of his propositions before all who may choose to attend."

Although public debating at the time was a popular attraction, many people, including Mr. Campbell, were aware such polemics often intensified rather than dissolved differences. Mr. Campbell also recognized that public "disputing," as he termed it, on religious matters tended to magnify the lesser aspects of religion and dwarf its essential nature. But he also realized little progress could be achieved in any field without controversy, a feeling bolstered by the fact his previous debates happily had furthered interest in the Movement.

The debate with Robert Owen took place in Cincinnati, Ohio, in April 1829, and attracted thousands from all parts of the country at each of its sixteen sessions which extended over eight days. It was held in the largest auditorium in the city, the old

Stone Church of the Methodists on East and Fifth Streets, the crowds so taxing the seating capacity of twelve hundred that people stood in the aisles, sat on the steps of the rostrum, and perched on the widow ledges at every session.

Morning and afternoon sessions of four hours each were held, but the afternoon sessions were generally prolonged until, as records of the event indicate, "candles were called for." Although each man was scheduled to speak for thirty minutes at a time, the procedure was not closely followed, and on the last three days Mr. Owen surrendered the remainder of the time to Mr. Campbell, who proceeded to deliver a remarkable speech of twelve hours, in two-hour periods, from ten to twelve in the mornings and from two to four in the afternoons, for three days.

Robert Owen proved to be a genial, witty man whom Mr. Campbell instantly liked despite the disparity of their views. The utmost decorum was preserved in their verbal encounters, and their deference to each other was marked by such exaggerated and polite terms the audiences were entranced. An astute observer of the scene who seemed to have attended every session, Mrs. Frances Trollope of England, an eccentric visitor to America who was conducting at the time a fabulous bazaar on the Cincinnati Public Landing, was so impressed by the friendly spirit of the two opponents she wrote of it later in her famous book, "The Domestic Manners of the Americans," remarking especially on the fascinating sight of the two men going off to dinner with each other like old cronies after each session. All of which, she said, "could only have happened in America." Mr. Campbell's admiration of Mr. Owen was such, indeed, that later he said of all the men with whom he debated, he found Robert Owen the most gentlemanly.

But Robert Owen was an infidel, and no holds were barred in his attacks on Christianity. And no quarter was given in Alexander Campbell's defense of it. No verdict was rendered at the conclusion of the debate, but when Mr. Campbell sat down after his final twelve-hour speech, the audience rose to its feet in a prolonged tribute to the Defender of the Faith. Almost overnight Alexander Campbell became a national figure, a man to be reckoned with in molding the thought of the country, a religious leader whose allegiance was to a Christianity that transcended all the clamorous and disruptive claims of the contending sects. His reputation spread like wildfire, and before he left Cincinnati at the conclusion of his encounter with Mr. Owen, he received a letter from a group of admirers in Brooke County, Virginia, urging him to become a delegate to the approaching Virginia State Constitutional Convention.

He acceded to the request. The rank infidelity exhibited by Mr. Owen seemed to him a reflection of the mood of the nation, a mood that expressed itself in a lowering of moral standards. Widespread abuses of public office called for the participation of Christian people, and he would do what he could. The court system of the Virginia commonwealth needed revision, more adequate support of public education should be allowed, and if in the new constitution for the state there could be inserted a plan for the gradual abolition of slavery, his work would not be in vain.

But it was in vain. His experience among the lawmakers was disillusioning. Political expediency was in the saddle, and not one of his reform measures was adopted. He left for home convinced he could better serve the country in other ways. He was a preacher, a religious reformer, as the eminent former President of the United States, James Madison, one of his fellow delegates, told him on the final evening of the convention. "You have the ability of a statesman, Mr. Campbell," Mr. Madison had said, "but you have made no mistake as to your calling. You are one of the ablest and most original expounders of the Scriptures I have ever heard."

It is quite probable the two experiences were strong factors in a decision Alexander Campbell reached when he returned to his home in the Virginia hills. He would discontinue the publication of the *Christian Baptist*.

The iconoclastic paper had circulated now for almost seven years. It had aroused thousands of God's children to break the bonds of sectarianism and seek a direct approach to the living Lord. It had never faltered in its warfare against the trappings of the professional clergy. But more was needed now than attacks on the established churches. A closing of ranks was needed by the forces of righteousness. The country was expanding; its problems were mounting; evil was in the ascendency; and every man of goodwill, every church, every Christian journal was needed to strengthen the bulwarks of the city of Zion. Furthermore, if his followers should eventually be forced to formalize their entity as a separate religious body, they would need a journal which clearly delineated the new doctrine, a constructive guideline to direct them in building up their new church rather than tearing down the old ones.

With the close of the year 1829 the *Christian Baptist* ceased to exist. The birth of the new year, 1830, witnessed the appearance of a new journal, dedicated to inculcating in men and women a faith in the promise of the future, a harbinger among the people of glad tidings, preparing mankind for the ultimate triumph of the Kingdom of God on earth. It would continue to expose error where Campbell saw it, raising dust if necessary in its removal of whatever rubbish it encountered, but it was to be primarily a herald of a brighter day. He called it the *Millennial Harbinger*.

The first issue of the *Millennial Harbinger* was off the press and creating acclaim as Alexander Campbell saddled his horse in August, 1830, for a trip to the Western Reserve. The annual meeting of the Mahoning Association was to be held in the village of Austintown, and he was scheduled to attend.

As he rode into the territory we have no record that he anticipated the momentous events which were to transpire at the meeting, events which would direct the Movement toward its ultimate destiny.

CHAPTER VI

"Good-bye to the Baptists"

In a sense it was Walter Scott's own mercurial nature that set in motion the train of events which, after his three explosive years of evangelistic activity, left him shaken and seemingly bereft of power; and hastened the mood of rejection which caused him to leave the Western Reserve.

Despite the opposition Scott had aroused among the entrenched religious bodies of the region, the preachers in the Mahoning Association of Baptist churches continued to rejoice in the harvest of souls he was winning. But the abandon with which he formed churches only to leave them unnurtured, seemingly indifferent to their disorganized, bewildered state, was now a matter of outspoken concern. Years later, William Hayden, who traveled during much of the three years with Scott as his "singing evangelist," was to point out: "There were no measures to call out and prepare men to preach and teach; no plan of insuring a reasonable support for them; no way of securing harmony of action among them; no means to take care of the converts; no provision for holding ground when it was gained." For the want of such measures, many of Walter Scott's churches soon languished to the point of dissolution.

When the first hint of such criticism reached the ears of Mr. Scott, he gave it scant heed; it was a cloud no bigger than a man's hand and would be borne away by the winds without giving rain. "Convert the people and give them the Holy Ghost, and they will be safe," was his rejoiner. He was not unmindful of the need of shepherding the flocks, but in his passion for evangelizing it was subordinate to the task of conversion. This view, however, was not shared by the more thoughtful of his brethren. Soon, to the thundering criticism of the orthodox bodies, and to the rumblings of the bewildered over his erratic ways, was added the frank opinion of his friends in the Mahoning Association that more supervision of Mr. Scott's work was needed. Some control must be exercised.

When Walter Scott finally realized the seriousness of the concern, he could scarcely believe it. Was his beloved Mahoning Association readying itself to assume the stance of an ecclesiastical tribunal? He had rebelled at the strictures of authority in the Scotch Presbyterian fold; was he now about to become the victim of an encroaching power of a Baptist body? The attitude of his brethren was clearly unscriptural. No passage in the Bible could they point to which gave to any man, or group of men, the right to dictate on church matters to others. Alexander Campbell, his mentor and guide, had pointed out the horrendous results of such a stance in the very first issue of the *Christian Baptist*. "That monster horrific, shapeless, huge, whose light is extinct, called an ecclesiastical court!" Campbell had written. "Whether such an alliance of the priest and nobles of the kirk be called a session, a presbytery, a synod, a general assembly, a convention, a conference, an association or annual meeting—its tendency and results are the same. Whenever and where such a meeting either legislates, decrees, rules, directs or controls, or assumes the character of a representative body, in religious concerns, it essentially becomes the man of sin and the son of perdition."

In defense of the Mahoning Association it should be said that that body, in theory at least, was innocent of any intent of exercising ecclesiastical control. Its constitution disclaimed "all superiority, jurisdiction, coercive rights and infallibility, acknowledging the independence of every church." Its role in relation to its member churches was that of an adviser only; the sole purpose it had taken unto itself was that of spreading the Gospel.

Walter Scott knew this, but as the criticism mounted he remembered that other Baptist associations, similarly constituted, had not been above exceeding their authority. Some, he recalled, had even passed on candidates for the ministry, and disciplined church members, and expelled churches. They sought to justify such actions on the principle that, since they were the only recognized authority in the Baptist hierarchy, when authority was needed they fulfilled the role.

But the Mahoning Association was Baptist in name only, and Walter Scott had felt safe in it. Its preachers for the most part had nullified the Baptist position. It had never sought to exercise any control over the churches within its fold, or supervise the activities of the preachers, or of himself. Was it now about to betray him?

Even before the annual meeting of the Mahoning Association was called to order on that August day in 1830, the little village of Austintown was thronged with preachers and laymen, mingling in happy fellowship. A new meetinghouse had been erected during the past year by the Reformers, the first commodious house of worship yet built by the new Movement in the Western Reserve, and when Alexander Campbell entered it late on the afternoon of his arrival, he found it filled to overflowing.

Austintown boasted over seven hundred inhabitants. It was an expanding trading center, and its single tavern could not begin to accommodate the hundreds of Reformed Baptists arriving by wagon, on horseback, and on foot. Benches in the meetinghouse became beds for many of the visitors; others slept in their wagons, or in the fields; the lucky ones occupied available space in homes of the townspeople. Alexander Campbell and Walter Scott, and a few other leading preachers, were given beds in the two-story home of William Hayden, who, with his two brothers Daniel and A.S., gladly resorted to pallets on the floor, honored to suffer discomfort for such distinguished guests. The Hayden family was a pillar of strength in the Movement. Not only was William Mr. Scott's singing partner, but a preacher of power himself; his brother Daniel had assumed oversight of Scott's tangled financial affairs, and his youngest brother A.S., also musically gifted, was active in both pew and pulpit.

The Reformers' Church in Austintown had been constituted by Scott only two years before from what had once been a strong Baptist church. Scott justified his "take-over" when he reported he found the Baptist brethren in a state of entire prostration. "All was delinquency," he had related to the Mahoning Association, "a perfect web of wickedness, the like of which I never had seen. It was an involved labyrinth of personal and family quarrels. For about three weeks I strove to disentangle the sincere-hearted, but in vain. When the threads and filaments of a quarrel have forced themselves like waves over the whole body ecclesiastic, that body should be dissolved. We accordingly looked upon this institution as entirely lost, and began to preach the Ancient Gospel, the word of the Lord as a hammer and a fire. All hearts were immediately broken, or burst, and of that sinful people there have been immersed nearly one hundred and fifty individuals."

The church these one hundred and fifty reconverted people formed was, according to Scott, "walking in the commandments and ordinances of the Lord, blameless," to which he added the wistful words, "I hope." It was under the joint care of William Hayden and a good friend, John Henry, who likewise possessed a remarkable singing voice which he often allowed to echo across fields and groves and in the meetinghouses to supplement that of William Hayden and further enhance Scott's preaching.

John Henry had joined the Reformers with his wife, Jane Kyle, from a Presbyterian background soon after Walter Scott had started his evangelistic trips in the area, and immediately attempted preaching himself. But it was for his music he was best known. He played nine instruments, preferring the violin and the clarinet, often accompanying himself as he sang. He likewise possessed the volatile temperament of a musician, and his lean figure, over six feet in height, and sharp nose and deep-set eyes had become a familiar sight among the churches along the Mahoning River, his rich voice and profound knowledge of the Bible opening doors and hearts to the new doctrine. His musical ability had created a common bond with Walter Scott, who often joined him in playing the flute, and an intimacy existed between them.

But despite the outward bustle of fellowship among the men and women gathered in Austintown, as the annual meeting progressed Alexander Campbell sensed an undercurrent of unrest. Walter Scott sensed it too. Even the exuberance which he mustered to make his report did not dispel his sense that all was not well. Dissatisfaction existed among the brethren; a cloud of criticism enveloped them. To his brooding mind, it took on the aspect of a first dreadful step toward ecclesiastical control.

Whether or not Scott communicated his apprehension to his good friend, the volatile John Henry, will never be known; there is no record of a preconceived plan. But on the third morning of the assembly, John Henry rose to his full six-foot height and introduced a startling proposal. He called for the immediate dissolution of the Mahoning Baptist Association.

The proposal must have taken the members of the Association by utter surprise, and, according to parlimentary procedure, it probably could not be debated. To a few minds it may have echoed the justification Walter Scott had expressed in dissolving the original Austintown Baptist Church—"When the threads and filaments of a quarrel have forced themselves like waves over the whole body ecclesiastic, that body should be dissolved." At any rate, the presiding Elder put the proposal to a vote. Within minutes the Mahoning Association stood dissolved.

Alexander Campbell was taken as nakedly by surprise as the others. If he had received from Walter Scott any intimation of such a radical move, he had not taken it seriously. Records indicate that almost in dismay he got to his feet. He stood looking over the assembled body, now bereft of any form of cohesive organization. The Mahoning Association had not been perfect, but it had been the only tangible framework for his Movement in the entire country. It was the only semblance of orderly endeavor in evangelizing and extending the Movement. Now, with it at an end, how would the Movement continue? What would become of it? Was the principle of concert of action dead? Struggling alone, isolated from each other, with no lines of communication between them, could the infant churches now aligned with the sprawling Movement survive?

"Brethren, what are you going to do?" he cried. "Are you never going to meet again?"

His distressed eyes may have singled out Walter Scott. If they did, in all likelihood he experienced a surge of conflicting emotion. The great talent for preaching possessed by his friend had fascinated him. In Walter Scott he thought he had found a Timothy, a preacher who could spread the word as no other, who could captivate crowds, convert the unsaved, dispel error in doctrine, and lay the foundation for a mighty ursurge in restoring the Ancient Gospel. Scott had seemed to grasp the essential truths of the "Declaration and Address" of Father Thomas as had no other man. But his nature was impulsive, his temperament erratic. Could he be depended upon now to continue to further those truths?

His questions to the group went unanswered in the first shock of the precipitate action. And then someone suggested a yearly meeting be held, a meeting with no powers, no evangelistic purpose, no reviewing action; an assembly of the brethren for fellowship only, and for mutual encouragement. Whether it would be a sufficiently tangible something to hold the floundering brethren together would have to be seen.

In a mood of bewilderment the men and women who had crowded the village of Austintown in such high expectancy went through the motions of their closing sessions. One by one they departed, on horseback, or huddled in wagons in hushed groups, leaving Walter Scott amid the ruins.

For a whole day after the meeting closed the evangelist lingered in the village, wandering the streets. Then he rode slowly back to Canfield, exhausted, a lethargy, an acute depression upon him. One thing only was clear to him—he must leave the Western Reserve; its open spaces, so symbolic of the freedom he loved, seemed a mockery. His work here was finished. Within a week after reaching his home, he packed his household possessions and moved his family to Pittsburg, the scene of his early life in America, the place of his conversion to the simple New Testament Gospel. He needed to reclaim the tranquillity he had known there.

But the peace he sought was not there. All autumn and into the winter months, Walter Scott brooded, restless, searching both his soul and the Scriptures for guidance. Early in 1831 he saddled his horse and turned its head south, riding through the intense cold of January with no clear plan in mind. He reached Cincinnati, and for two months felt something akin to his old buoyancy, his spirits revived by an encounter in the bustling settlement on the Ohio River with a dynamic young preacher of the new Movement, David Burnet, a man of a different cultural stripe than the preachers he had known in the Ohio frontier. But when Mr.

Burnet invited him one Sunday evening to deliver the sermon at his church at Eighth and Walnut streets, and he stood before the expectant audience, Walter Scott discovered he could not articulate his views. His power of oratory had left him. Haltingly he stumbled through his discourse, and the next morning, chagrined, baffled, he left to return to Pittsburg.

There, for a period, a curious mystical mood engulfed Walter Scott. He closeted himself in the rented three-room house into which he had moved his family, and when he emerged he had produced a penetrating document he called "A Discourse on the Holy Spirit." He sent it to Alexander Campbell. Campbell's sincere admiration of the piece seemed to Scott a sign that his future service in furthering the Movement lay in his early dream of editing a paper, a paper in which he could give expression to his passion for evangelizing. If his ability to sway crowds with his oratory had forsaken him, not so his burning zeal to win souls to Christ. While he was still deep in plans for starting his project, a blow from the cloudless blue sent him again into acute depression. His precious three-year-old daughter Sarah Jane sickened, and in a matter of days died.

The child had been the light of his life, the symbol of his vivid experience in the Western Reserve, a symbol now extinguished. In a compulsion to flee from the past, he once again piled the few household belongings of the Scott family in his creaking flatbed wagon and, with Sarah and their remaining children, drove across Ohio and back into Cincinnati, selecting the village of Carthage on the outskirts of the city as their home. Here he slowly regained a sense of normalcy. He secured the use of a small handpress and began issuing a paper he called the *Evangelist*, a journal that was to continue for thirteen fruitful years.

"The cause is still advancing," he wrote in the first issue. "I am persuaded that nothing but more zeal in our Disciples is necessary to make it triumph among men. I now reside in Cincinnati, and I have resolved, with the help of the Lord, to avail myself of the advantages afforded by the press."

He also afforded himself of some converts he had made, and organized a church, resuming his halting preaching as he was able.

It was also in a dispirited mood that Alexander Campbell left the Austintown meeting. The basic premise of the Movement he headed was the unity of divided Christian people; it was the *summum bonum*, the goal. But now his Movement was adrift on unchartered waters. To the world, his isolated churches, wandering in aimless fashion, susceptible to every speculative wind that blew, would appear as a ludicrous denial of his dream.

And the winds were already blowing. An incident had occurred as the members of the disbanded Mahoning Association assembled for the last time before leaving Austintown, which gave validity to his apprehensions.

Sidney Rigdon, the Baptist preacher who had called on him at Buffaloe in company with Adamson Bentley, and one of the first converts to the new Movement, had introduced a topic which Alexander Campbell well knew would have far-reaching disruptive consequences if allowed to gather momentum.

Sidney Rigdon was a heavy-jowled, heavy-paunched man, a spell-binding preacher given even more so than Walter Scott to visions and imaginative schemes. Rumors had reached Alexander Campbell of his attempt to induce the church for which he was preaching in Kirkland, Ohio, to advocate a system of community property. Now, during the closing hours of the Austintown meeting, as if enough trouble had not already been created, Mr. Rigdon raised the question: "Do not our pretensions to follow the Apostles require a sharing of our wealth, a community of our goods?"

Mr. Campbell had encountered the question the year before in his debate with Robert Owen in Cincinnati, but he had managed to ignore it, keeping the debate centered instead on Owen's militant atheism. Owen, he knew, entertained many radical schemes for society's reform, attempting to incorporate them in his colony at New Harmony, Indiana, and while Mr. Campbell was in sympathy with any attempt to alleviate the conditions of the poor, he was not convinced dividing up the wealth accumulated by rich men would do it. Such a notion was highly impractical. His political sense, however, warned him at the time of the debate not to allow Robert Owen to force him to take a position in which he seemingly opposed helping the poor. Yet neither was he prepared to advocate any radical solution.

Now, however, with the visionary Rigdon raising the same

questions in the assembly of preachers who looked to him for guidance, he could not avoid it. His appraising blue eyes measured the group.

"No," he said with a firmness which could not be mistaken. "On the other hand, Mr. Rigdon, there is clear precedent in the New Testament for the ownership of private property." He turned the talk to other subjects, warding off any further discussion of the matter.

But as he rode homeward he was troubled. He had quieted Sidney Rigdon on the matter of community property, but other speculative theories would arise, diverting his followers from their primary task. Most of the matters would probably be imaginative aberrations; but already there were outcroppings of a morbid interest in the prophecies of the Bible. He had heard much talk at the meeting concerning the imminent advent of the millennium. A New England farmer, William Miller, was foretelling the end of the world by 1843, when Christ would appear in the clouds to judge the world. Walter Scott had taken part in the discussions on the subject, his imaginative mind embracing the prophecy. To him, the wave of religious interest created by Miller's prophecy presaged the long-expected day of glory when Jesus would return and establish his kingdom; it foretold the time when the ransomed of the Lord would return to Zion with songs and everlasting joy upon their heads, and sorrow and sighing would flee away.

Mr. Campbell had tried to caution Walter Scott to calmness, but to little avail. Scott had insisted on talking of the millennial prophecies in Ezekiel and Isaiah, and had spoken ecstatically of the joy of mortals and immortals dwelling together in the millennium, quoting from the writings on prophecy of Elias Smith in New England.

As he rode along, Alexander Campbell admitted to himself that he, too, was influenced by the Miller prophecy. But he was not allowing himself to be carried away by it, certainly not to the point of determining a fixed date. True, the Lord would come again in the clouds of heaven with power and great glory, but the day or the hour, he was convinced, no man could foretell. Nevertheless the scriptural passages held meaning for him as well as for the more excitable Scott, and he realized that, overwhelmed as he often was with the mysteries of eternity, he had been influenced to voice his awe in the choice of a name for his new paper, the *Millennial Harbinger*. He prayed that God in his wisdom would allow it to become a worthy harbinger of the future.

As if the action of the Mahoning Association in dissolving itself had been a signal, other Baptist associations which had been infiltrated by the Campbell Movement in scattered areas of the country began breaking asunder, separating themselves irrevocably from the orthodox Baptist faith. The breaks also separated the churches comprising the associations from each other. As a consequence, hundreds of small congregations, newly born, found themselves standing alone, their only tenuous bond with other congregations which had accepted the new doctrine, that of a yearly meeting, or something resembling it. To most of the churches their new independent stance was frightening. But it was also exhilarating. They were now conforming, they figured, to the New Testament pattern of the independence and complete autonomy of the early churches, and for such adherence to literal Bible practices they were willing to pay the price.

Part of the price, their preachers soon discovered, was the lack of an assured income. Within the Baptist fold their salaries had been low, but at least they could be depended upon. Now there was no source to which they could turn except the spasmodic generosity of their loosely organized congregations.

"I was left in a destitute condition," John Schaeffer, a former Baptist preacher wrote years later. "My salary at the time [of his break with the Baptists] was $400.00, which, added to marriage fees and other perquisites came to near $500.00. My year was expired within two months when I 'came out' from among them. But my convictions of truth did not allow me to dissemble and preach and practice error two months longer for the salary. I had thirty acres of land, less than half paid for, without team or means to cultivate it. I was without money, forsaken of father and mother."

Another price which few had foreseen was the privilege each member now claimed for himself to advance his own interpretation of the Bible.

Obadiah Newcomb, a former Baptist preacher in Wadsworth,

Ohio, shared with Walter Scott a sense of relief in dissolving the Mahoning Association, convinced it threatened to become a supervisory body. His zeal for the total autonomy of each local congregation was exceeded only by his zeal for a rigid adherence to the letter of New Testament pronouncements. The Apostle Paul had spoken out clearly on the evils of personal adornment, and Mr. Newcomb was convinced that any ornamentation; any outward show of ostentation by a church member was evidence of lack of true conversion.

The bold action of the churches in shedding themselves of any supervisory power by dissolving the Mahoning Association gave courage to his convictions. During the closing session of the Austintown meeting his eyes fell reprovingly on a young preacher in the front benches. A flashy guard chain was across his vest. It is of record that Mr. Obadiah Newcomb had viewed the ornament in rebuking silence during the meeting. Now he strode across the room and in full view of the assembled brethren gathered the glittering chain from the man's chest and, dangling it for a moment before the eyes of the startled congregation, dropped it without a word in the owner's pocket and stalked back to his seat.

While men of such stalwart conviction were the seedbed of the new church, Obadiah Newcomb was not following any prescribed attitude of the Movement. The scattered groups had no firmly fixed standards of moral behavior, or of anything else, to serve as guidelines. Each was a law unto itself.

And that was exactly as it should be, sincere men said, as the groups began settling into a variety of church patterns. And that was exactly as it should *not* be, other sincere men began murmuring. The voice of the turtle was beginning to be heard in the vineyard.

BOOK TWO

Thy sea, O God, so great
My boat so small. . . .

Winfred E. Garrison

CHAPTER VII

"To Your Tents, O Israel"

It was October 1833. Golden sycamore leaves covered the ground as Alexander Campbell looked out the high, narrow window of the trim meetinghouse in Richmond, Virginia, averting his gaze for a moment from the faces expectantly turned toward him. The freshly varnished pews were crowded, and people were sitting on stools in the aisles. They were his followers; this new meetinghouse they had erected, two stories high and fully one hundred feet long, had an air of permanence about it which bore testimony to confidence in the continuing growth of what was still a nameless church.

He frowned at the thought of the dilemma over a name. The group before him had its counterpart now in hundreds of communities across the nation. Some called themselves Christian Churches, others, Churches of Christ; the public still referred to them as Campbellites. He continued to prefer the name Disciples of Christ, or Disciples' Church, and used it repeatedly in the *Millennial Harbinger*. But by whatever name, his followers were now a separate entity in the religious community.

He allowed his mind to revert to the series of recent events which had congealed them into a distinct body. The break with the Baptists occasioned by the dissolution of the Mahoning Association had been followed by groping efforts of the groups isolated by that action to find a firm footing; then tentative gestures of cooperation with each other in the form of yearly meetings; the recurring overtures of union with Barton Stone's "Christians," and in hundreds of cases actual union; and then, only one short year ago, the great, widely publicized merger in Lexington, Kentucky, of the two groups, a merger which seemed to formalize the two bodies as one.

Rallying about the Bible as their only guideline, the two had come together, not as a surrender of one group to the other but by way of a mutual resolve to meet on common, holy ground. It had been a dramatic event, the climax of years of working together, the culminating days preceded by a series of prayerful conferences between great-souled John T. Johnson and vigorous "Raccoon" John Smith, representing his doctrine, and Barton Stone and one of his strong followers, John Rogers. For four days, including Christmas Day, 1831, the four men had sat together in the high-ceilinged library of the Johnson home at Great Crossings, near Georgetown, discussing, analyzing, praying—dispersing only to come together again for another four days a week later, this time inviting leading preachers and laymen of both groups to meet with them at the Hill Street Christian Church in Lexington. Here, on the final, climactic day, January 1, 1832, Barton Stone and "Raccoon" John Smith had clasped hands, symbolically sealing the covenant of union; pledging themselves and their fellows to work and worship together hereafter as one body. It was the first statewide merger, the first to involve thousands of people and hundreds of congregations, and it had marked a milestone in the Movement's development.

Mr. Campbell had anticipated it but not without some misgivings. There were still points of difference between him and Barton Stone which were unreconciled. But he had felt swept along by a surge of events he could not control, and had tried to remember that faith was more important than opinion, and fellowship with all who received the Gospel and endeavored to live by it made unnecessary a meeting of the minds on all points of theological theory. Upon the simple truths of the Gospel, all followers of Jesus Christ could be united in one body if they would forego the luxury of speculation, and he and Mr. Stone were both committed to proclaiming that fact.

Since the merger of the two bodies in Kentucky, the learned John T. Johnson had joined Barton Stone in editing his paper, the *Christian Messenger*, sounding a single, confident voice for the new union. And "Raccoon" John Smith was riding the winding trails of the state in company with John Rogers, consolidating their two forces, realigning the groups in each community into a single body—some to stay together, others to separate at the first inevitable friction, but all to emphasize in the minds of the watching sects that a strong, united church had come into existence.

With the assumption by the Movement of a permanent character, the attacks upon it increased. The orthodox bodies were not of a mind to receive into their ranks a strong church whose avowed purpose was to uproot the existing order. Every facet of the Movement was scrutinized, and much of it heatedly denounced. To help meet the attacks, Alexander Campbell had begun traveling among the congregations, defending them, encouraging them, strengthening their conviction of the rightness of their course. Now, in the late summer of 1833, he was visiting the groups in eastern Virginia. With him on the platform was David Burnet, the young preacher Walter Scott had encountered in Cincinnati, and one who had long interested Mr. Campbell.

Mr. Campbell had met David Burnet seven years before when he passed through Cincinnati on one of his early trips to Kentucky. David was then a lad of only eighteen years, and was known as the "boy preacher." Mr. Campbell had been impressed by the fact the youth had declined an appointment to West Point Military Academy to enter the ministry of the Baptist church. He was a member of the cultured Burnet family of Cincinnati, considered one of the "first families" of Ohio. They served rather elegantly as nominal members of the Presbyterian church; and had been in turn annoyed and amused by young David's interest in religious matters.

This interest led him at the age of fifteen to reject his infant baptism by sprinkling, and join the Baptist church by immersion, an act in defiance of his father, Isaac Burnet, Mayor of Cincinnati, and against the judgment of his eminent uncle, Judge Jacob Burnet. For a short period young David considered law as his profession, influenced by working with his father and uncle in their law offices, and by his naturally incisive mind. But the call to preach won out.

Writing of David Burnet later, a biographer, W. T. Moore, says: "Surrounded by a large circle of influential relatives and friends who, if religious at all, had little or no sympathy with his views of Christianity; with wealth and worldly honors offered him without stint, he turned his back upon them all and, like the great lawgiver of Israel, chose rather to suffer affliction with the people of God than to enjoy the pleasures of sin for a season, esteeming the reproach of Christ greater riches than all the treasures and honors of the world. It is only now and then that a young man under such circumstances deliberately selects the profession of an humble preacher of the Gospel."

By the time David Burnet was twenty years of age he had assumed the pastorate of a small Baptist congregation in Dayton, Ohio. Within a year the membership doubled and worship services, overflowing the small meetinghouse, had to be held in the courthouse. But much in the Baptist doctrine bothered him; it was not all to his liking. He deplored its emphasis on its written creed; he did not agree with its view of the nature of baptism. Baptism, to him, was for the remission of a man's sins; it was not an initiation rite for entry into the body of Christ. That entry was made on the simple confession of faith, and was the only test of Christian fellowship.

When a copy of the *Christian Baptist* fell into his hands, he knew he had located at last a doctrine with which he could be in full agreement. Within months he led his Dayton Baptist church to reject its written Articles of Faith, and to withdraw from the Miami Baptist Association. It worried him that the new Movement had no visible framework with which he could align his church, but he was not daunted. A few years later contact with the Sycamore Street Baptist Church in Cincinnati gave him opportunity to introduce there, also, Campbell's doctrine; and from that church he led a group which subsequently formed what was now becoming a flourishing congregation at Eighth and Walnut streets in Cincinnati, known simply as the Christian Church.

Mr. Campbell had followed the situation in Cincinnati closely, remembering the boy preacher he had met, impressed by the leadership he was displaying. The young man had great potential. Now braving a current cholera epidemic, he had invited David Burnet to visit the churches with him along the eastern seaboard. The encounter confirmed his estimate of David Burnet as no ordinary young preacher. With rare astuteness the young man had already grasped the range of the Movement's problems. One matter that especially concerned him was the isolation of the churches. Their quick, shallow rooting must be counteracted, he felt, by some form of cohesive, helpful ties with each other. He had himself experienced the loneliness of isolation when he had first brought his church out of the Baptist fold in 1828. At that time he had anticipated that the Movement could not be long contained within the Baptist framework and, even though two years were to elapse before the formal break with the Baptists in the Western Reserve, he had formed his Cincinnati Christian church as a congregation independent of any other body. Bereft of any alignment, it had been forced, however, to grope its way for guidelines, and he knew the need for nurturing similar congregations now that the Movement was launched as a separate entity. The people were in hungering need of contact with others of like mind.

The meeting the two men were attending in Richmond was proof of it. It was the first "cooperative assembly" held in the state. Almost one thousand men and women were in attendance, coming from sixteen Campbellite churches established in isolated spots all the way from Fredricksburg to the seaboard, each welcoming the opportunity to undergird, and be undergirded by, the wisdom and strength of the others.

Another need which both men realized must be met was that of trained ministers. A cardinal principle of the Movement was that faith is founded on testimony; and testimony could come only by "hearing the Word." It could not be prayed for, nor received by revelation as other sects believed. As part of the doctrine which distinguished the followers of Mr. Campbell from other bodies of religious people, this made necessary articulate preachers who could rightly divide the word of truth. Yet in all Virginia, only one trained evangelist, a man named Peter Ainslee, was giving voice to the principle and oversight to the groping congregations which sought to live by it.

In his swashbuckling *Christian Baptist* days, Alexander Campbell had ignored the need of establishing closer ties among the churches not only because he felt such associations could easily assume decision-making powers, but because he had no desire to see the supremacy of the local church in any way diminished. Now, however, as the Movement assumed the posture of a separate entity, the practical problems of making its identity in the religious community significant, and its work effective, especially in the extension of any service beyond the local church, were crowding upon him. Soon after his tour with David Burnet in 1833, a change in his attitude toward the matter was apparent. President Andrew Jackson was imbuing the nation with a fresh and realistic concept of the relation of the several sovereign states to the central government, and perhaps Mr. Campbell's brush with public affairs during this and other tours suggested to him a parallel to the situation existing in the Movement. Or perhaps he realized that just as the authority of the church, as the body of Christ, was not necessarily vested in clerical roles, so the liberty and freedom of individual churches were not sacrificed but rather found fuller expression in acknowledging their membership in a larger body. At any rate, the next year he wrote in the *Millennial Harbinger*: "The church is not one congregation or assembly, but the congregation of Christ composed of all the individual congregations on earth. In the work of conversion, the whole church, by natural necessity, as well as by the authority of the great King, must cooperate."

The matter of a trained ministry also soon received his attention. In the days when he had inveighed against the pomposity of ministers, referring to them as "hireling clergy," his tirades were based on the conviction the ministry was not to be confined to the preacher alone; it was to be the task of the whole church. This conviction was still strong; he continued to maintain a strong stand against "clerical domination," reluctant to sharpen the line between the clergy and the laity, distrusting theology as a specialized tool in imparting the Gospel, holding firmly to the priesthood of all believers. But he had no intention of elevating the role of the people at the expense of reducing the status of the minister.

It distressed him that many sincere but uneducated men were considering themselves as preachers who had as their chief qualification, and often their only one, the ability to speak with a ready tongue. "It is not of the wisdom that comes from above to countenance every one who wishes to be heard in church," he was soon saying. "While we contend that every citizen has the right to be heard, as well as to hear, yet we have no idea that every disciple is to become a public speaker . . . at his own volition and by virtue of his discipleship." By 1840 he was so convinced of the need for trained ministers he was ready to embark on an educational venture, the chief purpose of which was to adequately prepare young men for the ministry.

David Burnet did not wait that long. Convinced the Movement must begin immediately not only to set men apart for its ministry but to supply them with ammunition, within a few short months after his return to Cincinnati from his tour with Mr. Campbell he began the publication of a journal he called the *Christian Preacher*. For five years this twenty-four-page monthly paper was to set a scholarly tone for the emerging leadership of the church, and a guide for its preachers. The eagerness with which younger preachers, especially, read it prompted him to make available soon thereafter some additional material which he, as a young preacher, had found of indispensable value—the main features of the pungent *Christian Baptist*. He published in a single volume the selected pieces which had first shed light on his path, featuring the dissertations which held the irenic flavor of Mr. Campbell's writing, and the compelling basic dictums that had shaped his thinking.

While this material soon put the stamp of greater competence on the preachers, both Mr. Campbell and David Burnet realized confusion continued regarding the more profound aspects of the Christian religion and the relation of these aspects to the Movement's doctrine. To offset this, Mr. Campbell prepared a logical statement of his own beliefs concerning the infallible, revealed truth of the New Testament and its bearing on the Movement's tenets. He entitled it "The Christian System."

The document clarified the thinking of scores of preachers, but it was greeted by other scores of them with a shock of disbelief. Any written statement of belief was to them a creed, and despite Mr. Campbell's hurried explanation that he had presented only his own views, they detected in the document a questionable note of liberal thinking. In it Mr. Campbell had implied that, for matters other than faith, worship and morality there existed a

"Law of Expediency" to care for things of vital importance to the well-being of the kingdom for which no precepts were to be found in the Bible. This was oddly at variance with the cherished dictum promulgated by Thomas Campbell, "where the Bible speaks, we speak; where the Bible is silent, we are silent." He had also implied that the pathway to heaven was so straight and simple that not even those famous five steps to salvation first profounded by Walter Scott and echoed by hundreds of preachers —not even these were in all cases necessary.

Plainly, Alexander Campbell was becoming less rigid in his views. And few people were greatly surprised when, a year later in 1837, Mr. Campbell answered the inquiry of a lady in Lunenburg, Virginia, as to who should be considered a Christian by stating:

"Who is a Christian? I answer, Every one that believes in his heart that Jesus of Nazareth is the Messiah, the Son of God, repents of his sins and obeys him in all things according to his measure of knowledge of his wills. . . . I cannot therefore make any one duty the standard of Christian state or character, not even immersion into the name of the Father, the Son and of the Holy Spirit, and in my heart regard all that have been sprinkled in infancy without their own knowledge and consent, as aliens from Christ. . . . There is no occasion, then, for making immersion on a profession of faith, absolutely essential to a Christian."

Reaction to what seemed such a radical departure from the concept of immersion as the only form of baptism was mixed. Some preachers rejoiced in the liberalizing of Mr. Campbell's views, agreeing in substance with the position that while immersion was for them the scriptural form of baptism, men who saw otherwise were not to be excluded from the household of Christians. Others were outraged; Alexander Campbell had departed from a basic tenet of the church he had set in motion. He was a beloved leader, but he was no longer to be considered an infallible one. Confusion over the Movement's doctrine, which had been somewhat clarified by Mr. Campbell's explanation of it in "The Christian System," again shrouded the churches. And it was in no way helped as, suddenly, dozens of preachers in all parts of the country, infected with the freedom with which Mr.

Campbell had spoken his mind, began looking about for means of amplifying their own views. They did not have far to look. Hand presses were flooding the country; printing devices were readily accessible. Church periodicals began sprouting like weeds after a spring rain.

In Indiana a red-headed Irishman named John O'Kane began issuing a paper he called the *Christian Casket*. In Ohio, Arthur Crihfield sent broadcast each month a journal entitled the *Heretic Detector*. A paper named the *Israelite* appeared in Indiana.

Since the growth of the Movement had created many issues, each editor of these and a score of other papers delighted to advocate his own idea of how things should be handled. They were self-appointed scribes, but on the whole they were men with a flair for vivid writing, and few people could resist reading their inflammatory approaches. As a result a habit of following the guidance of church periodicals took root among the people, and grew with the passing years, a habit that became a significant factor in the Movement's development.

The most controversial point at issue was that pertaining to the cooperative assemblies, or their counterparts, which were rapidly sprouting here and there. The innocuous yearly meetings were now being called "Evangelizing societies" or "cooperations." They were still loosely structured devices in no way designed to provide supervision of local affairs. True, they were "innovations," but since distrust regarding innovations had not yet made itself widely felt, many people welcomed them. They saw in them a means of better obeying the biblical command to "Go into all the world and preach the Gospel." Through such cooperative assemblies they could share with neighboring churches in sending missionaries abroad. The Bible made no reference as to how the task was to be done, so why should it be taken for granted it meant a single congregation rather than an organized group of churches should undertake it?

But the dread of "ecclesiastical control" lay like a brooding ghost over the Movement, and any action taken by a cooperative assembly met with the inhibiting cry, "Just so started the controlling bodies of the sects!" Many who voiced this warning had been conditioned in their thinking by Alexander Campbell's early caution in the *Christian Baptist*. "Every Christian who understands the nature and design, the excellence and glory of the institution called the Church of Jesus Christ," Mr. Campbell had written, "will lament to see its glory transferred to a human corporation."

In central Indiana the fiery, red-headed Irishman, John O'Kane, who had been teaching school and preaching as well as editing his caustic paper the *Christian Casket*, put aside his quill pen and reared his tall, commanding figure to its full height in order to better observe what was going on.

John O'Kane had migrated from Virginia ten years or so before, bringing with him notions implanted by his contact there with James O'Kelley in his flight from the dictates of the Methodist bishops. He also brought his wife. She was the daughter of a man named Joseph Thomas, known throughout the Virginia countryside as the "White Pilgrim," because of the long white robe he wore as he roamed the hills and vales expressing his religion in poetry and song, and his habit of retiring to lonely places for prayer and fasting.

John O'Kane must also have brought with him something of his fanatic father-in-law's absorption in religion and his courage. Although he had associated himself upon reaching Indiana with Barton Stone's followers, he was not silent in his criticism of the things he considered wrong with Stone's doctrine, and swung back and forth from the "New Light" position to the Campbell Movement. For a while he kept a foot in each household, uncertain where he belonged. When the merger of the two groups in other parts of the land began in earnest, sparked by the union of the Kentucky forces, he at last knew. The united body became his spiritual home, and to advance its cause became his passion. He became the employed evangelist for the Evangelizing Society of Rush County, Indiana.

In this capacity he invaded the surrounding territory. He strengthened dozens of struggling churches, consolidating their efforts with those of others, undergirding them until they could stand alone. In one instance he herded five wholly unrelated, independent congregations of the Movement, each on the brink of extinction, into one united body, merging the five streams with such adroitness they flowed together in harmony, and eventually formed one of the strongest churches existing today in that area, the Central Christian Church in Indianapolis. One of the leading layman of the united body was Dr. John Sanders, whose daughter Zerelda was to become a dominant figure in Indiana political and religious life. Zerelda married a man named David Wallace, a widower with three children, one of whom, Lewis, became a soldier and author, using Zerelda as the prototype of the mother in his novel *Ben-Hur*. When Zerelda's husband, David Wallace, became governor of the state of Indiana in 1837, she assumed a militant role in the fight against the liquor traffic, even stomping out of the morning worship service at the Christian Church in Indianapolis one Sunday because wine instead of unfermented grape juice was used in the Holy Communion.

John O'Kane's work became a demonstration of the possibilities of coordinated effort, and the whole brotherhood sat up and took notice. Was the glory of the local church, they asked, to say nothing of its supremacy, about to pass to human devices? Would the church have to admit to having a rival? Could it no longer claim to be the only missionary society?

On and on the questions ran, some voiced by sincerely concerned men, others by querulous troublemakers, until Mr. Campbell, listening and watching from his home in the Virginia hills, grew annoyed. "There is too much squeamishness about the manner of cooperation," he bluntly stated in the pages of the *Millennial Harbinger*. Soon he began openly and actively encouraging churches in all parts of the country to cooperate in keeping an evangelist at work among them. In his own bailiwick in Brooke County, Virginia, he set an example by promoting a plan for the county to undergird financially an evangelist, Henry Barton, who ministered to and for all the churches in the geographical area.

For a few years cooperative assemblies lingered at the county level, their only work that of evangelizing among the churches in their own county. Then, inevitably, neighboring counties sought fellowship with each other and, heedless of the mutterings of the fearful, formed themselves into regional assemblies. But fellowship at that level, it was discovered, needed the sustaining bond of a common task, and soon joint ventures of one kind and another were undertaken. The rumblings of the literal-minded grew louder.

But the joys and fruits of working together were too apparent and abundant to be resisted. Whether scripturally authorized or not, the method of bringing in the Kingdom by cooperative effort, even if it was what many considered to be a human organization, was proving effective, and for a time jubilation overcame misgivings.

In Illinois a group of churches took the next inevitable step. Assembling in Springfield, they put into operation a plan for the support of an evangelist, not by the county or by a region, but by the entire state. The action reverberated across the land, and in faraway Missouri, where many Kentucky people had migrated, taking their new religious convictions with them and raising the literacy level of the frontier communities, a group of recently planted churches, meeting at Bear Creek in Boone County in 1837, announced they were putting into operation the first of what was to become for them an annual statewide assembly. The purpose of the statewide assembly was for "fellowship and mutual encouragement," and if a few fearful brethren saw in it the makings of a controlling body, they were left in no doubt that some such purpose was in the minds of their sister churches in Indiana. When, soon thereafter these Indiana churches called a general statewide meeting of their own, the call was not limited to the usual "free interchange of views and the procuring and sustaining of efficient and faithful evangelists." It frankly stated part of the purpose was "to promote the general prosperity of the good cause in the state." At this meeting even resolutions were passed on matters of common concern. They were not binding on the churches, but the fact such action was taken marked a significant milestone.

Equally indicative of the change taking place in the Movement was the presentation at this meeting of statewide statistics. This seemingly innocent procedure was significant in that it acknowledged that the local church was not a complete entity in itself but existed as a member of a larger body. In the realization of that kinship, a new brotherhood consciousness was created and the seeds of pride in the Movement as a whole were fertilized. The statistics, largely a guess, placed the membership in the state of Indiana of what were increasingly being called the churches of the Disciples of Christ, at 7700. More enthusiastic and optimistic self-appointed enumerators judged it to be twice that figure, basing their assumption on the fact most of the churches carried the names of only adult males on their rolls.

The size of the new body in Indiana reflected the steady growth it had experienced in other parts of the land, and indicated the Movement was irrevocably launched as a separate church. The shallow roots deplored by David Burnet were going deeper. Only a few men sensed the fact that so were the seeds of discord.

CHAPTER VIII

"Captives of the Word of God"

David Burnet might have been content to continue his struggle for a trained ministry and his fight for a solid framework for the Movement from his pulpit in Cincinnati and through the pages of his widely read paper the *Christian Preacher*, if a circumstance in Kentucky had not catapulted him into another role, short-lived but significant, and again into the orbit of Alexander Campbell's watchful eyes.

Bacon College, in Georgetown, central Kentucky, was looking for a president.

The Campbell Movement, itself just emerging from infancy, had given only sporadic attention as yet to any such traditional task of the church as educating oncoming generations in the liberal arts. The training of men for its ministry was proving enough of a problem. Gestures toward establishing schools had been made here and there by ambitious individuals, but none of them had achieved recognized academic standing, and most of them soon fell by the wayside.

But the situation in Georgetown was different. The Baptist brethren had established a college there in 1831 during the height of their furious defense against the inroads being made by the Campbell forces. Since the school's purpose was to meet the enemy face to face, the Baptists had planted it practically on the doorstep of their most implacable foe, John T. Johnson. The close contact did not produce exactly the results the Baptists had in mind. Due to the proximity, its curious-minded mathematics professor T. F. Johnson had probed into the rival doctrine and had become imbued with Campbellite leanings, even to such an extent that he was inspired to put more emphasis on teaching the new doctrine than on his mathematical formulas. Soon he left the Baptist college, under what circumstances we do not know, and started a school of his own on almost adjoining property, aided and abetted by the wealthy, influential John T. Johnson, no blood relation but a brother in the faith.

His new school opened in 1836 with forty-five students. To offset the impression that it had been created primarily for a sectarian purpose, it was named for Francis Bacon, the eminent British scientist and educator. John T. Johnson not only gave it material aid, and the benefit of his time and influence as curator, but suggested as its president Walter Scott, whose classical learning he had come to admire.

Walter Scott was still burdened with poor health, as well as with the cold ashes of his extinguished oratorical powers, but his scholarship was sound. It was reported that he came to Georgetown and stayed at the embryo school only long enough to deliver an inaugural address before fleeing back to his haven in Carthage, Ohio, and his philosophical broodings. The report is not accurate, however, for there exist today copies of a journal he and John T. Johnson produced intermittently during the year 1837, from Georgetown, called the *Christian*. But its essays on Lockean philosophy must have proven too profound for the average reader of that day; at any rate it was absorbed at the end of the year by David Burnet's the *Christian Preacher*. The circumstance leading to its absorption was the acceptance by David Burnet of the presidency of Bacon College.

To David Burnet education was a matter of supreme concern. He was undoubtedly actuated in his acceptance of the position by his hope of establishing in the Movement a program for general education as well as one for preachers. He moved his family from Cincinnati to Georgetown, and took up the reins, continuing to edit from there his cherished journal the *Christian Preacher*. It had grown in influence and circulation, with subscribers in every state in which the Movement had churches, and when it absorbed the infant but more scholarly *Christian*, its booming prestige caught the startled gaze of Alexander Campbell. No similar threat to the preeminence of his *Millennial Harbinger* had ever before appeared.

What course David Burnet's role in the history of the Movement might have taken if the situation had continued will never be known. The fearful financial panic of 1837 descended on the Kentucky country; all banks suspended payment of specie, and Bacon College was put on the block to the highest bidder, which turned out to be the fashionable Kentucky watering place of Harrodsburg. The move to the more worldly climate of the resort area in 1839 held no appeal for the dedicated Burnet. He saw all chance of making the college a center of influence for the furtherance of the new doctrine go aglimmering, and he resigned, returning to Cincinnati. A man named James Shannon was secured for the vacated office, a man who was to play a role in the Movement later when the slavery issue came to the fore.

Back in Bethany, Alexander Campbell had erected a new study for himself in the cluster of towering pines he had planted west of the house. It was an eight-sided structure of brick, the only light coming from a cupola at the top. He needed the light from above, for he was wrestling with problems calling for divine wisdom. The problems were many and varied, but giving them all a cutting edge was a problem as old as man himself—that occasioned by personal pride. Mr. Campbell was to wage a constant war of his own in this sphere, and eventually emerge the victor; but in the process he was to lose several battles to his lesser self.

The matter of a threat to the standing of the *Millennial Harbinger* now called him to battle, and to expose some quite understandable human frailties by taking advantage of a set of circumstances too tempting to resist.

Mr. Campbell was an extremely busy man, but with the preeminence of his beloved paper threatened he knew he must give attention to enhancing its pages. He could not give more time to it himself; he was in constant demand to visit churches all over the land in need of his counseling visits; also the flood of criticism of his views required him to write prodigiously, analyzing his position, and settling disputes among the brethren. In addition he felt it his duty to personally supervise his lively household of growing children and bickering relatives, as well as to manage his farm and the breeding of his purebred stock. His eye fell on a brilliant young man who was giving needed help to Walter Scott in Carthage, Ohio, in publishing Scott's paper the *Evangelist*.

The young man's name was Robert Richardson; he was the student at whose home in Pittsburg, Campbell had first encountered Walter Scott sixteen years before. As Robert had grown to manhood, his friendship with Scott had deepened, and although he studied medicine at the University of Pennsylvania and became a licensed physician, his heart had been won to the simplicity of the Gospel as taught by Scott, and he determined to give his life to furthering its proclamation. In a burst of concern over the rightness of his course, he had ridden more than a hundred miles on horseback from his home in western Pennsylvania to Carthage in order to be immersed by Scott into the faith. He had lingered to help him edit his paper, relinquishing his medical practice, and at once began displaying remarkable editorial ability.

According to most records, the first overtures toward diverting his talents to Mr. Campbell's paper came from Dr. Richardson himself. He had long admired Mr. Campbell, probably as much as he did Walter Scott although his contact had not been as intimate. Correspondence between the two had been steady as the young doctor sought clarification from Campbell on doctrinal points, and it is not surprising that, in the course of their discussions, Dr. Richardson expressed the desire for wider fields for his editorial talents. At any rate, as the need for strengthening the position of the *Millennial Harbinger* grew apparent, and Mr. Campbell's other duties increased, Mr. Campbell wrote asking him to return north and settle in Bethany, promising him a home and an income in return for his assistance with the *Millennial Harbinger*.

The years were to prove this a significant development. Robert Richardson was perhaps the one man in the Movement peculiarly endowed with the combination of self-effacing qualities and intellectual brilliance necessary to work closely with Mr. Campbell. He accepted the offer, and for the remainder of his life, Robert Richardson served in Mr. Campbell's shadow—handling details, implementing ideas, tempering and balancing Mr. Campbell's proud temperament with his own humility, and eventually becoming the great leader's chief biographer. But of greater significance was the part he played in rescuing the Movement from the charge that it was a cold doctrine based as much on John Locke's philosophy as on the Bible. Robert Richardson was possessed of a profound awareness of spiritual realities, and as the years passed he breathed into the pages of the *Millennial Harbinger* a new recognition of the role played by the Holy Spirit in the conversion and life of a Christian, imparting to its readers such a comforting sense of the abiding nature of God's love the magazine embedded itself in the affections of the people, and its primary place as an influence in the developing Movement was never again seriously challenged.

There is nothing to indicate that the conscience of Mr. Campbell was bothered by depriving Walter Scott of the services of the talented Richardson. For the relationship between Mr. Campbell and his once close friend, Walter Scott, was showing evidence of strain.

At the time of the appearance of Alexander Campbell's "Christian System" in 1835 and his avowal of a more simple pathway to salvation than the five steps Scott had outlined, Walter Scott had published, as if in reply, a volume entitled *The Gospel Restored*. It was a scholarly work, and bolstered Mr. Campbell's position on many points. But it also had some other things to say.

In the book Walter Scott implied that he was the first man in modern times to proclaim the true Gospel. The time, he said, was 1827. Gratuitously he gave credit to Mr. Campbell for putting forth a plea for the restoration of a peculiar ecclesiastical order before that time, but the Ancient Gospel he, Scott, had restored. And it was the Ancient Gospel that made disciples; the Ancient Order, as enunciated by Mr. Campbell, merely kept them.

The year 1827, he explained, was the date which would be held in history as the red-letter day because it was on November 18 of that year that he, Walter Scott, had baptized a Presbyterian, a man named William Amend, at New Lisbon in the Western Reserve, the first person in modern times to publicly accept the new plan of salvation and receive the ordinance of baptism in accord with apostolic teaching and usage.

The absurdity of Scott's assumption of such a role in history appalled Mr. Campbell. Publicly, in the pages of the *Millennial*

Harbinger, he berated Walter Scott's invidious manner of fixing dates, places and persons for the restoration of the Ancient Gospel. The Ancient Order, yes, but he denounced any kinship with such an arrogant claim as "restoring the Gospel." Through all history, he reminded his readers, the restoration principle had fascinated religious leaders; spurts of zeal to return to the original church had characterized scores of groups in ancient and even in modern times. The rocky road of Protestantism was strewn with bodies of those who had conceived it their duty to reproduce the practices of the primitive church. The term "restoration" was in no way the unique possession of his followers, even as to method, and he had never advocated "express terms and approved precedents" for restoring the early church.

But Walter Scott was unimpressed. He did not then, or ever, waver in his avowal that he had found the plan of salvation which had restored the Ancient Gospel and would eventually bring all men together into one church. He persisted in using the exact term, and even when Mr. Campbell, exasperated, was provoked enough to publicly imply later in the *Millennial Harbinger* that Scott had actually hindered the basic purpose of the Movement to unite the churches by his precipitate action in dissolving the Mahoning Association, setting the new body adrift prematurely and thus creating another sect, Scott remained impassive.

"Granted that we have created another sect," he said, unabashed, "but it is a sect which, in its progress, will consume all others. As Moses' rod ate up the rods of the magicians, the true creed will destroy all others, and the true principles of union will consume all those of mere party origin. Our mission is Union, which means the annihilation of sects and parties, and the recovery of the church."

From his spirited reaction, it was evident to Mr. Campbell that a measure of Walter Scott's confidence in himself had been restored. In this he rejoiced; he was still mindful of Walter Scott's inherently true worth. In spite of their strained relationship, Mr. Campbell urged him to undertake preaching trips as he felt flashes of his old power return, and accompanied him on several of them, doubtless a gesture on the part of both men to regain their old friendly footing. But the differences persisted, and became more aggravated as time passed by their divergent attitude toward the handling of the slavery issue, an issue that was slowly obscuring all else.

Both men considered slavery a loathsome evil. But Mr. Campbell was mindful of the fact it had divisive tendencies which could split asunder families and friends, and certainly his churches if allowed to absorb men's minds. His experience as a delegate to the Virginia Constitutional Convention in 1829, when he had attempted to secure the use of government funds to finance the emancipation of slaves, and later in 1840, when he had endorsed a similar scheme advanced by Henry Clay, had convinced him a rational discussion of the subject was virtually impossible, serving only to solidify the forces on both sides. Since that time he had tried to avoid the topic, especially among the brethren. He realized the nation would have to deal with it eventually, but he was hopeful it could be delayed until his Movement was on a more secure footing.

But not so the volatile Walter Scott. He had no use for slavery and his refusal to keep silent about it sometimes obscured his position. As tensions mounted he annoyed Mr. Campbell repeatedly by his persistence in bringing up the subject. He was not content to denounce it but made it the subject of such painstaking analysis as to confuse many people. In 1835 he allowed himself to be drawn into a furious exchange of views in his paper, *The Evangelist,* and, in attempting to extricate himself he only became more deeply mired in a position which was interpreted by some as defending the horrendous evil.

The dispute started when he mentioned in his paper a fact which everybody knew, that the early Christians held slaves and were not reproved for it by the Apostles. Asked by a subscriber why this was so, he felt obliged to remove the stigma of sin from the practice. The ownership of one human being by another, he said, to the comfort of the slaveholding church members and to the consternation of those in the free states, was not in the category of sin. "Sin and evil are not always convertible terms," he said. "All sin is evil but not all evil is sin. Disease and pain are evils, but they are not sins; sorrow, degradation and servitude are evils but not sins."

With dismay Mr. Campbell read the reply of a man in Indiana, Nathaniel Field, to such reasoning. "I must confess that I have fears the leaders of the reformation are wanting in moral honesty as well as moral courage," Mr. Field wrote. "Of what avail will our reformation be if it is understood to sanction slavery? The Disciples in this part of the country are beginning to throw off their cowardice and their man-fearing spirit, and speak out boldly upon this subject. Silver Creek has resolved to hold no correspondence with associations that sanction slavery. Our church at this place of seventy members has resolved not to break the loaf with slave-holders, or in any way to countenance them as Christians."

Another problem which Mr. Campbell found more than mildly disturbing had to do with something he did not care to mention openly. The feeling was spreading that the fountainhead of the Movement was shifting slowly but inexorably from the hills of Bethany to the rolling country of the more centrally located and easily accessible Ohio town of Cincinnati. The feeling had started with the merger of the Campbell and Stone forces in central Kentucky, and had gained strength as such men as John T. Johnson and David Burnet had come into prominence as leaders, backed by able periodicals being issued in increasing numbers from Cincinnati. But its chief impetus had been supplied by the founding of Bacon College in Kentucky, the first institution of higher learning to be established by the Movement.

Evidence that Mr. Campbell had watched the founding of Bacon College with a wary eye is seen in the fact that it was not until December, 1837, almost two years after the school started, that he even mentioned it in the *Millennial Harbinger*. A flourishing educational institution, he was aware, would do more than anything else to localize a movement's strength.

"I have been backward hitherto to say much about the institution," he wrote then in partial apology, "until I could ascertain from its principal managers their views especially with reference to the discipline and moral culture under which the youth are to be placed. . . . I am happy to learn that such is the firm determination of each of the Trustees and faculty with whom I have conversed."

Mr. Campbell was doubtless sincere in the reason he cited for his belated commendation of the struggling Bacon College. He was profoundly concerned with the moral culture of the youth of the land as well as their academic training, a task which he felt could be accomplished only by a church-related institution. But he also had other reasons.

For one thing he was absorbed at the time in denouncing Catholicism in a debate with Catholic Bishop John B. Purcell in 1837 in Cincinnati. He had been drawn into the debate by circuitous circumstances. While attending a meeting of the Cincinnati College of Teachers in October the year before, at which he was a speaker, he had engaged in informal but agitated discussion on the use of the Bible in the common schools with a man born in Ireland like himself and possessing the same tenacious, fighting spirit, John Baptist Purcell, Bishop of the Cincinnati Diocese since 1833. The heated exchange was overheard by a group of prominent Cincinnati Protestant citizens. Already concerned over the strong Catholic flavor permeating their city's life, they prevailed upon him to engage the Bishop in formal debate.

Although such a procedure was contrary to Catholic tradition, Bishop Purcell consented, probably one of the few times a high prelate of the Catholic faith ever defended in public, open debate the validity of the church's faith against Protestant charges. The encounter took place in January of the following year, 1837, lasting from the 13th to the 21st of the month, audiences crowding the Sycamore Street Meeting House in Cincinnati for each session.

Mr. Campbell struck blow after blow at Catholic claims, convinced the Roman body was as mutable and fallible as any other sect, but his arguments were weakened by the fact he affirmed a series of negative propositions. "The Roman Catholic institution, sometimes called the Holy Catholic Apostolic Church, is not now nor was she ever catholic, apostolic or holy," he said, ". . . . but an apostasy from the only true, holy, apostolic and catholic church of Christ." He denied the validity of the apostolic succession as well as the boasted unity of the Catholic church, and equated the Roman body with "Babylon, the man of sin and the empire of the youngest horn on Daniel's sea monster." Mr. Campbell was also under the disadvantage of suffering from a severe cold, and spoke with difficulty.

No verdict was rendered, but at the conclusion of the debate the Protestant citizens of the city, led by the celebrated Dr. Lyman Beecher, president of Lane Theological Seminary, assembled and formally gave voice to the feeling that their cause had been ably upheld. It is doubtful, however, the debate seriously injured the Catholic church. Even Mr. Campbell, in referring later to the event, said, "Dr. Purcell is a bishop much nearer the papal throne since than before his victory at Cincinnati." And the reactions of two young interested observers, Peter and Glenn Burnet, members of a family which had enthusiastically joined the Campbell Movement, are revealing of the debate's effect. Glenn Burnet became a minister in the Movement and served for years in the brotherhood's expansion on the Pacific Coast. His brother, Peter, also went west, and became the first governor of California in 1850, but he left the Movement and joined the Catholic church, affirming he had been converted to it by his attendance at the Campbell-Purcell debate.

But a more pertinent reason for Mr. Campbell's attitude toward Bacon College was probably a feeling of chagrin. The college had usurped priority in the Movement's educational life.

He had dreams of establishing just such a school in his own bailiwick of Bethany, but the time to establish it had never seemed just right. Now, spurred on by the launching of Bacon College, and convinced by his encounter with Catholic thinking that the time had come to awaken the youth of America to an appreciation of Protestant principles, he began immediately to busy himself with plans to found a college of his own at Bethany.

If the founding of Bethany College by Alexander Campbell in 1840 also was timed to shift the eyes of the brotherhood away from Cincinnati and back to the hills of Virginia, it was successful beyond anybody's dream. For two years following the Purcell debate the proposed establishment of Bethany College was the topic of sermons, of discourses at cooperative meetings, of conversation at dinner tables across the brotherhood.

The uniqueness of the announced plan captured imaginations everywhere. The school was to be located on the Campbell farm at Bethany, and was to be a fourfold educational institution—a home school for boys, a college preparatory school, a college and a church. The church would be in session seven days a week, a laboratory of Christian living, influencing all other departments. The college would be the only literary college in America with a department of Sacred History and Biblical Literature, with the Bible a required textbook; it would be a college in which the formation of moral character and education were considered identical. "A scheme in which, in one word," Mr. Campbell wrote in the *Millennial Harbinger*, "the formation of moral character, the cultivation of the heart, shall be the Alpha and Omega, the radical, regulating and all controlling aim and object."

Although the original plan of a fourfold structure was soon abandoned, the central purpose of making the Bible the chief textbook, and the cultivation of moral character as essential as the inculcation of knowledge, held firm.

In 1840 a charter was obtained for Bethany College, and buildings erected on land donated by Mr. Campbell adjoining his farm. Mr. Campbell was elected president, as well as professor of Mental Philosophy, Evidences of Christianity, and of Moral and Political Economy. The school opened with 150 students enrolled in twenty classes, and almost immediately became a power in the life of the Movement. By the time of its first commencement exercises in 1843, over two thousand people journeyed from all parts of the land to witness the going forth of its first graduates, most of them embryo ministers armed with Bible truths, trained to eschew speculative theology and instead to exalt Christ and him crucified.

The attention of the brotherhood was turned again to Bethany as the center of the Movement. It would probably have continued there, and Mr. Campbell's worries on that matter put at rest, if all unwittingly he had not aroused David Burnet to action in another field which threatened to again divert eyes toward Cincinnati.

There was little of the self-assertive about David Burnet. If any conscious design formed in his mind or lurked in his heart to divert leadership of the Movement to his own area of Cincinnati, he gave no outward indication. He rejoiced in the founding of Bethany College; his communications to Mr. Campbell concerning it have the ring of complete sincerity. He even discontinued his cherished paper the *Christian Preacher*, recognizing

that with the establishment of Bethany College more adequate
means were now in operation for the training of the Movement's
leadership. But he had unharnessed zeal for promoting the cause,
and the energy to match it. Now that cooperative assemblies were
providing a framework for local and area-wide endeavors, and
preachers were provided means of training themselves, he turned
his attention toward another of the Movement's needs. The doctrine of the Movement was based on the Bible, and the brethren
therefore should all be "captives of the word of God." That meant
the Bible should be in every home. So, when Alexander Campbell
pointed out in a current issue of the *Millennial Harbinger* that,
"We can do comparatively nothing in distributing the Bible without cooperation," David Burnet seized on the statement as a
mandate for action.

He began laying plans for the establishment of a Bible Society
which would facilitate wider distribution of the Scriptures. In
his enthusiasm he wrote Mr. Campbell of his idea, confident of
his endorsement. Mr. Campbell was as ardent an advocate of
the wider distribution of the Scriptures as Mr. Burnet, and all
would doubtless have been well if Mr. Burnet had not mentioned
a seemingly trivial detail. The headquarters of the proposed Bible
Society would be in Cincinnati.

David Burnet was not the only young preacher on whom Mr.
Campbell was keeping an indulgent if watchful eye. A score of
able, dedicated and well-informed, if not well-trained, youths were
entering the ranks of leadership in the Movement, most of them
a source of pride to Mr. Campbell, a few a source of worry. Now
that Robert Richardson was helping with the paper, as time
allowed from his desk in his eight-sided study in Bethany, the
great leader undertook tour after tour in answer to pleas from
churches in all parts of the land in need of his counseling and
inspiring presence. He endeavored to make more profitable the
long stretches in his journeys by stagecoach or river steamer or
by horseback, by frequently securing as a companion a fellow
preacher with whom he could discuss the work of the churches,
preferring if possible a younger man.

Tolbert Fanning was a giant of a young man Campbell had
met on one of his visits to Nashville, Tennessee. He was six

feet six inches tall, ungainly, awkward, but with a bearing which
set him apart. Young Tolbert had been reared in a Baptist home
in rural Alabama but had disdained joining the church, rebellious
of its creedal system. In 1822 he first heard of the Campbell
doctrine, and was ripe for a reception of its emphasis on the
Bible as the sole source of authority. He was immersed five years
later in Cypress Creek in Alabama, near his father's farm home,
and in 1829 migrated to Tennessee and began to preach.

His ungainly height and his lack of education at once became
blocks in his progress. "You are neither called nor qualified to
preach; you will disgrace the cause," an irate Christian woman
told him. Another old lady put it more graphically. "You run
your legs too far through your breeches," she said. "Go home
and go to plowing."

But young Tolbert had determined on his course. The first step
was to get an education. He was without funds but he was not
without ingenuity, and he applied that quality not only to secure
the means of going on to school but to put into practice the
Christian ministry to which he felt called. He hired himself out
as a farm hand; he ran a cotton gin, he bred horses but he also
preached as he could gather people about him. Lacking a place,
he invented one. Men loafing about a saloon provided a ready
audience for him; Methodist camp meetings were made-to-order
occasions. At one such meeting he strode up to the "mourners'
bench" after watching a man agonize at it in an effort to be
assured of his salvation, and tore the seat and railing from their
moorings, explaining to the startled seeker the more simple route
to the Throne. Happening on a slave sale one day in Murfreesboro,
Tennessee, he mounted a nearby tree stump and began preaching
against slavery. He evidently embellished his sermon with vivid
language, for the surprised crowd turned from the sale to listen.
The owner of the slaves, left with no buyers, was incensed and the
next day filed suit against Tolbert Fanning, charging him with
"inflaming slaves to riot." It was a serious charge, and a long
trial ensued, but the court found Fanning not guilty as charged.

By 1833 Tolbert Fanning had accumulated sufficient funds to
enter the University of Nashville, graduating in two years, tele-
scoping the four-year course. It was during this time that he
attended what was once the First Baptist Church of Nashville,

but which had been brought over almost intact into the Campbell Movement under the leadership of a dapper, eloquent, sagacious man named Phillip Slater Fall.

Encouraged by Mr. Fall, and doubtless aware of the admiring glances of Mr. Fall's sister Charlotte, young Tolbert, now twenty-five years old, began to preach in earnest, snatching, as he later claimed, men as branding irons from eternal destruction. It is of record that he baptized hundreds, and started scores of churches in Tennessee, implanting in them a passion for the doctrine of the Movement. Such activity was not long in coming to the attention of Mr. Campbell.

Mr. Campbell invited the young man to visit him in Bethany, and to accompany him on a short tour. It was a congenial occasion, and a longer tour, one of over three months' duration, followed in 1836, extending into New England and on into Canada. The two men became close friends; they were seasick together on Lake Erie; they shared the same bed in villages where accommodations were limited; they read and relished the same books. Such intimate contact with the great Campbell left its mark, and Tolbert Fanning was never again the same.

If it was the purpose of Alexander Campbell to inculcate in the young preachers with whom he toured his concern that the Movement remain a Bible-centered movement, he succeeded remarkably well with Tolbert Fanning. The Bible became for Fanning not only the infallible source of all belief, but the only source. It was to be interpreted literally; it was to be believed word for word; it was to be adopted precept by precept. Those who did anything less were bordering on heresy.

Shortly after Fanning's return from his long tour with Mr. Campbell he married a young woman in Nicholasville, Kentucky, Sarah Shreeve, and may have intended settling in Kentucky. But within a few months the bride died, and Tolbert returned to Tennessee to assuage his grief. He was so successful that, on December 22 of the same year, 1836, he was united in marriage with Philip Fall's sister Charlotte.

In every way Charlotte was a match for her virile young husband. She was teaching in Nashville at the time of her marriage, and was possessed of a brilliant mind. She could read and write in six languages—Hebrew, Greek, Latin, French, German and English. She also had a remarkably fine singing voice. She was a year older than her husband, and more aware of social amenities; and their home soon became the center of much of the cultural life of Middle Tennessee.

For a brief time Tolbert and Charlotte Fanning lived in the village of Franklin, close by Nashville, operating a female school and aligning its curriculum so thoroughly with the doctrine of the new Movement that every subject taught, of whatever nature, was based on biblical passages. In addition, Tolbert Fanning ran a farm, experimented in crop rotation, bred fine animals, became a judge of thoroughbred stock at county fairs, and preached every Sunday and on many weekdays. His energy and zeal fore-shadowed the role he was to play in the Campbell Movement as it expanded. And so did his uncompromising nature.

CHAPTER IX

The Starting Flag Is Down!

Although churches of the Movement were appearing in the nation's larger cities as those urban centers developed, the brotherhood's strength continued during the nineteenth century to be centered in small towns and rural areas. Here doctrinal disputes and war on moral conditions of the times, dance halls and fancy women, "spot" cards and whiskey drinking, absorbed their time and attention. Political problems which dominated talk in every blacksmith shop and every crossroads store were left for the most part to the unwashed, the unsaved, the unimmersed.

But in 1842, triggered by news that one of the preachers of the Movement in Illinois, Edward D. Baker, had run for Congress, defeating a man named Abraham Lincoln in the Whig primary election in San Gamon County, a question was suddenly on everybody's lips: should a Christian take part in politics?

The answers were mixed. Some felt entanglement in political affairs was a trap to ensnare the unwary Christian with the lure of public acclaim; some were convinced it meant compromising a man's conscience; to others it threatened the diluting of Gospel preaching. A few of the more cautious preachers held the view that Christian preachers should avoid entanglement because of its dangers to their freedom. They knew something of the historic trials of the early dissenters, when even "entertaining dangerous opinions" on the part of the clergy had been the cause for civil punishment, and they were not inclined to risk any alliance with civil authorities, even in a land avowedly democratic. Political pressures could still be exerted, and such tactics did not coincide with their idea of remaining free in a free church.

But a more significant argument, one peculiar to the Bible-loving people of the Movement and one which was to echo later in louder tones, was advanced by Barton W. Stone, now living in Illinois, as the question gained momentum.

Where in the Bible did God give authority to any uninspired man, or set of men, to legislate or make laws for the governing of men? The question took root in the conscience of the brethren, and came to fruition in some remarkable conclusions. The making of human laws argues the imperfection of God's laws, men were soon saying; the task implies that human wisdom is superior to the wisdom of God and can frame a better government.

Mr. Stone had moved to the northern state of Illinois a year following the merger of his followers in Kentucky with those of Mr. Campbell, one reason being his desire to live in a slave-free state. He thus carried to his new home not only his passion for the unity of all Christians, but his abhorrence of the slavery system. And it was this feeling that prompted his reasoning.

"God alone knows what is right or wrong, virtuous or vicious," he pointed out in his *Christian Messenger,* which he continued to edit from his home in Jacksonville, Illinois. "God alone can detect the difference between virtue and vice. . . . God has given us laws sufficient to govern the world. Were all mankind obedient to the laws given by the Lord of heaven and earth, we should have need of no others to make us blest and happy."

It is not surprising that such sentiments soon involved Mr. Stone in the radical stand of calling for a denunciation of any law which a Christian considered immoral. Abolitionist sentiment was growing in the North, and he did not escape the contagion of its agitation. Did not the Apostles resist the civil powers when they were forbidden to teach? Did they not choose instead to obey God? As the pressure against him on such a stand increased, he relented only enough to say, "I am determined to support any earthly government and not resist the power under which I live, provided there be no collusion between their orders and the laws of God. If there should be, we will obey God rather than man at the loss of all earthly goods!"

Barton Stone was to live only a few short months after he took his stand. His death in the fall of 1844 silenced his voice, but its echo reverberated across the brotherhood and found lodgment in the hearts of Christians in both North and South. One of them was a young preacher in Warren, Ohio, named Isaac Errett who was to reemphasize Mr. Stone's radical position in regard to nullification of the law a few years later in a pamphlet he entitled *The Design of Civil Government and Extent of Its Authority*. It was to rock the brotherhood.

Walter Scott had continued not only to agitate the slavery question, but as the matter of the propriety of a Christian engaging in politically controversial issues gained momentum, he voiced the view that a Christian should not only take part in political life when a moral issue existed but should consent to hold office. In the course of his turbulent life, Mr. Scott was to put this principle into action by involving himself in several political movements, most of them designed to better the lot of the workingman. His intense nature compelled him to identify with every sufferer, to feel every hurt. But his passion for proclaiming the Gospel still held priority. Political solutions had their place, and political action was not to be ignored, but a better and more lasting solution was to be found in the Gospel of Jesus Christ.

As the problem of slavery inflamed the nation, abolitionist sentiment strengthened in his village of Carthage on the outskirts of Cincinnati. Mr. Scott witnessed his fellow Christians swept into the vortex of the clamor; he felt that preachers were relegating to second place their main task of preaching the Gospel. By 1844 he was in despair. His paper the *Evangelist* seemed a neglected cry in a war-maddened world. Almost on impulse he announced he was discontinuing the paper and moving back to Pittsburg.

For the next five, fruitful years the visionary, temperamental evangelist resumed his life in Pittsburg, glorying in the gladsome task of reminding men that the Gospel of Jesus Christ alone could offer lasting solutions to man's ills. He organized a small church and, as God gave him the strength, went into neighboring states, holding revival meetings. Occasionally he emerged to speak before larger groups, intermittently displaying flashes of his old oratorical power. But the days of his glory as a preacher to thousands were over, and he found satisfaction instead in trudging from house to house, carrying the Gospel in word and in deed.

"O, that God may water what I have planted!" he wrote in his diary one day after marching up the great slopes of the towering western Pennsylvania hills. "With firm elastic tread I marched to the mountain, and descended running; the entire length of the hill did not exhaust me." Other entries in his diary reveal his enlarging conception of the task of the minister. "A pastoral visit," he wrote, "discovers the sore and enables the shepherd to put his finger on it on the spot. Publicly, a minister can say more, but do less. Privately, his field is narrowed down to the smallest possible dimensions and, with the power brought thus near to the machinery, he acts with the greatest possible effect." Other entries indicate how he put his new concept into practice. "Sought to reclaim an erring brother. Visited another in reference to a family Bible. Called on a few families. Promised a Bible and Testament to a poor black woman. Saw a young wife who with her husband was six months only in this country. Spoke with a family touching a family Bible, and with an acquaintance, an alien, on giving us a hearing."

At the conclusion of Alexander Campbell's short excursion into political life in 1829, he had written a friend: "I am conscious that many are infatuated with the charms of political life, but it has none for me. I have more pleasure in thinking on man's eternal destiny . . . than in all the splendid schemes of earthly ambition and political grandeur." No evidence exists to indicate he agreed with Barton Stone as to the sin of such activity, nor with those who held that the strength of the church would thereby be dissipated, nor even with those who later justified abstaining on scriptural grounds. He was concerned at the time only with the need to avoid divisive controversy on public questions as long as possible within the ranks of the brotherhood.

This may have played its part, early in 1843, in Mr. Campbell's ready acceptance of an invitation to debate a Presbyterian preacher, Dr. Nathan L. Rice of Paris, Kentucky, on the issues which separated the two bodies. While he was profoundly concerned with illuminating the two positions, he also doubtless hoped the debate would turn attention back to doctrinal matters and away from the explosive subject of slavery, renewing and strengthening a sense of solidarity among his followers.

Leaders in all religious sects were seeking to forestall division over slavery within their ranks, and the Presbyterians in Kentucky were doubtless actuated somewhat by this motive. But they also had other reasons. The Movement had made alarming inroads on their churches; their members now numbered slightly over eight thousand, while the Disciples claimed over forty thousand members in the state. A debate exposing the Movement's errors would break its hold in central Kentucky and retard its progress.

The debate lasted sixteen days, and was moderated by the great Henry Clay, attracting thousands to the Main Street Christian Church in Lexington. It riveted attention for the time, as Mr. Campbell had foreseen, on matters other than political, but its eventual value was even more significant.

Dr. Rice was an able theologian, but he proved to be an opponent who confused religion and theology, and insisted on debating opinions. When Mr. Campbell realized the points of difference between the Presbyterians and Disciples could not be clarified as long as opinions instead of facts were called in question, he launched into a summary which, all unwittingly, consolidated for the first time in a single, penetrating statement the purpose and position of the Movement clarifying for its followers the direction it should take in history.

"It is not the object of our efforts to make men think alike on a thousand themes," he said. "Let them think as they like on any matters of human opinion. . . . I have learned not only the theory but the fact that if you wish opinionism to cease, you must not call up and debate everything that men think and say. . . . We receive men of all denominations under heaven, of all sects and parties who will make the Good Confession on which Jesus Christ built his church. . . . On a sincere confession of this faith we immerse all persons, and then present them with God's own book as their book of faith, piety and morality."

The debate, and especially the summary of the Movement's basic principles, served to solidify the bonds of brotherhood more strongly, even, than Mr. Campbell had anticipated.

The several hundred preachers attending the debate were thoughtful men; all of them carried a sense of responsibility for the furtherance of the Movement. Their allegiance to Mr. Campbell was total and sincere, and they rejoiced in his generally conceded victory in the debate. Now that he had clarified what they hoped was for once and all time the vague purpose and confused doctrine of the Movement, their concern turned to a similar clarification of what should constitute its organizational framework.

Several informal meetings of the preachers had been held during the time of the debate, all confined to mutual edification and profit. But toward the close of the two-week period another meeting was held of which only a scant record exists. It was convened in the basement of the Main Street Christian Church where the debate was held, and the fact that the name of Alexander Campbell is not included among the sixty-five men listed as present gives credence to the supposition that something was to be discussed involving matters he was apparently avoiding. The gathering included such leaders as David Burnet, John O'Kane, John T. Johnson, "Raccoon" John Smith, James Shannon, L. L. Pinkerton and others.

The single record of the meeting indicates that upon motion of Elder John O'Kane it was agreed "the organization of the brotherhood" be considered. A committee of five, headed by David Burnet, was appointed to present this touchy subject in the tangible form of a plan of action when the group reassembled the next morning at eight o'clock. But no further meeting was apparently held. What put a stop to it is still a matter of conjecture.

It is a matter of record, however, that almost immediately more pointed and urgent articles on various facets of "Church Organization" began flowing from the pen of Mr. Campbell. Other series of articles on this topic had appeared in the *Millennial Harbinger* from time to time, but none of them came to grips with an actual plan for establishing a connectional framework among the churches. Now Mr. Campbell boldly discussed a national cooperative assembly as possibly needful in expediting the work of the church, qualifying his seeming endorsement, however, with the proviso that it not be vested with authority to legislate for the churches.

In January, 1845, David Burnet's dream of establishing a Bible Society came to fruition with the organization of the American Christian Bible Society with headquarters in Cincinnati. It marked a significant milestone as the first national agency in the Movement. It presented an imposing constitution, a representative board of trustees and a shrewd selection of officers. David Burnet was president, and among the nine vice-presidents was listed the name of Alexander Campbell.

Mr. Campbell might have received the Bible Society with good grace, and possibly followed it with a plan for a nationwide organization to further other objectives, if Mr. Burnet had not proceeded almost at once to organize also what promised to amount to a brotherhood publishing house. It was called a Sunday School and Tract Society, a society Mr. Burnet conceived as necessary to print the Bible and other materials, which by their usage in the churches would establish a binding cord in the sprawling body.

The number of periodicals which had come into existence across the country had increased. Most of them articulated the particular views of a single individual, responsible only to himself. While Mr. Campbell realized that none of them, limited as they were in circulation, could ever threaten again in influence the leadership of the great *Millennial Harbinger*, he had no such assurance that other printed matter issued elsewhere would not challenge the preeminence of that which was pouring from the press he had by this time installed on the banks of Buffaloe Creek in Bethany. Pamphlets, books, sermons, tracts and songbooks were issued in an almost constant stream. As the fountainhead of literature for the Movement, the Campbell press at Bethany was taken for granted, and he had no wish to see it replaced.

A few months after the formation of the Sunday School and Tract Society, the *Millennial Harbinger* carried the first of its attacks, not directly on the publishing venture but hitting it by flank attack on the Bible Society.

An article by a well-known preacher, Aylett Raines, a close friend of Mr. Campbell's, denounced the Bible Society as unnecessary, claiming "more good can be accomplished through existing societies." As a footnote to the article, Mr. Campbell endorsed the view of Mr. Raines and supplemented it with a happy line of reasoning. His former friends, the Baptists, Mr. Campbell said, were endeavoring to distribute the Scriptures, and he wished his followers to cooperate with them. This would be a means of exhibiting to the world that a spirit of unity and goodwill prevailed between the two bodies, repudiating the well-founded rumor that a grudge lingered between them. The union of effort would go "to demonstrate that, while they have very unjustly reprobated and badly treated us, we have no desire to retaliate. . . . Such cooperation on our part will likely lead them to reflect upon their measures." He concluded by pointing out, "The Baptists are so shamefully opposed by sectarian pedobaptists that their former comrades should stand by them."

Mr. Campbell must have suspected that some knowledgeable people would not harken to that argument, for he supplemented it with another reason for his opposition to the Bible Society. It was because the brotherhood as a whole had not established it; hence, the brotherhood could not be called upon to support it financially. Especially, he went on to point out, since other institutions, such as Bethany College, had a prior claim.

The reference to Bethany College's prior claim brought an instant rejoiner from David Burnet. "Was there a convention of the churches to establish Bethany College, the claims of which must now be heard?" he wrote in angry reply. "And until they are heard, the Bible Society must die in despair? The Society, composed of hundreds, cannot ask aid of their brethren but Bethany College, called into being by one brother, may?"

The patronizing tone of Mr. Campbell's response was probably not designed to aggravate the situation, but it did little to mend it. He implied that Mr. Burnet appeared oversensitive and superexcited; that his manner of expressing himself did him injustice. "I shall not, therefore," he concluded, "respond in that spirit."

For a while the deepening cleavage between the two men was given time to heal by the departure of Alexander Campbell in May, 1847, for Great Britain at the invitation of the fledgling churches of the Movement which had come into existence in that part of the world. Mr. Campbell had not been back to his native land since his leave-taking as a youth of twenty, now almost forty years ago, but his message had penetrated many hearts, and churches there were numerous and increasingly influential. He sailed on the S.S. *Siddon,* and it is of record that David Burnet went to New York to see him off. What passed between the two men at the time is not known.

Mr. Campbell's two months in the British Isles were not without incident. He preached forty-three times in his travels through the length of the country, and was hailed everywhere as an acknowledged religious leader. And, much to his chagrin, he was also hailed in Scotland as a slaveholder, and a "defender of man-stealers" by an irresponsible but crafty former Baptist preacher who was at the time affiliated with the Morrisonians, the most intolerant of the sects in Scotland. In refuting the charge, Mr. Campbell was arrested for libel. Rather than accept bail offered by his friends, he spent ten days in a Glasgow jail. When the case came to trial, it was dismissed for lack of evidence, and his accuser fled to France.

In addition, he was ill much of the time, and while the trip was exhilarating it was also exhausting. The toll it took on his health was accentuated by news which greeted him upon his return home. His youngest son Wickliffe, of whom he was especially proud, had drowned in Buffaloe Creek. The blow was staggering, and for a time blotted out all else. It was feared by many that Alexander Campbell, now past sixty years of age, would never again be the same.

But with a resiliency which characterized him, he resumed leadership of the brotherhood, now generally being called the Disciples of Christ. It claimed 120,000 members and ranked sixth among the Protestant bodies in America. To relinquish the oversight of such a growing movement was not in his plans, and as if to combat the general concern over his health, he summoned strength to assert a more militant stance. Moral societies, and especially the Masonic Order, were increasing in number and influence in America, threatening, Mr. Campbell believed, to usurp the church and desecrate God with their religious rites and ceremonies. Along with many preachers in the Movement, he had taken a stand against them. An opportunity to denounce them, as well as avert the threat he feared to his leadership in the spreading influence of David Burnet, came soon after his return from Great Britain. He discovered David Burnet's name listed on a program for an address at the cornerstone laying of a Masonic Hall at Mount Pleasant, Ohio.

"My indignation burned at the appearance of Mr. Burnet's name in such a connection," he wrote in the *Millennial Harbinger*.

"I could neither understand nor believe it to be a proper representation of his position. I call for his defense!"

It is evident from his many references to Mr. Campbell that David Burnet loved the great man despite their differences. Whatever impulse he may have had to reject or simply ignore Mr. Campbell's demand for an explanation of what was in the nature of his own private business, he resisted. He was a proud man and cherished his own dignity, but he loved the church even more, and would allow no pride or place to interfere with its progress. The sparring and half-concealed hostility between him and Mr. Campbell must come to an end. Humbly, almost hat in hand, he wrote in reply: "My name was inserted in that program contrary to my request and without my knowledge. Consequently, the address was not delivered."

But Alexander Campbell was not to be so easily quieted. He made no further reference to the matter, but he did hit upon another grievance, perpetrated this time by one of David Burnet's close friends, Alexander Hall.

The man Hall had had the termerity to issue a statistical "Register" of the new churches, a factual if not wholly accurate listing, without Mr. Campbell's authority. With poorly concealed scorn, Mr. Campbell wrote in the *Millennial Harbinger*: "Mr. Hall has not done a good job; he has in fact meddled in too many things to do anything well. Furthermore there is too much of this uncalled-for and irresponsible editorship."

Such a skirmish might have little significance if it had not, through Mr. Campbell's subsequent embarrassment over it, contributed to bringing into existence the first national assembly of the brethren. For Mr. Campbell learned that the statistical matter in Mr. Hall's scorned "Register" had not been gathered with any help from David Burnet but had been furnished by his own close confidant, a man in his employ, one F. T. M. Arny.

This embarrassing incident, seemingly trivial though it was, displayed the nobility in Mr. Campbell's makeup which was at the essence of his being. He was a proud man but a quality of greatness transcended all else, and now he humbled himself. He took an honest and hard look at the conditions of the brotherhood he had brought into being which would allow such a lack of communication to occur.

What he saw was not too pleasant. Preachers were milling about at will, and churches were following a variety of patterns, each a law unto itself. The only points of contact afforded preachers with each other, or churches with other congregations, were the loosely formed cooperative gatherings which scrupulously avoided anything resembling the exercise of authority, and were tolerated only because they were without that authority. No means existed for the planning or execution of any task too big for a single church, or a small group of them, and benevolent impulses in the brotherhood of necessity died aborning.

This state of affairs may have been sufficient for the needs of the Movement in its early days, but it was functioning now in a changed nation, the conditions under which it was continuing to grow demanded change. The religious forces in the country had supplied a driving power to the nation's expansion, and had received a thrust from it. Back in 1834, when the Movement was evolving into a separate religious body, and its preachers labored for the most part under raw frontier conditions, each of necessity had to be a law unto himself. One such preacher, John Baugh, had pioneered at that time in the unsettled Michigan Territory, where the land had recently been wrestled from the Indians, "the footsteps of whom are yet to be seen in almost every direction," he had written Mr. Campbell in 1834. "But now they are gone, their cornfields laid waste. On the first of the month a church of Jesus Christ was organized within about one mile of Dubuque with eight members, and at candlelight they communed again, and two more were added to the little unit."

Now, in little more than a decade, a steady migration of people had invaded the land, and the little units, meeting by candlelight under simple rules and procedures of their own devising to fit the primitive circumstances, were being replaced by congregations feeling the influence of the rising sophistication of the people. Even geographical boundaries had changed to meet changing needs. One of the Movement's preachers, John Box, had lived for thirteen years in a log house on the Mississippi River, which shifted its political location during that time from Michigan Territory to Wisconsin Territory, then to Iowa Territory, and finally came to rest in the state of Iowa. Such preachers had developed a pattern of independent action, embedded in them by their circumstances and by the Movement itself. But as their experience widened, and their insight sharpened, their independent stance had been shaken by the discovery that the freedom every man cherished—social, political, economic as well as religious—was not to be obtained by allowing every man his way.

Within a few months Mr. Campbell began another series of articles in the *Millennial Harbinger* on "Church Organization," and came to grips with reality. Human ecclesiastical societies, he reminded his brethren, were unauthorized by the scriptures; they tended to infringe on the autonomy of the local church; their support could become a test of fellowship; their actions could be the source of divisive controversy. What did the brethren want to do? Did they desire to take the risks of creating a national clearing house? Did they wish to bring into being a brotherhood-wide cooperative organization?

The answers were mixed. Many were dubious of the wisdom of venturing to surmount the risks involved. But others felt the ends to be achieved outweighed the calculated dangers.

Braving the unsettled climate of opinion, Mr. Campbell finally said: "Nature's laws and powers, singly and alone, never operate. She completes nothing by single efforts. Atoms come together and mountains rise. Drops mingle into floods and oceans spread over immense channels. Planets circle around their suns and systems of worlds are formed. . . . Thus nature is one grand cooperative system."

And on this lofty note of authority from nature itself, he at last called for a meeting of the brethren, "to discuss and possibly set in motion" a national organization.

"A church in the aggregate," he said in substance with an eye to those still standing with reluctant feet, "is the same as the Kingdom of God, with officers belonging to the whole kingdom."

CHAPTER X

The City of Confusion

"One move from the Bible and its practices, and we are in the quagmire of party corruption!"

Leading the chorus of such warnings, as the call went out from Mr. Campbell for a national convention, was the voice of Tolbert Fanning in Nashville, Tennessee. Ironically, Mr. Fanning echoed convictions Mr. Campbell himself had planted in the young man's legalistic mind ten years before—convictions which had grown more rigid with passing time, but which, in Mr. Campbell's mind, had mellowed. To Tolbert Fanning the first giant step was about to be taken in departure from the Bible and its practices.

His warning was carried in the pages of the *Christian Review*, a magazine he had started in 1844 to combat what he sensed as a "creeping liberality of thought" among the brethren. The paper was to live only three short years, but in that time it accurately reflected a hardening mood in a segment of the brotherhood against a lessening of scriptural authority, and became the instrument of precipitating some pertinent questions. The demise of the paper was the result of an intriguing series of circumstances.

The plain-speaking Tolbert Fanning, with his talented wife Charlotte, had moved from Franklin, Tennessee, to another and larger farm closer to Nashville which they called Elm Crag. Here they again conducted a flourishing college, Franklin College, enrolling two hundred young men and a group of young ladies. For fourteen years this college was to continue as a powerhouse of strength for those who sought to restore the primitive church in literal form. The larger farm also enabled Mr. Fanning to indulge more thoroughly in his hobby of farming and stockbreeding. He had become a rigid perfectionist, and he advised all farmers to knock in the head all scrub cattle, sheep and hogs, and concentrate on thoroughbred animals. He introduced the Morgan strain of horses in the state of Tennessee, and enjoyed nothing better than breaking horses to harness and saddle on his training track. Blue ribbons won at stock fairs adorned the walls of his house, evidence of his pride in his heifer and bull calves, his stallions, boars and sows. He ran his school with the same goal of perfection he demanded on his farm, a trait that lent credence to his reputation for being a tyrannical man. Certainly he did not suffer fools gladly.

Soon after starting his paper, he found his duties so many and varied he sought help in editing it. His eye fell on Jesse Ferguson, a young preacher who had recently assumed the pastorate of the church in Nashville. In 1845 Mr. Fanning persuaded him to become co-editor of the journal. The young man was grounded in the Bible, and his sound convictions, Mr. Fanning felt, would emphasize the primacy of the Scriptures.

Jesse Ferguson was evidently possessed of a charm that captivated all hearts. He was six feet tall, lithe and graceful, with flowing black hair and a wide, ready smile; a man of vital energy with the gift of impassioned speech. His eloquence was attracting such crowds to the Nashville church that the members pitched in and raised thirty thousand dollars to erect one of the most commodious church structures yet to adorn Nashville's streets.

For a time all went well as the two Bible-based editors worked side by side, and Mr. Fanning congratulated himself on selecting such an assistant; it was evidence of his keen ability to judge men. He claimed he could hear a boy walk on the upper floor at his school and tell what kind of man he would make. "A bigoted fellow," he said, "takes long strides, lighting on the heels of his boots, making as much noise as an ass with his hoofs shod."

He soon became aware, however, that Jesse Ferguson was not using his brilliance and eloquence humbly, as a gift from God. But Mr. Fanning rationalized this shortcoming; it was the result of the tendency of churches to embrace what was becoming known as the "pastoral system," the system, advocated by David Burnet, of having a settled, salaried pastor in each congregation.

"The best preacher in the world," Mr. Fanning wrote in an early blast at what he considered this departure from apostolic practices, "preaching three times every Lord's Day to keep the saints alive, will kill them spiritually, and, without great care, eternally." A definite salary, such as Mr. Burnet advocated, was the ruination of a preacher; there was no need for a bargain to be struck between a preacher and his supporting congregation. Preachers should "plow in hope and walk by faith." A salary was corrupting in its tendency; it stifled exertion and begot habits of idleness. "Preachers who sell their chatty and pompous Sunday speeches for gold," he said, "rest as a deadly incubus upon all churches over which they preside. The system kills the congregation by inactivity, by spiritual stupor, by pride."

Holding such views, it was easy for him to place the blame for Jesse Ferguson's less admirable traits on the Nashville church, which had tempted him with a specified salary. But soon he realized Mr. Ferguson was showing other disturbing tendencies. He was inserting into Mr. Fanning's paper a version of Bible truth with which Mr. Fanning had not reckoned. It had to do with a belief in a second chance for each sinner after death. At first the references were mild, but as they became more specific Mr. Fanning became embarrassed. Rather than denounce Mr. Ferguson, however, he deemed it more prudent to simply dissolve the partnership. He withdrew, turning the paper over to the young preacher, who promptly renamed it the *Christian,* and began giving full utterance to other newfound truths.

After a few issues of the *Christian* had rolled from the press, even Tolbert Fanning conceded Mr. Ferguson's shortcomings could no longer in all fairness be attributed to David Burnet's heretical pastoral system. The man was advocating not only the view that salvation was possible for a sinner after death, but a belief in "spirit rappings," a doctrine utterly foreign to the Movement. Soon he claimed to be in communication with individuals in another world.

Mr. Fanning's confidence in his judgment of men suffered a severe jolt. He chose, however, to ignore Mr. Ferguson rather than rebuke him. But not so Alexander Campbell.

Back in Bethany, Mr. Campbell had for some time been viewing with a jaundiced eye the raucous clamor raised by such papers as that of Jesse Ferguson. He had rebuked Mr. Hall for issuing his statistical "Register," and now he turned his guns on others. "The unlicensed press in our Movement is the most fearful omen on my horizon," he wrote. "We have been most reckless in choosing our editors, our scribes, our elders and our preachers. We have a brood of periodicals the most irresponsible I have ever known. Some editors just out of the shell of conversion; a youth converted this year, the next a preacher, in the next a scribe, then an editor." And then he singled out the vulnerable Ferguson. "Mr. Ferguson assumes the Bible authorizes preaching to disembodied spirits," he wrote. "There is not one passage intimating that any Apostle ever did this—it is a figment of a daring imagination, as baseless as a dream of morning." Without mincing words, he called upon the Nashville church to repudiate Jesse Ferguson and his views.

The result was confusion compounded.

Jesse Ferguson refused to answer Mr. Campbell's criticism of his views until he was acknowledged to be within his rightful bounds of Christian liberty in holding them. He was as free, he maintained, as was Alexander Campbell to theorize without being accused of heresy. "When have opinions become a test of fellowship?" he asked. "Why does Mr. Campbell dare call on the church in Nashville to regulate my preaching?"

When his questions went unanswered, he shifted to biting personal comments, a form of attack designed to ruin the reputation of the opponent and not his arguments, and which set a pattern for much of the controversy that was to plague the brotherhood in years to come. Alexander Campbell, he said, could never be like the rest of mortals, partly right and partly wrong. Every opponent to him was a knave and a fool; he was always right. Yet he was never more wrong than when he assumed an authority over every man's conscience.

As the warfare between the two men continued, the great Nashville church, once filled to overflowing, began having some vacant seats. And in 1856 the congregation split asunder. Both groups claimed ownership of the fine building, and the matter was taken to the civil courts. The decision favored those who repudiated Mr. Ferguson and his strange beliefs as contrary to the doctrine on which the church had been built, and was binding.

But the emotions aroused, unfortunately, were not subject to civil authority. Soon thereafter the coveted structure mysteriously caught fire and burned to the ground one stormy night, and all that remained of the once proud building were piles of charred timber. Jesse Ferguson was referred to thereafter as the "Fallen Ferguson." He became a forlorn figure, an inglorious, wandering star among the brethren until his death in 1864. His significance in history is due solely to the fact the questions he raised did not die with him. The extent of the realm of opinion and the sufficiency of the New Testament to supply minute instructions for today's church became thereafter lively issues.

Now, as the call for a general convention rang over the land, came a chorus echoing Tolbert Fanning's warning, "Where is the scriptural authority for such a gathering?"

Alexander Campbell had a reply.

"To ask for a positive precept for everything in the details of duties growing out of the various exigencies of the Christian church and the world," he said in the *Millennial Harbinger*, "would be quite as irrational and unscriptural as to ask for an immutable wardrobe or a uniform standard of apparel for all persons and ages. . . . In all things pertaining to public interest, not of Christian faith, piety or morality, the church of Jesus Christ in its aggregate character is left free and unshackled by any apostolic authority."

They were brave words, but nevertheless, when the brethren assembled 156 strong at the Christian Church at Eighth and Walnut streets in Cincinnati on the morning of October 23, 1849, the high-backed chair on the platform reserved for Mr. Campbell was empty. William K. Pendleton, his right-hand man in the administration of Bethany College, and now co-editor of the *Millennial Harbinger*, explained his absence as due to illness. It was probably true, although Mr. Campbell was at the time striving to dispel the rumor that his health was failing and, according to records, was up and about his duties at Bethany within a few days. At any rate the historic gathering convened without him and resolved itself into a "General Convention of the Christian Churches of the United States of America," a cumbersome title that was soon discarded. It was not only unwieldly but, worse, it smacked of designating the convention as an official organization of the churches instead of a voluntary assembling of interested individuals.

For that is what it was. With the exception of a group from Indiana, those attending were self-appointed, a procedure contrary to the wishes of both Mr. Campbell and David Burnet, who had urged that only "chosen delegates" attend. This made of the first convention of the Movement a mass meeting with no authority, no responsibility, its actions advisory only. As the years passed attempts were made to transform it into a delegated body, but the attempts were futile and the mass convention established a pattern that was to continue for over a century.

Alexander Campbell's leadership of the Movement was duly recognized, despite his absence, by his election as president, a position he was to hold until his death. David Burnet was chosen first vice-president. Nineteen additional vice-presidents were elected representing such diverse schools of thought as Walter Scott, John O'Kane, John T. Johnson, W. K. Pendleton and Tolbert Fanning.

The presence of Walter Scott was especially gratifying. The death of his beloved wife Sarah a few months previously had aroused for him the sympathy of the brotherhood, and he was greeted upon his arrival from Pittsburg with a show of affection that indicated his early labors were not forgotten. The expression of affection was evidently contagious, for within a few months Walter Scott found himself another wife in the person of Miss Annie Allen of Mayslick, Kentucky. Together they moved to Covington, Kentucky, and began operating a school. But the new Mrs. Scott lived only three years, and again Walter Scott became a suffering, searching soul. His search led him to Mason County, where the following year he remarried, this time a wealthy but austere widow. Soon it became apparent to the watching eyes of concerned friends that the widow had little patience with her new husband's erratic ways, and Walter Scott's turbulent life closed on a discordant marital note in 1861.

A variety of pertinent matters consumed the time of the week-long convention, but it was the question propounded on the second morning by John T. Johnson that resulted in its most significant action.

"Is not the purpose of our being here," Mr. Johnson asked, "to form a missionary society?"

The question was deceptively simple. Everybody agreed that missionary work should be undertaken. But how? To the literal-minded there was a significant difference between "cooperation," which many, influenced by Mr. Campbell's position, had come to accept, and "organization," which thereby created a body not ordained by God to do the work of the church.

But tall, determined John T. Johnson was of no mind to permit such quibbling to forestall longer his determination to obey the Great Commission. The order was clear; the method of obeying it was secondary. In meticulous, legal phrasing he presented a resolution calling for the creation of a missionary society to spread the Gospel abroad.

A goodly portion of those who listened to his plea for passage of the resolution were conquered by his sincerity, if not convinced of the scriptural soundness of his plan. Before the convention adjourned, it formed from itself a working arm, an organization called the American Christian Missionary Society, to join the Bible Society and the Publication Society as another, and vastly more significant, national brotherhood agency.

The decision to come to grips with its missionary obligation had not been an impulsive gesture. The conscience of the brotherhood had been prodded for some time by a comparatively unknown man, a medical doctor named James T. Barclay.

James Thomas Barclay, born in 1807, was a member of a well-to-do Tidewater family of Virginia. He married into an even more well-to-do family in 1829, that of Miss Julia Ann Sowers, when she was but seventeen years of age. At the time of their marriage neither James nor Julia Ann were even nominal members of a church. But both possessed visionary natures and were of a religious bent. James had been educated at the University of Virginia and later finished a medical course at the University of Pennsylvania. He soon found medicine held little attraction for him, but dutifully set up in practice at Charlottesville, Virginia. And here a smoldering dream of James and Julia Ann to carry the cross of Jesus Christ to remote corners of the world burst into flame. They joined the Presbyterian church and offered themselves as missionaries to go to China.

For some reason the Presbyterian Board refused to send them, or it may be that the entreaties of the young doctor's mother, recently bereaved by the death of her only other son, prevailed. At any rate, the doctor and his wife gave up the idea for a time and tried to settle down to a life of comfort and complacency in a pleasant cottage in Charlottesville.

James Barclay's father, Thomas Jefferson Barclay, had been a warm friend of both George Washington and Thomas Jefferson. He served as Washington's first consul to France, and when Jefferson became President he appointed his namesake as Commissioner to the Emperor of Morocco. Mr. Barclay died while James was still a youth and his widow remarried Captain John Harris, but the youth was always aware of his father's friendship with the great Jefferson and cherished the association. He was aware, also, of Thomas Jefferson's financial troubles which began soon after the Embargo Proclamation dried up markets for grain and tobacco, and which were accentuated by Jefferson's continued high scale of living, the poor judgment of his overseers, and his carelessness in endorsing notes for faithless friends.

Following Jefferson's death in 1826 the famous house he had built, Monticello, and 3700 acres of the land he loved, was liquidated to settle his debts, and James Barclay bought the estate, paying $3000 cash for it plus the home he owned in Charlottesville, valued at $4500. The house remained furnished just as Jefferson had left it, even to the lamps on his tables, his iron bedsteads immovably attached to the walls, his herbarium filled with rare flowers. There young Dr. Barclay and his wife, Julia Ann, lived and there two of their three children, Robert and Judson, later to become the son-in-law of Alexander Campbell, were born and rocked in the Jefferson family cradle. But visitors and curiosity seekers constantly invaded the privacy of the Barclay family. After three years they were glad to accept the offer of a Mr. Levy of $10,000 for the estate, and left it. They were prompted in this also by the desire to make their lives more meaningful than that afforded by the social life of Charlottesville. They had heard some sermons by a Virginia adherent to the Movement, R. L. Coleman, and the logic and simplicity of his position appealed to them.

The dream of uniting the Christian world by spreading the Gospel message unadorned by creeds or man-made interpretations, possessed them. They were both immersed by Mr. Coleman in the James River.

In 1840 they moved to Washington, D.C., where, finding no church of the Movement, they organized one in their own home. This was later to become the National City Christian Church, and the pride of the brotherhood.

Records are obscure as to what prompted Dr. Barclay to address a letter to David Burnet as the corresponding secretary of the Bible Society in October, 1848, at the precise moment that Mr. Burnet was preparing to join with John T. Johnson in presenting to the brotherhood at the approaching convention the challenge to engage in missionary work. But the letter was no surprise as Dr. Barclay had been buttonholing any and every member of the brotherhood with whom he came in contact for several years, pouring into every listening ear his conviction of the need for such work. He was now forty-three years old and had evidently reached a plateau; from now on he determined to make his life count. "Should your deliberations result in the establishment of a foreign society or department," he wrote David Burnet, "or should it be deemed expedient to engage seriously in the cause of foreign missions . . . cheerfully will I say, 'Here am I; send me.' "

Negotiations were begun with Dr. Barclay, and a year after the American Christian Missionary Society was formed in 1849, the Barclay family sailed away as missionaries with the blessings and confidence of the brotherhood. Their destination was Jerusalem. The decision to "go first to Jerusalem" assuaged the conscience of any brethren remaining doubtful of the venture, and all felt secure in once more giving literal adherence to the commands of the Bible.

"It is the only legitimate standpoint at which to place our Jacob's staff," wrote Alexander Campbell later. "Had we no other object than to give publicity and emphasis to this capital point, it is worthy the cause we plead to erect and establish our first foreign mission in the identical city where our Lord was crucified, where the Holy Spirit first descended, where the Gospel was first preached and the first Christian church erected."

Unfortunately, it had not been previously ascertained that other equally devout missionary-minded bodies had the same idea. Dr. Barclay found upon his arrival in Jerusalem that the place was reeking with missions and missionaries. There also prevailed "a bitter hatred of everything called Christian on the part of the Jews," as he reported back to the brethren soon after arriving at his post. He was also amazed, he wrote, "to find such wide departure from the simplicity and purity of the faith once delivered to the saints on the part of those who not only styled themselves Protestants, but claimed succession from the Apostles!"

The family stayed at the task four years. A number of converts were made, and Dr. Barclay began the writing of what became a widely acclaimed book, *The City of the Great King,* dealing with his archaeological expeditions and discoveries, and which was credited with giving the Movement character and standing in the secular and scientific world.

The venture also sparked into life a missionary spirit in the Movement. Two years after the Barclays set sail, in an impulsive burst of enthusiasm, the new American Christian Missionary Society made a further attempt at fulfilling its purpose by giving its blessing to a project initiated by the church in Hopkinsville, Kentucky, of sending a freed Negro slave named Alexander Cross to Liberia, West Africa, to spread the Gospel among his own people.

The Hopkinsville church was under the ministry of Mr. Enos Campbell, a cousin of Alexander Campbell, who had followed his famous kinsman from Ireland to America, bringing his Irish fiddle and a burning desire to further his cousin's Movement. He had settled at the Campbell home in Bethany until Alexander's wife, Selina, let her irritation at his fiddle playing be known in such uncertain terms that he packed up and left. He wandered into Kentucky, a devout and dedicated preacher of the Word, serving various churches.

During the ten years he ministered at Hopkinsville, records of the church are typical of the sincerity with which most of the churches of that period took their responsibility. Membership was not granted lightly, and the Hopkinsville church did not hesitate to exclude a man as its record book states, "for want of interest in Christianity and neglect of its duties and obligations," or "for unchristian conduct." It also considered the Great Commission as a command not to be disregarded, and cast about not only for a worthy man to go forth but a suitable field to which to send him. With utter disregard for conventional procedure, they chose the man among them who gave the best evidence of good logic, ready utterance and burning zeal. He was a Negro slave. His owner was Thomas Cross, from whom the church, assisted by other small churches in the Green River area, purchased the slave, Alexander Cross, in April 1853, for the sum of $530.00.

He was placed for six months under the training of Enos Campbell and the elders of the church, and in October, according to the church records, "Alexander Cross, a free man of colour, was set apart by fasting and the imposition of hands to go into dark Africa as a missionary." A few months later he sailed with his wife and eight-year-old son, and settled near Monrovia, Liberia, West Africa. Soon he was wrestling against overwhelming odds, his limited qualifications impeding his attempts to communicate, but his zeal remained undiminished. After two years the long hours, the constant itinerating, the hot rays of the Africa sun to which he exposed himself, began taking their toll, and he contracted tropical fever and died in Monrovia.

The blow to the brotherhood was severe, but it was not the only reason the missionary enterprise soon ground to a halt, and its advocates began wandering in a desert for almost twenty years. With the exception of supporting for a brief time a former Congregational missionary, James Beardslee, in Jamaica, no further missionary work was attempted until after the Civil War.

The basic cause for this long pause stemmed almost directly from the choice of the brotherhood's first missionary, Dr. James Barclay. While the dedicated doctor was still struggling in the Holy City, it was discovered by his supporters at home that he had been at the time of his appointment, a slaveholder. The irony of sending a slave-owning man to preach brotherhood to the heathen did not escape many people, and the news triggered the explosion of the slavery issue among the churches.

CHAPTER XI

War of Words and Guns

The emergence of the slavery issue in the brotherhood at the beginning of the decade of 1850 was, of course, not as sudden as it appeared. It had been smoldering for years, its fires kept banked by Alexander Campbell. But now there was no side-stepping its impact.

As far back as 1819, when Thomas Campbell moved hastily and indignantly back to Pennsylvania after a short sojourn in Kentucky when he discovered a law in that state hindered his urge to preach to Negroes, Alexander Campbell began giving evidence of his hatred of the general injustice inflicted on people "whose skin is a shade darker than the standard color of the times," as he wrote in the first issue of the *Christian Baptist*. During his term in the Virginia Constitutional Convention in 1829, he proposed a plan of gradual emancipation for the Negro that might have prevented the Civil War if it had been adopted. It provided for the setting of any agreed upon date after which no person born would be considered a slave. Persuaded that in the climate of that day such a measure would tend to solidify the proslavery forces and do more harm than good, he withheld it, but during the next few years, until the peace and unity of the brotherhood seemed threatened, he did not hesitate to denounce the whole institution of slavery.

"Slavery, that largest and blackest blot upon our national escutcheon," he wrote in 1832 in the *Millennial Harbinger*, "that many-headed monster, that Pandora's box, that bitter root, that blighting and blasting curse under which so fair and so large a portion of our beloved country groans, that deadly gas whose breath pollutes and poisons everything within its influence."

Nevertheless, as fever over the issue mounted, Mr. Campbell's sentiments were suspect in the brotherhood. He had never quite rid himself of the stigma of once being himself a slaveholder. In 1819 he had, indeed, purchased two young Negro brothers to relieve their owner, a Methodist preacher, from the need to take them south when he was transferred to that territory. He kept both boys until they reached the age of twenty-eight and then gave them their freedom, and the two men, Charlie and Jim Poole, remained his good friends for life, Charlie remaining in his employ until Mr. Campbell's death. But the stigma of ownership remained to haunt him.

This was augmented by the seemingly conciliatory stand taken by the *Millennial Harbinger* as the crises drew apace. "To preserve unity of spirit among Christians of the South and of the North is my grand object," Mr. Campbell wrote almost wistfully in the paper in 1845 at the time he was trying to quiet Walter Scott on the subject. "And for that purpose I am endeavoring to show that the New Testament does not authorize any interference or legislation upon the relation of master and slave, nor does it either in letter or spirit authorize Christians to make it a term of communion." But the series of eight articles he wrote on "Our Position on American Slavery," although designed to keep the peace, seemed to many of his followers in the northern states to be in reality a defense of slavery as an institution. Mr. Campbell bravely attempted to maintain his neutral position by countering with the statement: "As an American citizen I neither assume to be an apologist for American slavery, a reformer nor an Abolitionist. The laws sustain it; and so long as the laws sustain it, abstractly right or wrong, it is the duty of every Christian man to respect it. . . . A Christian may, indeed, seek by his vote to have it annihilated or modified, but he cannot, as a law-abiding citizen or a Christian, violate or tempt others to violate existing laws without offending his Lord and becoming obnoxious to his displeasure."

His efforts to maintain his precarious balance were not helped by the stand taken by his associate, the learned Virginia aristocrat W. K. Pendleton. Mr. Pendleton voiced the view that the Caucasians had developed their moral feeling and intellectual powers to the highest degree of perfection which human nature has ever exhibited, while in the other races these characteristics were present to an inferior degree. He pointed out that Shem, Ham and Japheth, all sons of Noah, are represented in the ninth chapter of Genesis as heads of three races, their destiny prophetically determined by God.

This seemed to the northern brethren to hold the seeds of a denial of the brotherhood of man toward which they were supposed to be working, and suspicions deepened regarding the real sentiments held by Mr. Campbell and his friends at Bethany. Nevertheless, Mr. Campbell's efforts to pour oil on the turbulent waters might have been effective but for his attitude toward the Fugitive Slave Law of 1851.

The expansion of the Movement in the southern states, while not as great as in the North and West, had brought into the fold a large number of slaveholding members. According to the American and Foreign Anti-Slavery Society in 1851, the Campbellites owned 101,000 slaves, outranked only by the Baptists and the Methodists. But as the numbers of the Campbellites were fewer, it meant on a per capita basis they were the leading slaveholding religious body in the country.

To this segment of the brotherhood, Mr. Campbell's reaction to the Fugitive Slave Law was sweet music. He pointed out that the law was constitutional and should be obeyed. "Submit yourselves to every ordinance of man for the Lord's sake," he wrote, quoting the Apostle Peter. But it was music which did not produce harmony among the outraged northern brethren. Immediately the storm broke.

In Indiana an angry man named John Boggs began issuing a paper, the *Northwestern Christian Magazine*, pouring invective not only on the proslavery segment of the brotherhood but on all who clung to a moderate stand, especially Alexander Campbell. Even Mr. Campbell's brother-in-law, Matthew Clapp, an ardent Abolitionist, chided him in the pages of Mr. Boggs's paper for his stand. "How the mighty have fallen," Mr. Clapp wrote in derision. "Twenty-five years ago you [Campbell] raged against injustice. Now you are a conservative, and one would almost think from your frequent giving forth that you would, like an old Calvinist fogy, regard as incontestable proof of the divinity of any given doctrine that it outrage the sympathies and sensibilities and reason of men."

In a clash of Bethany College students over the issue, a group of ten young men with northern sympathies left the campus in righteous wrath, declaring it a proslavery camp. They added fuel to the flames by enrolling in a rival institution, Northwestern Christian University in Indianapolis, which had come into existence a few years previously with strong Abolitionist backing, and with a noticeable lack of support from Mr. Campbell. In fact, he took the occasion of its founding to say he hoped it would not encourage others to create "ill-begotten, misshapen, clubfooted, imbecile schools under the name and title of schools and colleges."

But perhaps the most significant reverberation to Mr. Campbell's seeming endorsement of the Fugitive Slave Law was a sermon preached and sent broadcast in pamphlet form, under the title "The Design of Civil Government," by the young minister at Warren, Ohio, one Isaac Errett.

Isaac Errett's depth of religious conviction had been tried and not found wanting. He was the son of devout parents, whose home in New York State was the center of religious influence in the small community. When the father, Henry Errett, died in 1825, Isaac was only five years old. His mother remarried, and the family soon moved to New Jersey, Somerset County, and then into Pennsylvania, settling at Saw Mill Run near Pittsburgh. No schools were nearby, and as the stepfather needed young Isaac and his brothers to work in his sawmill, their schooling was neglected. But the millwork was disagreeable to Isaac and he soon became a journeyman to a printer. He not only learned the trade, but wrote occasional pieces for publication, and eventually edited a small paper, finding an unsuspected release in putting his rambling, disturbed thoughts into words. The absence of formal education was soon more than compensated by the training life was providing. A vague urge to "do good" led the youth by pure chance into preaching a sermon one Sunday morning for a small church of the Movement in Pittsburgh, and he discovered he had found his work in the world.

The broad spirit of toleration which lived in Isaac Errett, and

which was later to come to fruition to the everlasting blessing
of the Movement, met its first test when he assumed the pastorate
of the small Smithfield Street Christian Church in Pittsburgh soon
after his marriage in 1841 to the beautiful Harriet Reeder. The
members, he discovered, were of that group of adherents to the
Movement who accepted every word of the Bible as having the
force of positive law. Soon after he came among them, he
witnessed one of the Elders one Sunday morning publicly call
to account a member for marrying outside the church. "Be not
yoked with unbelievers," was the Scripture on which the reprimand
was based. He also discovered some of them insisted on going
through the ceremony of foot washing, and a number practiced the
holy kiss. "Greet ye one another with the holy kiss," an Elder
would call out as a service concluded, and before the astonished
eyes of Isaac and his bride, the congregation would obediently
start kissing.

The experience in attempting to persuade the church to abandon
such literal notions of Christian behavior, as prejudicial to the
church's witness in the modern world, implanted in Isaac Errett
an awareness, which increased with the years, of the need to
discriminate between the essential truths of the Bible and its
incidental teachings. It also developed in him the quality of
patience, a quality which was needed when he accepted the call
to the New Lisbon, Ohio, church in 1844. This group had been
brought out of the Baptist fold in 1827 by Walter Scott, and
was more imbued with the need for doctrinal correctness than for
other virtues. The good people promised him a salary of five
hundred dollars a year, considered a livable income for a family
of four—himself, his wife and two babies who had arrived in his
home. He threw himself into the work with abandon. But crops
were bad that year; other demands on pocketbooks took preced-
ence; and the church members, with no visible qualms of conscience, paid their young preacher only $250. They did consent,
however, for him to use what free time he had left after serving
them in working at other tasks. The following year he was forced
to raise his entire income from outside sources.

He stayed with the little church under these circumstances for
four work-filled years, and then, in 1848, piled his household goods
and family into a covered wagon and moved on to North Bloom-

field, Ohio, fifty miles distant, attracted by the plight of a struggling congregation there with whom he felt his labors could be more effective. The spirit of the members there was willing, but their leadership was weak; they had clung together for twenty years, meeting in storerooms or private homes, unable of themselves to erect a meetinghouse of their own. Within a year Isaac Errett organized the congregation on a working basis, and saw the foundations laid for a simple house of worship. The roof was still lacking on the structure when the brethren of the area sought to encourage Mr. Errett by selecting the spot to hold their yearly meeting. The encouragement turned out to include the invasion of Isaac and Harriet Errett's own three-room house to "sleep" the visitors when rain drove them from the unroofed meetinghouse. More than sixty people crowded into the small space and spilled over into the loft, where Harriet spread straw on the floor and strung sheets from the rafters to divide the men's pallets from those of the women.

This gesture of Christian hospitality was not lost on some visitors from Warren, fifteen miles away, and the young Erretts were given a call to that larger and more potentially fruitful field. It was from the pulpit of the Warren church that Isaac Errett's voice first resounded over the brotherhood.

Isaac Errett was just thirty-one years old, and fiercely opposed to slavery. But in his answer to Mr. Campbell's defense of the Fugitive Slave Law he indulged in no sentimental yearning over the suffering slaves; he did not resort to words of anguish over man's inhumanity to man. That moaning he left to lesser minds dependent on arousing emotional fervor. Instead, step by brilliantly logical step, he explored a conflict as old as Socrates, the conflict between individual conscience and the state, the conflict that had aroused Barton Stone to take the same radical stand a decade before for the supremacy of conscience. Barton Stone, however, had spoken before the brotherhood's ear was fully attuned to the impending crisis, nor had he spoken with the clarity with which Mr. Errett presented the matter, a clarity which at once made the young Errett a marked man, a preacher of rare sense and sobriety, and one to come under the watchful eye of Alexander Campbell.

Although Mr. Errett's address evoked the first serious public rumbling of the brotherhood's aroused conscience on slavery, its more immediate effect was to catapult him into an ironic situation.

A few months following the publication of his address, the Ohio brethren assembled in Wooster, Ohio, for their second state-wide convention. The year before they had organized themselves into a state association, aligning themselves enthusiastically with the new American Christian Missionary Society, imbued with missionary passion and delighted to have the cooperative means of expressing it on a national scale. But now, stirred by Mr. Errett's condemnation of slavery, they became more imbued with taking a forthright stand against the slavery evil, even to the point of withholding their support of the missionary task and the American Society. For the news was out that the Society's very own missionary, Dr. James Barclay, had been at the time of his appointment a slave-owner.

"In the name of religion and humanity," one of the delegates, John Kirk, shouted, "can we consistently sustain Brother Barclay as a missionary in ancient Palestine? How can we cooperate with a missionary society that sends such a character, guilty before high heaven and all good men, of such ungodly conduct?"

Isaac Errett listened, appalled. By his emphasis on the evil of slavery in his famous address, he had unwittingly provoked his brethren into a mood of withdrawing from what he considered the most forward step yet taken by the Movement, the creation of the American Christian Missionary Society. In his early pastorates he had experienced the frustrations of local churches unable of themselves to undertake the monumental tasks confronting the religious community on the frontier. With joy unrestrained he had watched from the distance of his youth and his obscurity the formation of the national cooperative framework, rejoicing that the churches had at last embarked on creating a means of all working together. His cheers were among the loudest, and he anticipated joining with heart and hand in advancing the American Christian Missionary Society.

Now, at the risk of seeming to condone slavery, he rose to the defense of Dr. Barclay and the Society. The good doctor had indeed owned slaves, he explained. He had inherited a family of black people, and when he was preparing to sail for foreign shores he had offered them their freedom if they would leave the slaveholding state of Virginia and forage for themselves in the North. They preferred, however, the security of a home with a local preacher who had offered to buy them, and the sale was made after Dr. Barclay assured himself they would be given a good home and fair treatment.

The explanation must have served to quiet the fears of the Ohio brethren. At any rate, they did not withdraw from the American Society. But the experience marked Isaac Errett as a man of granite integrity. He had been put to the test and he had emerged a fearless spokesman. The walls of his church at Warren suddenly no longer contained him; he became a debater, a counselor, a spirited lecturer, his voice given carrying power as he contributed the working of his logical, incisive mind to the solution of problems ranging from slavery to spiritualism. His six-foot, muscular frame and his massive head, with its thick, auburn hair combed high above a wide forehead and crinkling gray eyes, became a welcome sight on platforms within the religious community and without its gates. A brief interlude as a partner in a milling enterprise in Michigan contributed to his understanding of workingmen and the harsh realities of competitive industry and, while the experience was not an especially happy one, it gave him satisfaction in later years to remember he had helped in establishing the town of Muir, Michigan, carving a pleasant town out of the wilderness.

But he knew his destiny lay elsewhere; it lay in imparting to men his own vivid awareness of the reality of God, a need more essential to human happiness than economic security, more rewarding than earthly power and social glory. He had identified himself with the Disciples of Christ brotherhood because it promised freedom from sectarian shackles in proclaiming that reality, but when he returned to the ministry from his business venture he was troubled by the legalistic attitude he sensed as developing among his brethren. Many were perverting passages in the Scriptures into harsh and stern instruments; preachers were inclined to drive their converts rather than lead them into the presence of God. He realized they reflected the temper of the times. Hovering war clouds were threatening to shape every institution, including the church, into battlefields for man's folly instead of instruments of God's love. In 1855 he accepted an offer from the American Society to serve as its chief executive, an office known as corresponding secretary, and thus he stood at last at the center of the Movement's national stage.

The surging waters of passion engendered by the approach of the war tossed other young preachers on the Movement's national scene, some to sink into obscurity as the tide ebbed, others to linger and continue in high leadership.

James Shannon, who had succeeded David Burnet as president of the bewildered Bacon College in 1840, was an ardent pro-slavery man, militant in his defense of the system. He was a graduate of the University of Belfast, Ireland, with an unsurpassed record for scholarship, and when he came to America in 1820 to assume charge of an academy in Georgia, his reputation for learning, coupled with his commanding, erect presence and his appealing Irish brogue, soon led to an invitation to join the faculty of the Theological Baptist Institution at Newton, Massachusetts. He accepted the new post, but he had not realized how thoroughly he had been captured by southern ways of life, and returned at the first opportunity to become professor of ancient languages at the University of Georgia. A stint as president of Louisiana State College followed. It was while he was in Louisiana that he first encountered the teachings of Alexander Campbell. He embraced the Movement as ardently as he had embraced the southern way of life. And as ardently the Movement, weighted with unlettered frontier preachers, embraced him, a genuine scholar and a gentleman. When the Movement's first college, Bacon College, beckoned, he accepted its presidency at half the salary he was receiving in Louisiana, evidence of the fervor of his commitment, a fervor which characterized his intense nature.

At the base of Mr. Shannon's proslavery position was the unalterable conviction that bondage for some people was a blessing. It was part and parcel of the divine plan of God for his world, and it had been so recognized by the Jews, and never questioned by Jesus. Such views were tolerated when he voiced them in the border state of Kentucky, but in 1850, when he took them to

Missouri upon his assumption of the presidency of the new Missouri State University, they met with a different reaction.

Missouri was a battleground, split into openly belligerent camps on the slavery question. And when the attention-capturing Irish voice of James Shannon resounded from the high elevation of his office as head of the state's proud new seat of higher learning, denouncing the North, consternation followed. Political ranks in the state were rent asunder. Worse, the Movement with which he identified himself, and which had been so proud to claim him, now found itself embarrassed. Frequent blasts from the anti-slavery press directed toward "that damned Campbellite Democrat" did little to enhance the status of the new religious body. Nor did Mr. Shannon's uninhibited replies. A warmonger of the first order, he did not hesitate to incite to violence. "The right of property in slaves is sanctioned by the light of nature, the Constitution, and the teachings of the Bible," he shouted. "A deliberate and persistent violation of that right, even by Government, is as villainous as highway robbery, and when peaceable modes of redress are exhausted, is a just cause of War!"

Understandable pressure forced James Shannon to resign his academic office in 1856. But his church stuck by him, reluctant to admit every man did not have the right to his own opinions, but more reluctant to forego entirely the brilliance of his valid scholarship. A new college had been started by the Missouri brethren at Canton, called Christian University, and, happily for Mr. Shannon as well as for the college, the office of president was seeking an occupant. It was perhaps a benign blessing that his duties in launching the new school so engrossed him that he had little time left to agitate his proslavery views, and his death three years later, in 1859, removed the dilemma of the Missouri churches.

The approach of war was, indeed, placing the churches, not only in Missouri but throughout the nation, in a dilemma. Men with moral convictions on both sides of the issue were faced with the choice of keeping silent concerning their convictions, or rending asunder the body of Christ. To uphold a fixed position meant separating themselves, perhaps in mortal combat, from their brethren on the other side. Their dilemma was aggravated by a sobering sense of the sinfulness of war itself. Even aggressive, spirited Tolbert Fanning in Tennessee was moved to write: "The grand distinguishing characteristic of Christianity is, men shall not return evil for evil."

But not all of the Movement's leaders were emotionally stable. Few were farsighted enough to look beyond the immediate issue of slavery to the deeper moral problem of Christian participation in war itself. John Boggs, in his rabid *Northwestern Christian Magazine*, was instrumental in 1856 in calling into being a rival Christian Missionary Convention in Indianapolis, which was to endure until 1863. The immediate purpose of the rival society was to do what the American Christian Missionary Society refused to do—lend sanction and support to an Abolitionist evangelist from Indiana who had invaded the bleeding state of Kansas preaching hell fire and brimstone on proslavery forces there. His name was Pardee Butler.

Pardee Butler was as rabidly antislavery as James Shannon was proslavery. He had entered Kansas as an evangelist in 1855, hoping for eventual support from the American Society. He did not apply at once for such support, however, for the American Society was again in difficulties. In attempting to counteract its near-disastrous first venture in sending a slaveholder out as its missionary, it had inadvertently become embroiled again in the slavery issue, and Mr. Butler suspected it was not of a mind to singe its wings so soon again. The involvement had to do with its support of its second missionary, this time one to Jamaica, J. O. Beardslee.

Mr. Beardslee had been a missionary some years before in that island under the Congregational Board. But he was converted to the Movement and left the island to serve as pastor of the Christian church in Bedford, Ohio. When interest abruptly ceased in the work of Dr. Barclay in Jerusalem, the American Society, casting hurriedly about for means to rekindle it, offered to return Mr. Beardslee to Jamaica. He accepted, but before he left, wrote a series of articles for one of the church papers telling of his work in seeking the emancipation of Jamaican slaves. The magazine refused to print the articles, naïvely explaining, to the chagrin of many, that any such allusion to slavery would alienate the slaveholding members from the American Christian Missionary Society as Mr. Beardslee's sponsor. The statement was unfortunate, and in the ensuing uproar the American Christian Missionary Society was forced to deny it had any notion of practicing a deception upon the slaveholding church members by keeping quiet about Mr. Beardslee's antislavery work. But the shadow had been cast on the venture, and Mr. Beardslee's tenure as a missionary was brief, terminating in 1858.

Pardee Butler was without doubt a dedicated, if an overzealous, Christian. When he went to Kansas in 1855 from Indiana, he carried with him the same outrage over slavery that prompted another man of the same name, but no relation, Ovid Butler of Indianapolis, to promote the founding of the antislavery college in that city the same year, Northwestern Christian University, which embraced the fleeing Bethany College students and thus brought down upon itself Alexander Campbell's ire.

Pardee Butler, however, was geared to more action than seeking justice for the Negro through the slow process of time and education. He deliberately settled near the center of strong proslavery sentiment around Atchison, laying out the town of Pardee, establishing seven churches nearby which promptly began echoing his views. The troubled Kansas people, beset by agitation from both the proslavery advocates and the antislavery forces, now augmented by Mr. Butler, were in no mood to roll with such punches for long. Soon they made Pardee Butler the target of their venom. In August 1855, while he was in Atchison preparing to return to Illinois on a visit, he was cornered by a group of Border Ruffians, who demanded he retract his endorsement of the Kansas-Nebraska Bill. Upon his refusal the group excited a mob, and Mr. Butler was saved from hanging only by the intervention of a local dentist, himself a slaveowner, who proposed instead a more novel punishment—that he be set adrift on a flimsy raft on the treacherous Missouri River. Pardee Butler's hands were tied behind his back, his arms tarred and "cottoned," there evidently being no feathers handy, his face painted black with a large "R," for Rogue, inscribed on his forehead, and he was hoisted on a raft of two rotting logs tied together, at the end of which his tormentors erected a pole with a crude flag depicting him as a "nigger thief." As he floated away, it is recorded that he called to the men watching in high glee on the bank, "Gentlemen, if you are not ashamed of your part in this transaction, I am not ashamed of mine. Goodbye!"

Somehow the fiery preacher managed to free his hands and pull down the flag. He made a paddle of its staff and steered his way in the swift current filled with dangerous "rack heaps" of driftwood about twelve miles down the river to Port William.

One reason Pardee Butler did not apply for support from the American Society before going to Kansas, and postponed doing so for a year after working there, was that a man named Benjamin Franklin, who was suspected of holding southern sympathies, was serving at the time as its chief executive.

Benjamin Franklin was of the sturdy, pioneer brand of preachers who had characterized the Movement in the early days, and were still numerous in Indiana. He was essentially a man of the people, forthright, able but withal plodding. He was without formal education and was an avowed pacifist who decried participation by the church in any public question, and especially the burning question now before the country. But he possessed an irresistible urge to preach, an urge which led him, in 1840, to give up a gristmill in Indiana in which he had invested his life savings, and devote himself to the Gospel. He had known he would suffer, but perhaps not quite so much. For years he and his growing family lived a hand-to-mouth existence, but his path never altered.

After a few experiments in "sermonizing," Mr. Franklin evidently recognized and became resigned to his limited pulpit ability, for he turned to editing a succession of journals to expound his views. Ironically, early in the 1850's, he joined forces with the polished, aristocratic David Burnet in publishing a weekly paper, the *Christian Age,* in Cincinnati, a paper which soon became the organ of the American Society and which brought Mr. Franklin within the periphery of leadership of the Society. The partnership with David Burnet was dissolved in 1854, largely due to the disparity in temperament and social background of the two editors. The dissolution was not entirely friendly. Its terms dictated that Benjamin Franklin was not to edit another journal within the brotherhood for at least two years, and for that period Mr. Franklin contented himself by serving as secretary of the American Society.

When the ban on Benjamin Franklin's publishing ventures expired, he hesitated only briefly before relinquishing his post with the American Society to Isaac Errett, and entering again the fray of journalism. He started a weekly journal in Cincinnati, which soon became a monthly magazine, the *American Christian Review*, a journal which was to play a significant role for twenty years in shaping the thought of the Movement, and one in which Mr. Franklin's caustic manner of expressing himself came to full fruition.

Almost simultaneously another journal destined to play a significant role, was being launched in Nashville, Tennessee, by Tolbert Fanning. Mr. Fanning had continued to be disturbed by the spreading liberality of thought among preachers of the Movement, and felt the urge to again give expression to his fears. His disillusioning experience with Jesse Ferguson had not caused him to lose faith in all men, and he enlisted another young man to assist him as co-editor, one of his former students named William Lipscomb. The new paper he called the *Gospel Advocate*; it was to advocate the Gospel according to the Scriptures, and nothing else. As the years passed, it was to join with Benjamin Franklin's *American Christian Review* in recalling the Movement to its historic purpose of restoring the Ancient Order, denouncing all trends which would lead it astray, and eventually the two papers were to champion, and in a sense create, the cleavage between their followers and the readers of the more liberal paper which Isaac Errett was to edit, the *Christian Standard*, and sanction the resulting open break.

But little of this was foreseen as Benjamin Franklin left the Society's employ. The war years mercifully shrouded whatever suspicions of the American Society's creeping theological heresy present in his heart and mind, and it was not until the hostilities had ceased that he began voicing his distrust of the Society as an unscriptural appendage, and a threatening one, to the church.

To Mr. Franklin's credit, however, he foresaw while still working with the Society, a danger in it which was unrelated to its scriptural soundness. If worst came to worst in the civil strife, the very existence of such an organizational framework would provide the machinery for a visible division. "A general division cannot take place," he pointed out in 1855, "while . . . the congregational plan prevails. But combine the churches in an association, and then let some difficulty occur among the leading men, and they will sunder the churches from one side of the country to the other." His prophecy all but came true when, in 1861 and again in 1863, the Society left its neutral position and sided with the North in preserving the Federal Union.

In 1856 Mr. Burnet's languishing Bible Society and his more thriving Publication Society voluntarily dissolved in order to merge their interests in the American Society. The "anniversary meetings" of the three societies, however, continued to be held on three successive October days each year in Cincinnati. They had become occasions of such happy fellowship that few preachers voiced whatever forebodings they might have in creating a now potentially powerful single society. Certainly it presented, as Benjamin Franklin pointed out, a tangible body of such dimensions that, if it cracked apart in the tug-of-war between the opposing political forces, a break in the brotherhood would have to be acknowledged. That it did not crack apart during the crucial war years was due in large part to the leadership given it by the great-souled Isaac Errett.

Everyone breathed a sigh of relief when, in the midst of the confusing situation, Mr. Errett was called to become corresponding secretary. His popularity was at a peak; furthermore his well-known antislavery views immediately offset the rumor that the Society, so self-consciously neutral, was leaning toward southern sympathies; sympathies that Alexander Campbell, its nominal president, and Benjamin Franklin, Errett's predecessor, were suspected of harboring. On the other hand, the southern churches remembered Mr. Errett's stand at Wooster, Ohio, in defending the missionary slave-owner, Dr. James Barclay, and felt confident his determination to maintain the unity of the brotherhood would permit him no overt allegiance to the "higher law" which might, in his judgment, call for a repudiation of the institution of slavery. This confidence of a continuing neutral stand was soon justified when Pardee Butler, aware of Mr. Errett's antislavery views, now hopefully applied for the Society's support in his antislavery crusade in Kansas.

"As an anti-slavery man myself, I sympathize much with you," Mr. Errett wrote back to the fiery Butler. "I share your feelings. But in the missionary work I know nothing of slavery or anti-slavery."

They were plain words, and the brotherhood seemed satisfied. Neutrality would be maintained. Few foresaw how the emotional tides would rise and crash on the shores of the Movement two years later when the guns fired on Fort Sumter in April, 1861.

On that April day the hosts of the faithful were widely scattered, going about the Lord's business. Alexander Campbell and Isaac Errett were on tour in Virginia, raising money for Bethany College. The news sent both men scurrying back to their homes. In Cincinnati the music of fife and drum heralding the stirring event broke up an evangelistic meeting in progress at David Burnet's church at Eighth and Walnut streets. Together with R. M. Bishop, mayor of the city and one of the church Elders, Mr. Burnet and the visiting preacher, W. H. Hopson, drove through the thronged streets, agreeing to close the meeting that night. In northern Ohio, where a new school of the Movement, Western Reserve Electic Institute, was getting under way at Hiram, the young president of the school, James A. Garfield, petitioned for a commission as lieutenant colonel. He formed the 42nd Regiment from the students and was given full command. In the South, Tolbert Fanning was on a tour through the Deep South territory of Louisiana and Mississippi, where the people were experiencing such wild excitement the Lord seemed forgotten. Back in Tennessee, his beloved Franklin College was succumbing to the war fever, almost the whole student body of young men destined for the ministry leaving its halls to join the Confederate army. The mails were soon stopped, and the *Gospel Advocate* had to be suspended, not to be resumed until 1866.

For a time it seemed communication between the churches in the North and in the South would cease. Sectional loyalty came into play, and while some stalwart Christians refused to display sympathy with either side, holding war and the participation in it in any form to be evil, most of the brethren took firm positions. Even many of these, however, tried to hold to a sense of kinship in God's love with their fellow Christians on the other side. But one or two less inspiring characters emerged to shame the brotherhood by succumbing to hatred.

A well-known preacher, B. F. Hall, was one of these. Mr. Hall was a six-foot, two-hundred-pound giant of a man with a passionate nature and many idiosyncrasies. He had been converted in 1823 after hearing Alexander Campbell debate on baptism with W. L. McCalla, and was set apart for the ministry by Barton Stone two years later. He preached for a while in Philadelphia, then roved into Kentucky, and thence on west to Arkansas, where he brought the Baptist church in Little Rock over almost as a body into the Movement in 1832. The attention this feat accorded him was heady wine, and thereafter he displayed a marked talent for taking the center of any stage he found himself upon. He hated cats, and enjoyed the attention he created by demanding their explusion from the range of his vision whether he was in the pulpit or out of it, displaying no regret that the trait set him apart from the earthy, frontier church people to whom animals were a part of everyday life. An inveterate user of tobacco, he attempted time and again to forego the use of the weed but never quite made it. Discipline was not one of his virtues, nor was modesty. His love of fine trappings soon led him to seek a means of supplementing his scant income from preaching, and he became a dentist by a route which is obscured by time. But he continued to preach with a vividness that attracted hundreds, in Arkansas, in Memphis, and eventually wandered into Texas with his commanding presence and his more commanding message.

Here the Civil War found him. He became chaplain of a regiment of the Texas Rangers led by Captain Barton Stone, Jr., the son of the well-known gentle Barton W. Stone, now deceased and saved from the horrors of war.

At the battle of Pea Ridge near Fayetteville, Arkansas, his regiment was engaged in battle under General McCullock, and ingloriously routed. But the taste of blood was evidently sweet to Dr. Hall, and the desire for revenge obsessed him. It was reported that he behaved more like a fiend than a Christian gentleman. His total concern was to kill. His stated ambition, legend has it, was to catch every Yankee soldier he could find and cut off his right hand, and then send him back to his command with the severed hand tied to his saddle.

By October of the first year of the war, 1861, the conflict settled down to a jogging pace, and the Movement's leaders turned their attention to carrying on a semblance of the Lord's work. This included meeting together in Cincinnati for the usual annual convention of the American Christian Missionary Society. The meeting proved to be a testing ground for the unity of the brotherhood.

Cincinnati was in northern territory, and while a few brethren from the South ventured to attend, the preponderance of delegates were from the northern states, their sympathies with the Union forces plainly visible. Nevertheless, few were prepared for the bombshell dropped by a layman whose voice commanded a hearing. He was Dr. J. P. Robinson of Ohio, a member of that state's senate, and an influential figure in the political, civic and religious life of the state. In calm, measured tones Dr. Robinson introduced a resolution clearly nullifying the American Society's carefully preserved neutrality. It called upon the brethren to support the Union; to put down the "current Rebellion" peaceably if possible; if not, then to subdue it with bayonets.

Isaac Errett was presiding for the aging president, Alexander Campbell, who sat in the audience, the years so heavy upon him he seemed to only dimly comprehend the import of the resolution. Mr. Errett was forced to pound his gavel with resounding whacks to preserve decorum. In the confusion, political maneuvering came into play, and, to the consternation of many fair-minded men who favored the intent of the resolution but felt it placed the brotherhood's unity in jeopardy, the Society went on record as siding with one segment of its constituency against the other.

The southern churches were stunned; they received the news with disbelief. They had been betrayed by their fellow Christians; their cause had been denounced by the only tangible symbol of their family connection. Thereafter until the end of the war, the unity of the brotherhood hung in the balance. Two years later, in 1863, the convention passed an even stronger resolution, affirming the loyalty of the Society to efforts to preserve the Federal Union. But by that time the southern segment, prostrated by the conflict gave scant heed.

The war's end saw the image of the American Christian Missionary Society, the only evidence of the brotherhood's solidarity, reeling. But the organization did not dissolve. To many this was evidence that while sectional strife had taken its toll among the churches, an unbridgeable gulf had not developed. The Movement had survived; it had been saved for a purpose. A new depth of comprehension of the wonderous ways of God invaded the churches. By tacit consent they began ignoring their former differences; brethren who had refused to fellowship with each other, again embraced. It was as if they had seen Jesus Christ, the crucified, plainly, and had been baptized again by His Spirit. And soon everybody found other things to think about.

BOOK THREE

We interrupt this story to bring you an important word from Saint Paul:

O, you dear idiots of Galatia, who saw
Jesus Christ, the crucified, so plainly,
who has been casting a spell over you?
I shall ask you one simple question: Did
you receive the Spirit by trying to keep
the law, or by believing the message of
the gospel? Surely you can't be so idiotic
as to think that a man begins his spiritual
life in the spirit, and then completes it
by reverting to outward observances?

Galatians 3:1–4 (Phillips translation)

CHAPTER XII

The Long, Dark Tunnel

Even before the nation rose from the ashes of war and braced itself for the stormy days of Reconstruction, it was apparent a new generation in the Movement had come to maturity. Congregations, even in small towns, found themselves infected with a sense of urbanity and sophistication. This reflected the general rise in the cultural and social level of the nation, but it had more immediate roots in changes taking place in the Movement itself.

A slow trickling of wealth was finding its way into the pockets of the people, and a new class of "white collar" members, including not a few men of substantial means, was in the pews. The colleges which had sprouted here and there were lending an intellectual flavor to the Movement, most of them of valid accreditation, and respected college graduates were more frequently seen in the pulpits. The numerous periodicals flooding the brotherhood, if not erudite at least entered practically every home and stimulated a habit of reading. Lecture courses were popular in small communities and the churches sponsored frequent debates, both of which disseminated knowledge; rallies and conventions brought church members into contact with new people and new ideas, and emphasized the social niceties. Soon the Movement, which had once been a sect imbued with nothing but zeal, began conforming to standards of polite social decorum, and its leaders began feeling the first faint pressure of vested interest and the stirrings of denominational pride.

But the basic cause in the rise in cultural sophistication in the Movement was Alexander Campbell himself. Mr. Campbell had acquired land and its inevitable riches, and as early as 1840 had ceased equating godliness with poverty. This was fortunate.

In the early days he had inadvertently encouraged mediocrity and almost succeeded in setting its stamp on the Movement. He had openly scoffed at wealth and the pretensions of elegance. He had not hesitated to pour ridicule upon preachers who sought adequate salaries, and had urged that church structures be kept humble; they could be commodious, he conceded, but should be free from all the splendor of this vain and sinful world.

As time passed the realities of the expanding Movement altered for him many of such notions, but at heart he remained a man of the spirit, deploring until his death the tendency of the church to conform to ways of the world. He continued to decry, for instance, the use of the Lord's Day for anything but worship, pointing in scorn to families "whose most essential sanctification of that hallowed day was a clean shirt, a good coat and a more sumptuous dinner."

But as his own wealth increased his home at Bethany began reflecting a cultural level that attracted both the wealthy and the learned. High thinking permeated every occasion. Although the appointments of the "mansion" were not ornate, they were a far cry from the crude cabin furnishings of his followers in the early days. Imported French wallpaper and gleaming silver tableware, fine linen and polished mahogany were a background for the conversational badinage of alert minds, and table talk no longer centered on the breeding habits of sheep, but ranged into metaphysical discussions, especially when distinguished visitors were present, as was the case most of the time when Mr. Campbell was in residence.

In his travels the great leader became the showpiece of the Movement. He was rich and famous and brilliant, and he was entertained by the great and near great of every community he visited. Of his appearance and bearing while in his prime, a revealing glimpse is obtained through the eyes of one of the most severe critics of his doctrine, Dr. Heman Humphrey, who had this to say upon hearing Mr. Campbell speak in 1850 in Louisville, Kentucky:

"Dr. Campbell made his way up through the crowd and took his seat in the pulpit. He is somewhat above the middle stature, with broad shoulders, a little stooping, and though stoutly built rather spare and pale. He has a high, intellectual forehead, a keen dark eye, somewhat shaded, and a well covered head of gray hair, fast changing into the full bloom of the almond tree. I think he must be rather over than under 65 years of age. [He was 62. Ed.] He looks like a hard working man, as he has been from his youth. Very few could have endured so much mental and physical labor as has raised him to the commanding position which he occupies, and so long sustained him in it. His voice is not strong, evidently owing in part at least to the indifferent state of his health, but it is clear and finely modulated. His enunciation is distinct; and as he uses no notes, his language is remarkably pure and select. In his delivery he has not much action, but little of that fervid outpouring which characterizes western and southern eloquence. There is nothing vociferous and impassioned in his manner. I think he is the most perfectly self-possessed, the most perfectly at ease in the pulpit of any preacher I ever listened to. . . . No gentleman could be more free and unembarrassed in his own parlor. At the same time there was not the least want of deference for his audience. . . . In listening to him you feel you are in the presence of a great man. He speaks like a master of assemblies who had entire confidence in the mastery of his subject and his powers, and who expects to carry conviction to the minds of his hearers. . . . He held the great congregation for an hour and a half in that profound stillness which shows that his listeners are not aware of the lapse of time."

Although Mr. Campbell became one of the wealthiest men in Virginia, with land holdings extending as far as the eye could reach from the portico of his mansion in Bethany, the roots of his life went deeper than the soil he owned, and as the years passed the grandeur of earth faded in contrast with the riches of heaven. More than walking with the princes of the earthly realm, he yearned in all sincerity to "walk with God." In letters which have come down to us this note is repeatedly struck, lifting the thought of his family and friends from things of the earth and time to the realm of heaven and immortality.

The death of his father, Thomas Campbell, in 1854 at the age of ninety-one left Alexander Campbell bereft. And the tribute paid the older man by his famous son reveals the son's poignant regard for the glory accorded the saints of life. "I never knew a man in all my acquaintance," he said, "of whom it could have been said with more assurance that he 'walked with God.'"

During the period of the cultural transition of the Movement, the early leaders, one by one, were taken to their rewards. Barton Stone's death in November, 1844, was followed by that of Thomas Campbell in 1854 and John T. Johnson in 1857. Four years later, in 1861, Walter Scott died in Mayslick, Kentucky, a withdrawn, sensitive man to the last. And in 1866 Alexander Campbell passed away, followed in death the next year by David Burnet.

Strangely, the passing of none of the leaders created more than a ripple of consternation, least of all that of Alexander Campbell, despite the fact he had dominated his followers as had no other religious leader in America, and that it had been predicted the Movement would fall apart without him. Since the onset of the Civil War in 1861 the great leader had lived in a world of unreality, the ghost of his former personality, relinquishing in all but name the reins of leadership. Indeed, some say that after his return from Europe in 1847 he was never the same. At any rate, during the war years his mind roved his childhood, indulging in fantasy, acknowledging the present only in the experiences of his daughter Decima, which he projected as his own. Decima had married Judson Barclay, the son of the church's first missionaries to Jerusalem, Dr. and Mrs. James Barclay, and had gone with her young husband to live on the island of Cyprus upon his appointment there as American consul. Her frequent letters home were vividly descriptive, and as the Civil War raged, Alexander Campbell more and more retreated into the world they created in his imagination. It may be that in some curious undiscovered area of his great mind he was seeking this merciful escape, not only from the holocaust of the war but from what he could foresee in the nervous brotherhood he had brought into being.

If he did, he could not be blamed. For trouble was developing.

The new leaders taking command in the Movement reflected the less happy mood of the times. It was a mood of distrust. Not only was the political life of the country infected with it but it permeated the religious community. Every orthodox church body, its activities curtailed during the war years, now seemed determined to make up for lost time. In the rush, the eternal verities were often subordinated to churlish rivalry between the sects and petty grievances within the several households of faith. The mood of bickering over relatively unimportant matters among the Disciples of Christ might be personified by the attitude of a querulous woman in Tennessee whose grandson was to become a great churchman, N. B. Hardeman. She worried for years, her grandson later recalled, over the several versions of what became of Jephthah's daughter. She never got it settled in her mind, and it eventually assumed an importance that obscured all else.

The mood, however, gave rise to more serious matters as the tempo of the Movement's life increased. The cultural and economic rise of the churches caused them to replace many of their humble meetinghouses with more pretentious structures, and to introduce pieces of art and windows of stained glass. The pews became polished and padded, and soon sophisticated musical ears were no longer satisfied with a tuning fork. Eventually and inevitably, although the brethren continued to walk with God, they found themselves out of step with each other. For the rolling cadences of the organ began sounding over the battlements of Zion.

The trouble had its origin ironically in the simple early dictum expressed by the gentle Thomas Campbell: "Where the Scriptures speak, we speak; where the Scriptures are silent, we are silent." This seemed not only a simple but a safe guideline for unity, and for almost a generation few suspected it carried the seeds of unity's destruction. And certainly no one foresaw that in the pursuit of the sacred right to interpret the silences as well as the speech of the New Testament, a situation would be created calculated to cloud the thought of the Movement and consume its energies for the rest of the century.

In the climate of the day a matter which had troubled successive Protestant groups since the time of Martin Luther occurred to some of the brethren. Nowhere in the Bible was there authority for the use of musical instruments in worship.

John Calvin had been aware of this, and in his rigid adherence to literal truth had silenced the organ in St. Peter's Church at

Geneva, Switzerland, and ordered its pipes melted and molded into cups for the communion wine. His spiritual descendants through the years had followed his example with more or less enthusiasm, and as they congealed into religious bodies in the frontier stretches of America, many of them, lacking an organ to forbid, had demonstrated their adherence to the principle involved by excluding the whistle.

The Disciple brotherhood was saved in its early days from miring itself in the matter because many of its frontier congregations were too poor to afford even a whistle. Otherwise, it is probable the question would have become an issue sooner than it did in view of the dependence on scriptural authority inherent in the makeup of the Movement. This is seen in the fact that when printed notes as aids to singing were first introduced, a few watchful guardians of scriptural authority pointed out that they were unauthorized as elements of worship. It so happened, however, that one of the most sincere advocates of adhering to the silences had, in all innocence, begun publishing hymnbooks with music in round notes. Four "parts" singing had come into use, and Augustus Damron Fillmore, a talented young preacher-musician, had sought to encourage the harmonious blending by putting into the hands of as many of the sweet singers of Israel as he could reach, copies of three hymnbooks he compiled which carried the helpful round notes—the *Christian Psalmist*, the *Harp of Zion*, and the *Christian Psaltery*. These became widely used and acclaimed, and as nobody was prepared to discard them, the propriety of using round notes was soon ignored.

One of the first recorded instances of a Disciple church venturing to use such an innovation as a musical instrument occurred shortly before the Civil War started. In Midway, Kentucky, the pastor, L. L. Pinkerton, not only agreed to but encouraged the installation of a hand organ in the sanctuary in 1859 for use in the worship services. As its plaintive notes pealed from the small sanctuary on a cloudless blue October morning, they seemed to reverberate across the length and breadth of the brotherhood. But the drums of war were also beginning to reverberate, and they soon drowned out the uproar the organ created. Not until the conflict was over did the question again raise its head.

L. L. Pinkerton was a tall, warm, glowing man, a doctor

of medicine and an able preacher. His credentials as a dedicated Christian were above question. He had demonstrated his faith by many good works, especially his almost single-handed establishment of a school for orphan girls near Midway, Kentucky, which had become known far and wide as an example of Christian concern for those in need. He was a pulpit orator of excellence, a counselor firm and impartial, a scholar whose knowledge and wisdom were reflected in an uncommonly keen sense of humor, and a man whose popularity was balanced by a humility which compelled him to refuse several college presidencies. And he enjoyed a good ear for music. He was not about to forego blending his voice with the harmonious chords of an organ when singing his beloved hymns because the Bible had not anticipated such an instrument and sanctioned its use.

Following the close of the war, with the nation settling down to more or less normal living, musical instruments began appearing in public markets. Melodeons, harpsichords, wind-propelled organs with foot pedals began gracing parlors of the well-to-do church members in the Movement, providing a relieving center of mirth and melody from the raw memories of the conflict. Inevitably people who loved their churches began coveting their use as aids to worship. Taking courage from the example of the Midway, Kentucky, Church, congregations here and there began installing them.

The controversy over the organ's use in worship services was at first accentuated by the peculiar position in which the Movement found itself at this period in its development. The rise in its cultural level had been experienced by its city churches, and by those in the larger towns, and to a lesser extent in the rural communities. But a number of churches resisted it. They insisted on keeping their meetinghouses unadorned, and their preachers rewarded with a side of hog meat because they entertained a deep-seated suspicion of wealth. Somehow they connected organs with fashionable society and ostentatious show. To them an organ was a symptom of wayward, worldly inclinations that boded evil. That the use of the instrument was also a violation of scriptural silence, did not at first loom large in their objections, and it is possible that the all-out war that eventually resulted over the matter could have been mercifully dissipated by time and Christian forbearance as cultural tides engulfed the rural areas, if various spokesmen had not assumed the task of fanning the question of scriptural authority into flames. Most of these self-appointed monitors were the editors of small and not-so-small periodicals, but the tremendous impact of their combined bristling editorials gave evidence that the encroaching worldliness so dreaded by their rural and small-town readers had been accompanied by an even more encroaching, insidious power of the church press.

During the dispute over slavery, the editors of the church papers published in the North had the advantage of the attacker. This gave them more temerity in speaking out on the issue. Their southern counterparts, as spokesmen for the slaveholding region, were expected to defend it, but somehow found it embarrassing, as Christian journals, to do so. They were saved, however, from acknowledging this conflict of interest by the harsh fact they were all soon stony broke as well as deprived of paper, ink and mailing facilities. Only one church paper in the South, the *Christian Intelligencer*, edited by John G. Parrish in Richmond, Virginia, was able to keep afloat during the war.

But now their work could be resumed, and the itching fingers of the editors again had something to write about. In the North, South, East and West periodicals claiming to speak for the Movement jumped on the issue of innovations with alacrity. Among them the *American Christian Review*, founded in 1856 with the articulate, earthy Benjamin Franklin at the helm, carried the loudest voice. Mr. Franklin had maintained its existence in Cincinnati during the war by holding to a neutral position. This enabled him also to hold on to subscribers in all sections of the divided nation. Although this stance was interpreted by some cynics as evidence of the shrewd nature with which Mr. Franklin was endowed, all agreed the editor was sincerely dedicated to the belief that participation in war by a Christian was wrong.

"We will not take up arms against, fight and kill the brethren we have labored for twenty years to bring into the Kingdom," Franklin announced at the war's start. And he stuck with it. As the war fever mounted and public emotions heightened, he was threatened with bodily torture; he was ostracized, ridiculed, denounced as a creator of constructive treason. But he refused to retreat. Given the choice by military authorities of fighting or working to defend Cincinnati, he limped painfully to the hills back of Covington and arduously, relentlessly worked with pickax and shovel, erecting barricades, living on army rations, suffering exposure and near starvation. But he refused to kill his brother man.

Now, with the war over, the same stubborn cast of mind prompted Mr. Franklin to come to grips with other things he considered wrong. The increasing acceptance of such an innovation as the organ suggested to him that possibly the basic structure of the brotherhood was being corroded. Accordingly he undertook a personal tour of the churches to ferret out other insidious "expediences." He met with much success. In fact, he unloosened a whole Pandora's box of potential disputes which he felt obliged to publicize in his paper. Among other things he learned that preachers were discussing the probable mystic indwelling of the Holy Spirit in aiding sinners to believe and accept Christ, without recourse to the Word. Mr. Franklin was convinced speculation on the Holy Spirit as an operating agency in conversion would dissipate, if not undermine, the concept of the all-sufficiency of the Bible to convert upon which Alexander Campbell had founded the Movement. This bit of theological hairsplitting did little to throw light for his readers on their pathway to heaven, but it did impart to them a fear that infidels were lurking in every church. The identification of such interlopers need not be awaited, Mr. Franklin implied, until their views could be ascertained on such an abstract matter as that of the work of the Holy Spirit; heretics could be located quite readily as those who accepted the use of the organ in worship.

Such a test, superficial and devoid of spiritual meaning, might have borne the seeds of its own undoing if allowed to stop there. But it took on the aspect of a visible symbol of the basic "poles apart" attitude toward a question that had become vital among the brethren. Did the silences of the Scriptures bind them to abstain, or loose them to perform? One group of men held that where there was no prohibition there was no transgression. Another group saw things differently. Where there was no clear command to act there was no justification for action, and any step in that direction was a violation of God's word.

The long, dark tunnel of controversy over what constituted an "opinion," which any man was free to express and act upon, and what constituted "an addition to God's plan for his church," and was therefore sinful, had been entered, and cast its spell over the children of God.

CHAPTER XIII

"The Saints Their Watch Were Keeping"

The outcry against the use of the organ raised by the articulate Benjamin Franklin was soon echoed by equally articulate Tolbert Fanning, who was inspired to give rebirth to his suspended *Gospel Advocate* as soon as he could get around to it after the war's close. The paper was reborn in Nashville, Tennessee, in 1866 with a vigor and fighting spirit that reflected the stance of another young man Mr. Fanning enlisted at his side. The young man was David Lipscomb, a younger brother of William, who had worked previously with Mr. Fanning but whose health would not permit him to reenter the fray.

William and David were the only sons of first cousins, Granville Lipscomb and his wife Nancy. The family's roots were in Virginia, but Granville and Nancy had migrated to Tennessee with their small sons, and here Nancy soon died. As a man needed a wife in the frontier country, Granville remarried within a year, a woman named Jane Breeden. Eventually seven children were born to them, and the family became a happy unit. But between William and David existed the close tie of their common parentage and, although they differed widely in temperament, they became inseparable. William was less rugged than his younger brother and prone to illness, but he was the one always sent by the father to the gristmill as "David would get into mischief," the father explained.

The two brothers entered Franklin College near Nashville together in 1846, the school conducted by Tolbert Fanning. The institution was in its second term and still maintaining a forbidding schedule. Each student was required to give nine hours a day to study and five hours to working in the garden. The faculty also participated in this program, teaching nine hours and working with hoe and pitchfork for five hours. The scheme was abandoned the next year, but it would have worked, Mr. Fanning was convinced, if it had not been for the fact the faculty rebelled.

Both boys had attended regularly the Bear's Creek Church near their home in Owl Hollow in Middle Tennessee, a church which subscribed to the doctrine of Alexander Campbell. But not until they came under the craggy eye of the towering Tolbert Fanning did they join. Even then they dipped into the world of religion with caution. It was six years after they graduated from Franklin College before they embarked on their lifework of preaching, eventually finding in the task the satisfaction all men discover when fulfilling their destiny.

In a sense the Lipscomb brothers personified as much as any men who participated in the Disciple Movement the freedom-loving spirit of America. They relished freedom with a passion. Any inroads upon it met with instant and violent rebuff. Before the war started, copies of Benjamin Franklin's paper the *American Christian Review* had fallen into their hands, and his contention that all war was wrong, and that no Christian should engage in it, convinced them that the government was embarked on a course that violated individual freedom. His stand gave them courage in a position they both took as the war engulfed the nation—they would never take up arms against their fellow man.

Tolbert Fanning agreed with them. But when he was forced to discontinue his paper in 1861, his stand against the conflict took a less belligerent form. It was that of a despising aloofness from the whole sorry mess. He went about his business as if the war was not raging, winning blue ribbons at the Tennessee State Fair for his ewe sheep and trotting stallions, and his harness mares. His attitude infuriated his neighbors and, with the Lipscomb brothers, he was persecuted at first by the Confederate sympathizers and then by the Union forces when they swept down the Cumberland River valley. The Confederates took his horses and farm tools, and the Federals occupied his house. He was arrested for treason when Andrew Johnson became military governor of the state, and his remaining buildings were burned to the ground.

William, now married, had made room for David in his household, and the two brothers had bought a five-hundred-acre farm from Mr. Fanning for $16,275, near White's Bend on the Cumberland River. Mr. Fanning had thrown in two wagons, an assortment of farm and carpenter tools, household furniture, two mares, forty-five head of cattle, five yoke of oxen, a number of hogs and all the wood crop on the place. All this was lost to the invading armies.

William, in poor health, was forced into a silent acceptance of the outrage but David had a toughness that would brook no such treatment. In appearance he was not a prepossessing man. His stocky frame and round head set on a short neck seemed built more for the rough life of the open than the pulpit or schoolroom, and a habit of blunt frankness in his speech did little to ease the unfavorable impression he often created. But he had the courage of a lion, and now he tramped into Nashville and presented himself to Governor Johnson, demanding retribution. None was forthcoming, but he refused to be silenced. He demanded an honorable exemption from military service and, when this was denied, he drew up a petition and sent it to Richmond, the Confederate capital, declaring his opposition to the war, refusing to have anything to do with it.

His defiance was no mere gesture. Whereas at first he had been opposed only to participation in the war, now he determined to have nothing to do with civil government of any kind. Never again would he even vote. He became convinced a Christian's first and only allegiance was to God. The church needed no help from human governments; it was destined by God to form governments of its own according to its own views of right, and for the accomplishment of its own ends.

David married in 1862, while the war was still on, a fine young woman as vital and determined as he, named Margaret Zellner. Owning no possessions after the destruction of his property, the young couple kept house in a log cabin near Lawrenceburg, Tennessee, cooking over an open fire, their improvised furniture an assortment of rough-hewn logs and cornhusk mattings, enduring ostracism and privation. Around them the war raged. When their infant son, the only child they were destined to have, died suddenly one stormy midnight, David went out and cut down a cedar tree by the light of occasional flashes of lightning, to fashion a coffin. By dawn, friendless, bereft, they loaded the precious bundle in their wagon, maneuvering with difficulty to get through the picket lines to reach the Zellner family burying plot in Maury County.

To such a man Tolbert Fanning knew he could entrust the pages of the *Gospel Advocate;* here was a man able to fight the battles for which Fanning was being forced by his increasing years to wage with lessening vigor. So it is no wonder that, when the war was over and Mr. Fanning was casting about in 1866 for a co-editor to replace the ailing William Lipscomb, his choice was the aggressive, determined, committed, dedicated and articulate David Lipscomb.

Within a year David Lipscomb was virtually in control of the paper.

The appeal of the Movement for David Lipscomb lay in its avowal of freedom—freedom of interpretation of the Bible, freedom of conscience, freedom from ecclesiastical control, freedom of every man to his own opinion, and of every congregation to go its own way. For him, Tolbert Fanning exemplified that freedom.

When Mr. Fanning had returned from Cincinnati in the late fall of 1849, after attending the formation of the American Christian Missionary Society, and had voiced his first mild apprehension that the autonomy of the local churches might be threatened by the creation of the national organization which he already considered unscriptural, the seeds of suspicion of all such innovations were planted in David's youthful mind. There they took root, and grew and flowered with rapidity and vigor.

Later, the passage of resolutions by the American Society, especially those in 1861 and in 1863 concerning the preservation of the Union, supplied for him the final evidence that trust could no longer be placed in the national agency. He had questioned before its scriptural soundness and authority, as he did that of the organ; now he questioned its motives. It backed political issues; it was itself political. The dread of such a body assuming authority over the freedom of the local church obsessed him.

By this time Benjamin Franklin, once a servant of the American Society, also had come out against the organization. His opposition to this innovation had emerged slowly despite the vehemence of his stand against the organ. He had viewed the Society in its beginning days as a necessary agency to extend the work of the church, but now he saw it as displacing the church as a working force. "We have tried to construe things we have seen among us in a favorable light, but all in vain," he said. "The conviction is there, deep and strong . . . that evil, most ruinous and mischievous evil, is intended." He seemed to write more in sorrow than in anger, but the anger was there, and soon began expressing itself against the Society in the same strong terms he employed against the use of organs in church services. Both lacked scriptural authority.

Again and again the two editors—David Lipscomb in the *Gospel Advocate*, and Benjamin Franklin in the *American Christian Review*—struck with horrendous force, and the brotherhood reeled. "It is our solemn conviction that the adopting or substitution of any society or plan for Christian work," David Lipscomb stated plainly, "is an insult to God and a disgrace to the Christian profession." The American Christian Missionary Society, he went on to point out, was a human institution. It was organized by men instead of by God to do the work God gave the church. It was a reflection on God's wisdom, on the adequacy of the church, and on the Bible as a guide sufficient for all Christian men.

This the two able, influential editors believed with utter sincerity, and this they boldly and persistently proclaimed. Conciliatory overtures were made by supporters of the American Society in the interest of peace, but neither Mr. Franklin nor Mr. Lipscomb was impressed, and many cheered them on. "Do you wish to make the impression that there are no differences when differences exist?" David Lipscomb chided a reader who questioned his belligerent course. "That would be to perpetrate a deception upon the public, to act a falsehood."

Among the voices cheering their perseverance were two from Kentucky, their cutting edges as sharp and incisive as a surgeon's scalpel. They belonged to Moses Lard and John McGarvey, once students together in Bethany College, now bound in lifelong affection by their common interests and by a high caliber of intelligence.

Moses Lard was eighteen years old before he could write his name. He was tall, as straight and as formidable as an Indian, with flashing gray eyes, black hair and a protruding chin. The poverty of his family had prevented any formal education for him in the backwoods of Missouri, where his parents had migrated in the late 1820's from Tennessee after the birth of Moses, and in this he differed from his close friend John McGarvey, who was born in Kentucky and also reared in Missouri, but in the more cultured atmosphere of an aristocratic stepfather, Gürdon Saltonstall.

Moses Lard never lost the scars of his early poverty. It implanted in him a bitterness that flavored his life. He became a tailor, indifferent to religion, at times antagonistic to the Calvinistic preachers he occasionally encountered. He was lanky as a young man, loose-jointed, all muscle and tough sinew, strong as the mules which tilled his father's poor soil. But a restlessness he could not define haunted him; a feeling that his life was drained of meaning, and when he came into possession of the document written by Walter Scott entitled "The Gospel Restored," his interest and his untapped intellect were captured. He had married and was the father of two children, but he determined upon an education that would equip him to preach and to restore this same Gospel to its primitive simplicities. He entered Bethany College in 1845, and graduated in three years as valedictorian of his class, and returned to Missouri to preach.

John McGarvey entered Bethany College a year later, in 1846, graduating in 1850. He was ten years younger than Moses Lard, but the friendship that developed between the two students was deep, and was resumed when John returned to Missouri following his graduation.

John McGarvey stood scarcely more than five feet tall, and beside the towering Moses Lard he seemed even smaller. But in eloquence and in intellect they were matched as giants. For ten years they preached in neighboring Missouri communities, and when John McGarvey was called to Lexington, Kentucky, in 1862 to placate the Main Street Christian Church there, in its growing tendency to divide over the slavery issue, Moses Lard soon followed.

There Moses Lard began issuing in 1863 a quarterly journal

which stands without a peer for brilliance and incisiveness in the early literature of the Movement. The paper, called *Lard's Quarterly*, had for its stated purpose the proclamation of the claims for primitive Christianity, and was dedicated to the uncorrupted Gospel. That meant, in the climate of the day, that its chief purpose was to present an implacable resistance to any inroads of liberal thought in the brotherhood. It was not surprising, therefore, that in one of the first issues Mr. Lard turned his guns on the sinful innovation of using a musical instrument in worship.

"Let every preacher resolve at once that he will never enter a meetinghouse in which an organ stands," he said. "Let no brother ever unite with another using an organ. Let brethren remonstrate in gentle, kind, but decided terms and, if unheeded, let them abandon the church. Thus these organ-grinding churches will be broken down and the sooner they are in fragments the better for the cause of Christ."

Not only the organ but any innovation became the victim of his vitriolic condemnation. Of such a blight, he wrote, "No term but fiendish will describe it. It comes in humming the sweetest notes of Zion; it goes out amid the ruin it works, howling like an exorcised demon. . . . No more has it an ear for reason, argument or Scripture than the image of Baal. Argue with the spirit of innovation, indeed! I would as soon be caught cracking syllogisms over the head of the man of sin. Never! Rebuke it in the name of the Lord; if it go not out, expel it. This only will cure it."

Mr. Lard was not a man to mince words. He was committed to the unity of all Christians, but in his dedication to the Movement he conceived of unity being achieved only by all others joining the followers of Mr. Campbell. When, in 1864, the Baptists made overtures toward reuniting with the Campbell forces, Mr. Lard viewed the proposition with scorn. "During the last forty years we have been persistently denounced by the Baptists as a 'pestilential sect,' as 'baptized infidels,' and as less entitled to their respect than the infant-sprinkling parties," he wrote. "It is an insult to the name of Jesus Christ which we wear to even confer with any body of people claiming to be Christians who deny us that honor. . . . I am much inclined to think the Baptists look on us as apostates from the church of Christ, and as

having forfeited our claim to be held as Christians, and that what
the vast majority of them now seek is that, in penitence, we
shall return to them, be tried by them, and if deemed Christians
that then we shall be so treated, and not before. . . . Paul on
one occasion bore himself proudly in Philippi. We like his Roman
spirit. As a people we owe to the Baptists nothing."

An obituary notice he wrote upon the passing of a friend likewise reveals an astonishing frankness not often found in polite
church circles. After expressing a few words of regret, his honesty
broke through.

"There was not an intellectual feature in his face," he said
of the departed one. "Indeed, his expression and appearance
would generally have ranked him as standing none above the very
common level. He was not deficient in excellent sense, and his
abilities were respectable, but when this is said I believe the
most has been said that can be. His face was unfortunate; it
was pinched and dull. It was the face of a third-rate Presbyterian
preacher, of a man who had died in melancholy. To live, I should
say, gave him little pleasure; to die, but little pain."

In Mr. Lard's battle against the use of the organ, his friend
John McGarvey rallied to his side. Mr. McGarvey was also a
formidable adversary, but he had a personal grace denied Mr.
Lard, a charm that made him deeply beloved, even by those who
disagreed with him. He was a curious mixture of courtesy and
ferocious intolerance; more inclined to dally with the amenities
than his friend. His first efforts toward combatting the use of
the organ were directed toward enlisting the wavering *Millennial
Harbinger* to join in denouncing the use of such an innovation.

But the *Millennial Harbinger* was desperately trying to maintain a neutral position on the matter, under the editorship of
William K. Pendleton. Alexander Campbell was in his final days,
and his failing health muted his flamboyance. Although he had
questioned the use of the organ in his early days, referring to it
once as being as distasteful as "the sound of a cowbell in church,"
he was now weary and in no state of mind to enter the dispute.
Doubtless he hoped it would meet the eventual disinterest that
had been the fate of the issue of "open" versus "closed" communion. That knotty question had lifted its head quite a few
times. Was it consistent for the Disciples of Christ to permit

the pious unimmersed of other churches to the Lord's Table? The question hung unanswered, for nobody wanted to challenge the undeniable truth that the Lord's Table belonged to the Lord. So, by tacit consent, the churches agreed their only task was to spread the Table, and let every man examine his own worthiness to partake.

Mr. Pendleton took no sides on the organ matter, but he did open the columns of the still influential *Millennial Harbinger* to a discussion of the subject. And for two years John McGarvey used those columns to take on any man so daring as to advocate, or even defend the use of a musical instrument in worship, replying in increasingly harsh terms. Soon the issue obscured all else. It raged in the columns of the *Gospel Advocate* and the *American Christian Review,* growing out of all proportion to what many considered its importance. But sides were so markedly drawn few men dared withdraw from the fray, or suggest it be left to the healing hand of time.

By a curious bit of reasoning both Moses Lard and John McGarvey made a distinction in their war on innovations, between an innovation for "work," such as the missionary society, and an innovation for "worship," such as the organ, and they refused to join David Lipscomb and Benjamin Franklin in opposing the missionary society. But all four men stood shoulder to shoulder in their battle against corrupting the purity of the New Testament pattern of worship by the use of a musical instrument. They likewise were as one in advocating the view that the Disciples of Christ had the perfect plan for uniting Christendom and they shared the conviction that eventually all men would accept it. The crying need, as they saw it, was for the church colleges to prepare ministers who considered that their primary task was to proclaim that doctrine and annihilate the wayward, misguided denominations.

John McGarvey's devotion to the Movement was based on its emphasis on the Bible as an all-sufficient guide. Studying the book, teaching it, defending it, became with him almost an obsession. A steady stream of commentaries on the Bible's various books came from his pen. To instill in young men a passion for preaching the Word, he championed in 1865 the founding of what was to become the College of the Bible in Lexington,

Kentucky, a name and an institution which became famous, and eventually he relinquished the pulpit of the Main Street Christian Church in that city to join its faculty, weathering many storms which raged about it.

The plain-spoken ways of these four stalwarts had an influence on many men in the Movement less gifted in their felicity of expression, but who were equally endowed with their fighting spirit. They, too, felt free to speak their minds without mincing words. A clamor ensued that drowned out all else and, until the brotherhood developed a seemingly unlimited capacity to absorb dissension, the body of people which had come into existence to bring peace to a divided Christendom appeared to the rest of the religious community as more bent on war among themselves.

A group of concerned men in northern Ohio were watching the display of hostile bickering with increasing apprehension. They had formed themselves into a group during the war years to discuss the need for a mouthpiece that would assure the world the Disciples of Christ were behind the preservation of the Federal Union. When a lack of unanimity on that stand became all too evident, the discussions were dropped for a time.

But in 1864, when the enormous influence of the critical journals edited by Mr. Lard and Mr. Lipscomb and Mr. Franklin, and others who followed their leadership, reached alarming proportions, they came together again to discuss the founding of a journal which would combat that influence. They evisioned a paper which would focus attention on the things upon which the brethren agreed, ignoring as far as possible the points on which they differed. It would emphasize the spirit and not the letter of the law, imparting a sense of the need for God's guidance in all disputes. It would breathe forth the spirit of Jesus Christ in which the Movement was seeking to reconcile the world. With the promise of national peace around the corner, the need for displaying a similiar peace within the growling brotherhood seemed urgent.

The first decisive step toward this worthy end was taken on December 22, 1865, when four brothers—Charles, Thomas, Isaac and John T. Phillips, oil barons and dedicated members of the Movement, rich in spirit as well as in this world's goods—invited to their home in New Castle, Pennsylvania, about a dozen equally prominent and concerned men to explore the idea.

The Phillips home was a commodious structure of large rooms and lofty ceilings. It was set on a sloping knoll in a grove of cedars, well back from the white picket fence that edged the graveled roadway leading into the village of New Castle. It had been the center of many festive occasions in the life of the Movement, and as the group of men assembled on this day the scene must have taken on the aspect of good fellowship as well as serious business.

The serious business eventuated in the firm conclusion that the present aspect of affairs in the Movement required a new weekly paper edited by a strong, fair-minded Christian man, and launched and given direction by men wise in efficient business methods. Too many papers had been founded by well-meaning individuals in a haphazard fashion, to sink without a trace in a sea of debts. This was not to be one of them.

During the next few weeks the group assembled frequently, sometimes at New Castle, sometimes in nearby Cleveland. Holding firmly to business methods, a charter was obtained under the name the Christian Publishing Association; capital stock was set at $100,000, and shares were offered at ten dollars each. The paper was named the *Christian Standard*, and, again holding firmly to the plan, a strong, fair-minded Christian man was selected as editor. His name was Isaac Errett.

Isaac Errett was at the time preaching for a church in Detroit, Michigan. He had relinquished his post as corresponding secretary of the American Christian Missionary Society when war restrictions made travel among the churches all but impossible, and for a brief time had associated himself with the *Millennial Harbinger*, using its columns to urge toleration and forbearance among his war-fevered brethren. They now comprised a brotherhood of over a half-million members, their churches penetrating forty states and spilling over into England, Australia, Wales, New Zealand and Jamaica. Their preachers were numbered in the thousands. But their numerical growth had not been accompanied by a corresponding growth in harmony, and Isaac Errett saw more clearly than perhaps any other man in the Movement that the unity the founders of the Movement had sought would never, and perhaps never should, encompass uniformity of thought.

He was enlightened in this view by his experience after leaving the *Millennial Harbinger* to assume the pastorate of a small church in Detroit. The congregation he was called to serve was the so-called liberal wing of a larger group. It had broken away when the more conservative element in the group insisted on demonstrating the Movement's adherence to the simplicities of worship, by holding its services in the basement of the City Hall. As if to emphasize that such austerity was not part and parcel of the Movement's doctrine, the "come-outers" had purchased and renovated a structure formerly occupied by a Congregational group, transforming it into a thing of beauty with a steeple which dominated the community. The project stimulated public curiosity. What was the doctrine of these people who called themselves Disciples of Christ?

Isaac Errett was not long in telling them. He wrote and circulated a concise statement, enumerating step by step the Movement's position and its beliefs and practices. It was a lucid statement, compelling in its logic, and he entitled it "A Synopsis of the Beliefs of the Disciples of Christ." It explained the doctrine so clearly that not only did the public become aware of the position of the Movement, but many of the stragglers left in the City Hall rejoined their erstwhile brethren, convinced of the error of their ways.

But others, watching from afar, were equally convinced Mr. Errett had fallen into grave error himself. He had committed the grievous sin of forming for the Disciples of Christ the very thing they had come into existence to destroy—a written creed. The Bible alone outlined their position, and Christ alone was their creed. Within a fortnight the guns of Benjamin Franklin, David Lipscomb and Moses Lard were turned upon Mr. Errett.

"There is not a man in our ranks who has not felt scandalized by it," Moses Lard wrote in his *Quarterly* concerning Mr. Errett's "Synopsis." "It is a deep offense against the brotherhood, an offense tossed into the teeth of a people who, for forty years, have been working against the division and evil tendency of creeds. We still cry it is a creed, a creed, a creed without the appropriate label, a genuine snake in the grass, wearing a honeyed name."

But the group of men who had been scanning the horizon for the best possible editor for their new paper thought otherwise. Here was a man who knew intimately the doctrines of the Movement, and would hold high its standards. And the outcry must have convinced Mr. Errett himself that, while speaking for a Movement had its frightening aspects, it also had an irresistible challenge. For when the group approached him, they found him in a receptive frame of mind.

In proceeding in what seemed to be a sound, businesslike manner, the founders of the paper were aware they were blazing a new trail. The birth of no other paper in the brotherhood had been so carefully blueprinted, so painstakingly calculated. As the months rolled by they discovered also that few other papers had been forced to cling so precariously to life.

Almost at once unforeseen expenses were incurred. Debts began mounting; subscribers were not forthcoming; buyers for the shares of capital stock were scarce. Within a year of its founding, the disillusioned stockholders were of a mind to discontinue the venture. Isaac Errett had moved his family to Cleveland, and continued to work tirelessly, disheartened but still hopeful. He pled for time, for another year's trial. But the next year conditions did not improve, and the founders agreed to give him not only time but presented to him the paper itself, the whole business, run it if he could.

The first issue of the *Christian Standard* had come from press in April, 1866, and its front page carried the news of the death, on March 11, of Alexander Campbell. There is no record that Isaac Errett felt this strange coincidence was intended by divine providence as evidence the mantle of the great leader was being laid upon his shoulders, but the thought may have occurred to him. At any rate, something compelled him to hold on to the paper. He had no personal funds to carry it on; its continuance promised only more trouble and disappointment. On the other hand, his popularity as a preacher was such that almost any pulpit in the land would have welcomed him, affording him opportunity to give full voice to the Gospel he loved to proclaim, assuring him a life of usefulness and purpose, and relative ease.

He held on only by what is known today as "moonlighting."

He accepted a salaried position as president of nearby Alliance College in Ohio, and for a few desperate months met his classes in the daytime, and by night wrote, edited, read proof and helped mail out the paper, often working around the clock. The situation was precarious, and at the end of the year he was on the point of abandoning the whole project.

What would have happened had he done so is, of course, conjectural. The smoldering atmosphere of intolerance was plainly threatening a break in the ranks which, at that still formative period in the brotherhood's life, might have been fatal. Neither segment was yet in a position to stand alone. Other voices were urging caution, but none carried the weight of Isaac Errett's, and not even his was strong enough to completely dissipate all fears. But that he was kept in a position in which he could help mightily to forestall a break at the time suggests to many that, in deed and in truth, the saints their watch were keeping.

A printing executive in Cincinnati, R. W. Carroll, not a member of the Disciple brotherhood but a keen observer of the times and of men, sensed the potential value of such a journal, and of such a man as Isaac Errett, and offered to take over the financial management and continue publication of the paper. Mr. Errett gratefully accepted. What equipment and files had been accumulated were hastily packed and moved to Cincinnati, and on July 31, 1869, the *Christian Standard* appeared from that location.

The eyes of the brotherhood, and especially those of the editors of the other existing journals, had been watching the developments with mixed reactions. To many the new paper was a welcome spokesman for truth, tolerance and trust. To others it had assumed the stance of a creature bent on combat with those of its brethren daring to expose the heresies and departures from scriptural authority. And when it moved to Cincinnati, and began a new existence under the ownership of R. W. Carroll, David Lipscomb refused to publish the "prospectus" sent him. Mr. Carroll, he had learned, was a Quaker. Any paper issued under his aegis, Mr. Lipscomb viewed as one being published by "a company of infidels."

Moses Lard was surprisingly more merciful in his *Quarterly.*

But his brilliantly edited paper was to last only a short while longer, succumbing to financial difficulties itself in 1868. The next year he joined with John McGarvey and three other preachers in issuing another journal, the *Apostolic Times*, dedicated to the primitive faith and primitive practices. It breathed a more genuinely tolerant spirit of goodwill toward those of differing opinions, and might have even rallied to the support of Mr. Errett in his crusade for harmony, but it was caught in the financial panic of the early 1870's and lasted only a brief time.

Almost simultaneous with its demise another sheet was making a small stir in the Midwest which was to have a significant impact on the Movement. It bore the timid name the *Gospel Echo*. No man foresaw that this unpretentious paper, later renamed the *Christian-Evangelist*, would eventually join with the *Gospel Advocate* and the *Christian Standard* in serving as spokesmen for three divergent and distinctly separate segments of the Movement as it stumbled on its pathway toward unity.

No man foresaw this, for at the time the *Christian Standard*, freed of its financial worries, was beginning to sweep all before it. As the kindly spirit of Isaac Errett began permeating its pages, thousands were won to its tolerant point of view. Soon it became the nerve center of that group of the brethren who, merciful in their judgments, sought to perserve the brotherhood from the tragedy of division.

CHAPTER XIV

"Into All the World"

Despite the doctrinal disputes raging in the brotherhood, God's love and his redemptive plan of salvation were still primary in the hearts of the people. Most sermons dealt with the deeper matters of faith, and for thousands "life continued luminous under the Spirit's power." Among them was a group of women.

"This is a flame of the Lord's kindling," was the utterance of Thomas Munnell, corresponding secretary of the American Christian Missionary Society, when in 1874 he first learned the group was bent on organizing itself for missionary work. "And no man can extinguish it!" he added with an emphasis that indicated his own weariness with doctrinal disputes.

The remark contained a rebuke not only to the bickering disputants but to the men who had allowed their missionary zeal to languish. Yet nobody, least of all the women, allowed so much as a flick of an eyelash to reveal they knew all too well the men deserved the rebuke. The men felt it, too. As word spread of what the women were up to, it met with a variety of reactions. Women would only be playing at the job, one guilt-ridden preacher scoffed; they were amusing themselves; they would tire of their plaything in a year and abandon it. Another advised them to invest their time instead in giving attention to their dress, to the hooking, lacing, strapping, cramping, loading, painting and curling that deformed their bodies and dwarfed their minds. Others saw in the project a threat to the laws of nature; women were getting out of their natural sphere. "Let the women keep silent," they said in effect.

But all were equally futile in putting out the flame.

Such reactions were not surprising to the women. The Woman's

Rights Movement had not yet won for them equal treatment in the land, nor equal recognition of their abilities. They were still hobbled by tradition, immobilized by their position on a pedestal. Few were allowed more than an elementary education; experience in speaking in public was generally denied them; the intricacies of organizing more than a household routine were a mystery for them; and in most states married women, denied legal access to the family purse, had no experience in handling money. These handicaps make all the more remarkable the courage of the churchwomen in not only undertaking a piece of public work at a time when the country was still in the grip of the financial panic of the early 1870's, but in plunging into the waters of an enterprise in which the only other existing national organization of the brotherhood had mired itself twenty years before, its efforts now sunk almost without a trace.

The women did not exactly plunge in, nor were they without the backing of many wise and farsighted men. The possibility of the women undertaking such a task had arisen intermittently ever since the American Society's Missionary efforts had dwindled and died, and in 1869, five years before the women took action, Thomas Munnell had publicly proposed such a step when the churches met in convention in Louisville, Kentucky. No action was taken on his proposal, however, for at the time the churches had other troubles. A new plan of national cooperation, later to be called the Louisville Plan, was being adopted that year. It was a conciliatory gesture toward the brethren who were critical of the American Society and its way of doing things. The plan corrected some of the Society's more blatant defects, but it created others; it was cumbersome and unworkable. The critical brethren were not impressed, and it became a mound of ashes within a few years. From the ashes, however, arose an agency which was to continue for a generation. Organized as representative of the churches rather than of any individuals who found it convenient to attend and participate, it was called the General Christian Missionary Convention. It was while this assembly was being held at the Richmond Street Christian Church in Cincinnati, in October of 1874, that seventy-five inspired and inspiring women quietly congregated in the basement of the church.

The meeting was by cautious prearrangement. Its inception had taken place in the mind of an Iowa woman, Mrs. Caroline Neville Pearre, six months before when, as she later recalled, the impulse to organize the women had come to her with the force of divine backing after her devotional hour on the morning of April 10. She had learned of the frustration of some women in the nearby Des Moines church, who had formed themselves into a missionary group in February of that year, only to sit looking at each other, shrouded in an atmosphere of timid uncertainty. Other groups had formed elsewhere with the same result. Mrs. Pearre determined to know why. She formed a group in her own church in Iowa City, and soon learned firsthand. The futility of a single, unorganized gesture was all too plain. Alone, a local group of women could do practically nothing; united, the world could be won to Christ.

Letters to women over the country began streaming from Mrs. Pearre's quill pen—to Elmira Dickinson in Illinois, to Mrs. Joseph King in Pennsylvania, to Mrs. R. R. Sloan in Ohio, to Mrs. Otis A. Burgess and Mrs. Maria Jameson in Indianapolis, and to others. Mrs. Burgess and Mrs. Jameson, both prominent Indianapolis women, took the letter to a meeting of a sewing circle being held in the mansion of Governor Wallace, whose wife, Zerelda, was an ardent Disciple. Here, as Mrs. Jameson later reported, the women became inspired to "pick up the crumbs, as it were, the pennies and nickels that are being wasted and thrown away for naught and scattered for trifles, and devote them to a good cause."

By fortuitous circumstance, Isaac Errett visited Iowa City that summer and, learning of Mrs. Pearre's dream, went back to Cincinnati and promptly wrote an editorial in the *Christian Standard* entitled "Help These Women!" in which he proposed they organize during the Cincinnati convention that fall. His call rang with compelling urgency, penetrating every home, hearthside and kitchen in the brotherhood. A letter Mrs. Pearre wrote to her friend Mrs. J. K. Rogers in Columbia, Missouri, was tucked into Mrs. Rogers's best new envelope and taken as fast as the post office could deliver it to the St. Louis office of the Christian Publishing Company on Main and Olive streets, where the alert editor of what was once the *Gospel Echo*, now renamed the *Christian*,

James Harvey Garrison, quickly fulfilled the paper's early name by echoing Mr. Errett's fervent commendation of the proposed organization.

Caroline Pearre had been a schoolteacher, presiding over her one-room Iowa school with a timid hand, but her disarming air of sweetness belied a strong will. Her brown hair fell from a center part in soft waves, and only a close observer would have noticed it was caught at the back of her neck in a hard, solid bun. She wore the ruffled lace of feminine delicacy at her throat, but it edged a stiff collar caught by a secure brooch. If patient resignation was conveyed in her expression, her eyes also held a level gaze and her mouth could form into a firm line.

In preparing for the meeting she was assisted by the two Indianapolis women who had inspired their group, both even more forceful personalities than herself. Mrs. Maria Jameson, her hair a mass of fluffy white-spun silk, was the daughter of the wealthy Indianapolis attorney Ovid Butler, who had been instrumental during the war in founding Northwestern Christian College, which was later to bear his name as Butler College. She was plump and jolly with a still youthful bounce, but with the toughness of her father's mind, a trait that enabled her to lead the new national society as its first president for sixteen years. During a spell of illness, the reins for six months of that time were relinquished to Mrs. Otis A. Burgess, the wife of one of the most prominent educators in the brotherhood, a more severely plain woman with steel-rimmed spectacles astride her thin nose, whose ability as a leader and devotion to the work were soon apparent. In 1890, when Mrs. Jameson's health would no longer permit her to continue, Mrs. Burgess again assumed command, serving as president until her death in 1902.

It was these women, and seventy others like them from nine states, who listened with close attention to Caroline Pearre that October afternoon in the basement of the Cincinnati church, as she outlined the plan she had in mind. The discussion which followed was long; every woman had her say. They were not sedate matrons in need of a cause, nor were they given to short bursts of enthusiasm. Before they separated they committed themselves to uniting in the bold endeavor, and set in motion various wheels, including the appointment of a committee to complete a tentative constitution the Indianapolis women had prepared. The committee must have worked all night, for the next morning a detailed blueprint for a national society was approved, a document so competently drawn it was able to withstand, with few changes, the ravages of the next seventy years as a solid platform for a far-flung work. The organization was given the name Christian Woman's Board of Missions; national officers were named; and the city of Indianapolis was selected as its headquarters.

It is revealing of the spirit that was to reign in the organization that Mrs. Pearre, its acknowledged founder, did not allow herself to be named its first president but accepted instead the less conspicuous but perhaps more demanding post of corresponding secretary. Despite the popular notion ascribed to the female of the species, no hint of jealousy appears in the records of the organization, and as the years passed few personal rivalries developed among its leaders, and those few dissolved before the all-consuming demands of the task they had undertaken.

The task was nothing less than sending the Gospel of Jesus Christ to the uttermost parts of the earth. If the more immediate idea was to shame the men of the church who had wilted at the helm of a similar undertaking twenty years before, they succeeded with stunning and satisfying swiftness.

The following day the General Convention recognized the formation of the new organization, and sat in polite if not enthusiastic attention as one of its leaders, Mrs. J. M. B. Goodwin, spoke from the platform, one of the first women ever to address a general brotherhood assembly. The women had been wise in selecting her to speak for them. She had the gift of expressive language, and while she was not a militant woman's rights worker, she was aware that many brothers saw heresy in women speaking from the pulpit or praying in public, and she did not hesitate to mention that fact. She also mentioned that churchwomen so far had been allowed only to do such things as prepare floral offerings and sing praises in corporate worship, but now they were determined to increase the sphere of their usefulness. That included chiding the men to themselves get busy. "The brother who contributes less to the missionary cause than he spends for tobacco, has not the true missionary spirit," she said. She also had a word for the women. "The sister who thinks more of the lace on her handkerchief than the enlightenment of the soul of her washerwoman's child, has small conception of her religious duties," she said, closing her speech with the injunction, "Be faithful then, dear sisters, among a faithless generation, and go forward in this noble cause. And if you have a truth to utter, speak; and leave the rest to God."

Many felt her rebuke was justified. "In all honesty," said Joseph King after she had finished, "we are the only people not obeying the Great Commission, and not even trying!" And Thomas Munnell added the sobering thought, "Perhaps we are not worthy to do missionary work. We may be depending too much on ourselves. We are not strong because we are not weak."

Before the General Convention adjourned it extended to the Christian Woman's Board of Missions not only recognition but hearty approval, "assured that it opens a legitimate field of activity and usefulness in which Christian women may be active co-operants of ours in the great work of sending the Gospel to the world. We pledge ourselves to help these women who propose to labor with us in the Gospel."

The resolution was well intended and sincere, but it made embarrassingly obvious the fact that before the women could be "active co-operants" they needed something to cooperate with, certainly more than the vacuum then existing in the way of a missionary program on the part of the rest of the church. Accordingly, at the General Convention of the churches the next year, 1875, few dissenting voices were raised when a plan was proposed to create another national agency, a church-wide Foreign Christian Missionary Society.

Before the women adjourned in Cincinnati they passed the collection plate. Into it fell the sum of $430. It was a magnificent offering, considering the group consisted of fewer than one hundred women whose own money was doled out to them in measured amounts. It was evident the offering represented their "egg money" or its equivalent, hoarded since the first inkling of the plan was heard in remote farm kitchens, and was testimony that each woman had weighed the small sacrifices against the giant satisfactions of being a part of the undertaking, and were entering into it with a determination and dedication which those with hearts attuned knew was a gauge to the future.

Their first field of service, they decided, would be Jamaica. Undoubtedly the pressing needs of the island influenced the decision, but it is not unlikely they partook of a certain unspoken satisfaction in "picking up the pieces" and carrying forward work in a land the men had forsaken. Certainly the men were painfully aware of it as the women began, nursing their nest egg of $430, adding to it all they could spare plus the monthly dues of ten cents asked of each member. For by the end of the next year a fund of over $1,700 was in hand, sufficient to send to Jamaica in 1876 their first missionaries, Mr. and Mrs. W. J. Williams of Platte City, Missouri.

The Christian Woman's Board of Missions was destined to lengthen its cords and strengthen its stakes with a rapidity that amazed the watching religious community, and infected its own brotherhood with enthusiasm for the cause. The procedure it adopted for conducting its work set several precedents for other religious groups. Since 1861 women's missionary societies had existed in other Protestant bodies, but the CWBM claimed to be the first managed entirely by women, and the first in which women used their own methods of creating, organizing, promoting and developing their plans. No man held membership on its policy-making committees, although they were engaged as employed workers.

But perhaps the most significant precedent set was the stance the Board assumed of ignoring with a silence more loud than any utterance the doctrinal disputes absorbing the rest of the brotherhood. In 1883 a four-page paper was started, the *Missionary Tidings*, and almost as a rebuke to the other brotherhood journals it stood steadfastly true to its name, refusing to engage in controversy, carrying only the glad tidings of missionary work. The completion of the Board's first decade of service was celebrated at the General Convention in St. Louis in 1884. The whole brotherhood "raised its Ebenezer" and inscribed thereon its grateful praise. By that time, the women reported, they had raised and dispensed over sixty thousand dollars. They owned property around the world valued at forty thousand dollars, and had thirteen missionaries at work.

The conscience-stricken men who had launched the Foreign Christian Missionary Society in 1875, a year after the women started, watched the progress of the women with something akin to envy. Their own frail craft rocked along for seven years with little to justify its existence. A gesture toward undertaking foreign work was made in 1878 by sending a preacher, W. T. Moore, to England to cultivate churches there, but no enthusiasm resulted for the task. England was a Christian land, and changing people from one Christian church to another conformed to nobody's conception of carrying out the Great Commission.

Isaac Errett had been elected president of the Foreign Society at the time of its founding, and the office of the *Christian Standard* commandeered as its headquarters. But Mr. Errett's time was of necessity almost wholly consumed with editing the paper and, while a succession of corresponding secretaries were engaged to get the organization off the ground, enthusiasm was lacking. Mr. Errett, troubled by the situation, realized a spark would have to be supplied.

The need for a spark was apparent also to a young man serving as pastor of the Christian Church at Mount Healthy, Ohio, near Cincinnati. His name was Archibald McLean.

As a fun-loving youth on Prince Edward Island twenty years before, Archibald McLean's imagination had been captured by stories related by a visiting missionary. The man must have had imagination himself, for one of his stories concerned the potential power of a missionary ship which would roam the high seas, carrying the message of redemptive love to the benighted hosts in distant lands. Whether such a missionary ship ever materialized, Mr. McLean never learned, but he never forgot the dream it implanted in him, nor the joy of extracting from a fish bucket in which he kept his meager savings a treasured sixpence, which he put in the collection plate with his small, grubby hands. The incident left an indelible yearning in him to share with others his luminous dream.

Archibald McLean was of Scotch descent. His parents, Malcolm and Alexandra McLean, had been brought to America as children from the Highlands of Scotland, their families settling on neighboring wooded tracts of fertile soil on Prince Edward Island. Here they married and here, near the village of Summerside, Archibald was born on September 9, 1849.

A period of solid but uninspired schooling prompted him to

forsake book learning to follow the carriage trade. The father, a stern Scotch Presbyterian, was imbued with a sense of the exclusive nature of God's grace, which Archibald accepted without question until he heard the visiting missionary's plea, and later came in contact with a man named Donald Crawford, an adherent of the Campbell Movement. After that he rebelled, as Alexander Campbell had done before him, at the Presbyterian practice of excluding from the Lord's Table those whom the Elders deemed "unworthy to partake." Other points in the Presbyterian doctrine began bothering him as he listened to Mr. Crawford's manner of magnifying the Word of God above all human authority, and when he learned of the new body of Christians who thought of themselves "not as a church, nor as 'the' church, but as a Movement within the churches for the union of all Christians," he was won to its Plea. He was immersed on a June Sunday in 1867, and from the moment of his baptism resolved to spend his life shepherding flocks in the new Movement. To that purpose he entered Bethany College in 1870, graduating four years later with honors.

He was at once called to the pulpit of the Mount Healthy church, and it was destined to be the only pastorate he would hold. The Mount Healthy church had been organized by David Burnet in 1839, but the imprint of Mr. Burnet's gentle spirit had taken wings before the holocaust of the war. Members refused to speak to each other, and a complete breakdown in cooperation prevented the erection of a planned building, forcing the congregation to meet in either the Free Meetinghouse or abandoned warehouses. For five years after the war no services of any kind were held. When a few members became sufficiently ashamed of themselves, they rounded up a few others and began reassembling once a week for worship. But memories of the war were still raw, and when the youthful Archibald McLean assumed the pastorate a month after his graduation from Bethany College in 1874, the emotional atmosphere was still so highly charged the Elders regularly voiced their divergent views on the conflict when presiding at the Lord's Table.

Although he did not realize it at the time, the experience Archibald McLean gained in pouring oil on these troubled waters was heaven-sent. For he was to need it later. He preached from the Mount Healthy church pulpit for eleven years, leading the members back into the practice of the love of God, and of their fellows, guiding them in the erection of a suitable house of worship; stretching the horizons of their minds and hearts with his dream of taking the Gospel to distant lands. When sermons voicing his outrage at the missionary lethargy of the church reached the ears of Isaac Errett, Mr. Errett knew the spark he was seeking to ignite the zeal of the brotherhood had been found.

Time was to prove Mr. Errett correct. For the next thirty-eight years, with an interlude of only two years when he was persuaded to serve as president of Bethany College, Archibald McLean led the forces of the expanding brotherhood of Disciples of Christ in deadly combat with heathen forces, his unique personality and his passion for the task scarcely equaled in missionary lore.

Archibald McLean never married, and his tall figure, gaunt and ungainly, his clothes rumpled and unkempt, became the embodiment of the missionary enterprise for two generations of Disciples; his work the foundation stone upon which it rests today. He traveled tirelessly among the churches in behalf of the Foreign Society. His voice was shrill, his laugh was a staccato bark; his eyes, an intense blue and deeply set, fixed themselves in embarrassing focus on each individual before him. As he spoke he jerked at his coat collar and swept impatiently at a lock of stubborn hair. But five minutes after he began describing conditions in pagan lands, few in the audience noticed such things.

Within a year after he assumed leadership of the Foreign Christian Missionary Society a stream of workers began sailing to distant lands. Each volunteer was personally and meticulously examined by him, and their worthiness attested to his shrewd judgment. It is of record that during the term of service of the several hundred missionaries sent out by Mr. McLean, each of them received a personal letter from him every month they were in the field.

He studied with the scrutiny of a statesman every development in foreign lands which might affect the missionary enterprise. No change in world conditions escaped him. Like a shrewd general in charge of an army, he outlined the strategy to be employed in attacking the citadels of the heathen faiths. He selected the base of the attacks, choosing always a spot in the center of a land at the heart of the nation. In India, it was in the Central and United Provinces; in Japan, Tokyo, the capital city; in China, it was the

great city on the Yangtze, Nanking; in Africa, it was a village
where the Equator crosses the Congo River the second time; in the
Philippine Islands, it was Manila. And when the decision was
made to enter Tibet, the forbidden land at the roof of the world,
nothing less was contemplated than entering its remote capital of
Lhasa.

The venture into Tibet, which eventually inflamed to its highest
degree the brotherhood's missionary passion, started when a man
in Holland, Petrus Rijnhart, conceived the idea of entering Tibet
from the China side to spread a Gospel plan strikingly similar to
that the Movement was espousing. He was convinced not only that
the New Testament contained all a man needed to attain salvation,
but that his task was to take it to the uttermost. The uttermost
was the far and vast interior of China. He had studied the means of
reaching that part of the world and had learned the ancient antip-
athy to foreigners, manifest in the heavily guarded passes of the
Himalayan frontier, did not exist to any appreciable degree on the
stern border between outer Tibet and China. Hence, in 1892, he
crossed the Chinese Empire and lived for ten months in the village of Lusar. There he was kindly received by the priests in the
Tibetan lamasery as a "white Lama from the west," and went about
doing good, distributing the Bible and explaining the simple plan
of salvation, unsponsored by any missionary board. The experience
confirmed his conviction the Lord would open the way to further
penetrate Tibet, and he came to America to arouse interest by
lecturing, and to secure funds.

His lecturing proved profitable, and among those whose interest
he aroused was a young woman, a member of the Disciple
brotherhood in Canada, who was just finishing her medical training. Her name was Susie Carson. He persuaded her to join him
as his wife and helpmate.

It evidently did not take much persuading, for Susie Carson
had joined the Ontario Christian Woman's Board of Missions
and had already determined to place her life and her medical
skills at the disposal of needy people. She was aflame with enthusiasm for the venture, as well as love for Petrus. They married,
and together she and her husband enlisted another dedicated
Christian, William Neil Ferguson, to join them. In the early

autumn of 1894, laden with medical supplies and Christian faith, and given the blessing of the Disciple churches who had heard of the project, but as yet no financial undergirding by either the Women's Board or the Foreign Society, the little party of three sailed from San Francisco. They were four months on their unchartered journey, reaching the village of Lusar, where Petrus had formerly lived, the middle of January, 1895.

Lusar at that time was a single street lined with flat-roofed mud houses in which one thousand Mohammedans, Chinese, Tibetans and Mongols lived in more or less amicable accord. At the end of the street the Rijnharts and Will Ferguson built their own flat-roofed house, as well as whatever furniture they felt essential, and for two years the intrepid missionaries surveyed the land, itinerating among villages in the mountainous country, mapping out their course. In the spring of 1897 a halt of necessity was called by the Rijnharts when, in June, Susie gave birth to a beautiful baby boy. They named him Charles Carson Rijnhart. Mr. Ferguson, probably impatient at the enforced halt, started itinerating on his own, and eventually left the Rijnharts to continue his work alone.

Central to the plans Petrus Rijnhart had in mind were preaching and teaching, not only in the immediate community of Lusar but, probably influenced by what he had by now learned from his wife of Archibald McLean's strategy in capturing the heart of a nation, he envisioned entering Tibet's capital, the forbidden city of Lhasa. To this end the couple started out when the baby was scarcely more than a month old, in the direction of the sacred city. They had two pack mules, a Mohammedan helper named Rabim, a box of medical supplies and a bag of Bibles. They preached, taught, doctored and distributed the Scriptures from village to village until they reached the settlement of Tanker. Here they pitched their tent for the winter, surviving the icy blasts of the mountain winds. At the first hint of spring they moved on, penetrating deeper and deeper into the interior. This time they traveled with more equipment. They had six pack animals, and their one helper, Rabim, was assisted by two Mongol guides who knew the country. But after two days they reached bandit-infested regions, and the guides deserted them. For weeks they wandered, eluding robber bands. When the storms of midsummer came, the mountain trails were turned into slippery, treacherous slopes, and their pack animals and much of their equipment were lost in the flooded, raging rivers. They sought to gain refuge in the snowclad Dang La Mountains but as they neared its slope the baby, now a year old, became sick. In two days the infant was dead.

Dr. Susie reported later that her grief was all but overwhelming as she wrapped the small body in a towel and placed it in a drug box. Petrus and the faithful Rabim dug a grave on the winding mountain trail, and carefully, prayerfully, they lowered the tiny bundle into the bleak and barren Dang La mountainside, pushing a boulder over the grave to prevent wild animals, which abounded in the area, from devouring it. The next day they picked up their remaining equipment and the pieces of their lives, and trudged on. Two months of torture followed. They were forced to hide for days in caves and in riverbeds from roving robber bands. Rabim, their one helper, grew weary of the seemingly endless traveling and left. And a few days later Petrus Rijnhart, reconnoitering up the Tsa Chu River, waved to the still griefstricken Dr. Susie before he rounded a bend. He never returned. Dr. Susie kept vigil alone in the mountain fastness for four days and nights before she began wandering, limping her painful way into camps of curious nomads, skirting hostile bands, making her way as best she could to the border town of Ta Chien Lu. No trace was ever found of Petrus Rijnhart.

Two months later Dr. Susie walked into the courtyard of the China Inland Mission at Ta Chien Lu, her sheepskin clothing ragged, her face almost black from exposure. An Englishman named John Moyes greeted her in the first English words she had heard since her husband had disappeared; he was the first white stranger she had seen in almost two years.

When the story reached America, it sent a shock through the Disciple churches. And when Dr. Susie Rijnhart herself returned to her homeland to regain her health, the brotherhood took her to its heart, and Tibet became the focus of its missionary passion. The lonely baby grave on the mountainside was engraved as an indelible picture on its conscience. There was little question but that the task begun by the Rijnharts would now be taken up and supported by the brotherhood. So nobody was surprised when a young medical student in Kansas, Albert Leroy Shelton, volunteered to resume the work of storming the battlements of the forbidding land of Tibet.

Archibald McLean, himself stirred to his depths, studied all the elements in the situation. Was it expedient to send missionaries into such an inaccessible spot without government protection? Would it not be better to wait awhile? But Christ, he remembered, did not tell his disciples to wait, but to go. "We are not to choose conditions; we are to meet them," Dr. Susie joined him in saying. The work was great, so great that beside its greatness any sacrifice would seem small.

The year was 1903. Under cloudless blue September skies, and with the blessing, and this time the financial support of the Foreign Christian Missionary Society, Dr. Susie Rijnhart again set sail from San Francisco, in company with young Dr. Leroy Albert Shelton and his wife, Flora Beals. The saga they were about to write would add to that started by the Rijnharts, and live forever in the annals of missionary lore.

It was not until the party reached Tachin Lu, China, that Dr. and Mrs. Shelton realized romance was in the air. They were welcomed by Mr. John Moyes, the first white person Dr. Susie had met after her experience in wandering alone in the mountains. As Mr. Moyes told Dr. Shelton later, when he had first seen the bedraggled but heroic woman, knowing not from whence she came or who she was, he knew by some mysterious alchemy that she was the one who must someday be his wife.

Following their marriage at the British Consulate in Chentu, Dr. Susie and her new husband returned to Tachin Lu to work with the Chinese and Tibetan people, a work they were to continue for three years until her health made necessary their permanent departure to America. But her task had been accomplished; she had sparked into living flame an interest in Tibet, an interest that now focused on Dr. Albert L. Shelton.

The Sheltons stayed in Tachin Lu for two years, learning the language, teaching and healing the sick, before venturing into the interior toward Lhasa. Two baby girls were born to them while they waited, and the Foreign Society, inspired by their determination, sent out another missionary couple, James Ogden and his wife, to reinforce them. Soon after the Ogdens arrived the small band proceeded to the isolated village of Batang, selected as their first way station on the road to Lhasa, and which was to be the scene of much of the unfolding high drama.

"We were strangers in a strange land," Dr. Shelton wrote wistfully later, concerning their arrival in the remote village. But God was with them, guarding his own. Within a short time Dr. Shelton encountered a former patient from Tachin Lu, on whom he had operated for appendicitis while preparing to move on into the interior of Tibet. The encounter was providential, reminding the lonely Christians they were not without friends in the vast land. "These patients," Dr. Shelton was able to write later, "I was to meet from time to time through all the country."

For the next ten years he was not only to meet them but literally thousands more. Batang and its Christian doctor became the focal point of interest for dozens of wandering tribes. They crowded his makeshift office, drawn by his winsome personality as much as by his medical skill. And when it became apparent his work had increased beyond the capacity of one man's endurance, Archibald McLean responded by sending out another physician to assist him, Dr. Zenas Loftis of Nashville, Tennessee. "We were all overjoyed to meet him in Batang," Dr. Shelton wrote later in his diary. "We had waited and prayed for years for this promised help, and it was at hand at last. He was a man much superior to us in training; his consecration and spiritual force were an inspiration."

But Dr. Loftis was not destined to render service in the faraway land. Six weeks after his arrival he developed typhus fever, and within hours death claimed him. The grave site selected was one facing the road leading to Lhasa, the goal toward which the missionary venture was still hopefully headed.

When the cable announcing Dr. Loftis's death reached America, the brotherhood was stunned. Was disaster to haunt the Tibetan venture? A call went out from the Foreign Society, and another Nashville physician responded, Dr. William Hardy, just finishing his medical training at Vanderbilt University. He was unmarried, but enroute to Batang he stopped in Nanking, China, to claim as his bride Nina Palmer, a missionary stationed there. By the time Dr. Hardy reached Batang, Dr. Shelton was showing signs of extreme exhaustion, and as soon as the work could be transferred to the new doctor the Shelton family started on its badly needed furlough home. They traveled for three slow, torturous weeks on foot and by horseback on the narrow, winding mountain trails, and were almost in sight of Yunnan Fu where they could secure better traveling equipment when robbers accosted them. Their escorts fled, and while Mrs. Shelton and the two daughters took refuge in a nearby ditch, Dr. Shelton faced the bandits. He was captured and forced to join them. He was not to be heard from for seventy-one days.

Mrs. Shelton and the girls managed to reach Tachin Lu, and the machinery of the capricious and graft-ridden Tibetan government was put into operation. The robber leader, Yang, had a well-organized band of two hundred men, and recognized the value of his prize hostage. Two months were to pass before negotiations could be started between him and the governor of the province. To the captive Shelton the time seemed interminable. He developed a tumor in his neck; sickness racked his exhausted body. He was unable to sit on his mule, and had to be carried much of the time on a sagging blanket hung between two poles. His clothing became rags, his shoes worn to flapping strips of leather; his only nourishment was the uncooked flesh of wild animals; his only shelter that afforded by rocky ledges under which he slept at night. Writhing in agony, he was abandoned to die in the loft of a decaying barn. And here, miraculously, he was discovered by a minor government official traveling the territory by chance. An escort of soldiers was secured and he was carried to Yenmo and thence into Uting and on to Yunnan Fu. There native doctors recognized the neck tumor and other conditions as requiring more skill than they possessed and, joined by Mrs. Shelton and the girls, Dr. Shelton at last sailed for America.

The Foreign Society had by now become doubtful of the wisdom of the Tibetan undertaking. But as Dr. Shelton slowly regained his health he insisted upon returning. Almost impatiently he took the few months' additional rest insisted upon by the now dubious Archibald McLean, before he and Mrs. Shelton again sailed for the hostile land. Upon arrival Mrs. Shelton decided to remain for the time in south China while the doctor proceeded on to remote Batang, his mind clinging to the dream of again storming the city of Lhasa. He reached Batang just before Christmas, and immediately began preparations to push on to Lhasa.

By the middle of February he was ready. Starting for the forbidden city, he reached Drubalong. There a messenger from the Tiji informed him permission must be obtained from the Galon Lama to enter the surrounding country. He was retracing his steps to Batang to prepare the communication when shots fired by marauding tribesmen rang out. Dr. Shelton was standing in the middle of a narrow trail and whirled about, mortally wounded. He was carried into Batang, but was beyond human help.

The news of Dr. Shelton's death was a personal blow to thousands of watching, anxious men and women. And the saga of Tibet became a living legend among the churches. For a number of years the work was carried on intermittently by other missionaries, but political difficulties increased to the point it became impractical, and it was eventually closed. But the story of Dr. Susie Rijnhart and Dr. Shelton continued to lift minds and hearts to tasks that transcended doctrinal differences. And for a time it even diverted the hammering punishment of a new weapon that had come into the hands of critics of the missionary enterprise—the battering rod of biblical criticism.

CHAPTER XV

Approaching the Eye of the Hurricane

While the drama in Tibet served to unite the brotherhood in Christian concern, it served also to magnify the role of organized missionary work, and thus kept in the forefront that divisive topic. No one was opposed to carrying out the Great Commission; the opposition was to the methods employed. By consigning the task to a human organization the brethren were not only departing from scriptural authority but the church was being robbed of its glory.

Neither Tolbert Fanning nor Benjamin Franklin, early critics of such departures from scriptural soundness, lived to witness the full expansion of the missionary enterprise. Benjamin Franklin died in 1878, four years after he relinquished his editor's chair at his militant *American Christian Review* to John Rowe, forced into financial straits by the panic of 1873. He retreated thereafter into relative silence, a ghost of his former self. Tolbert Fanning died in 1874, the victim of an accident on his farm near Nashville.

The farm had become a showplace for fine animals. Only the year before, in 1873, Mr. Fanning had entered a pony-sized Morgan horse, Little Dave, in the Wilson County Fair. The horse won the stallion class and then was entered in the trotting race. The betting odds against the horse were high because of his small size, and the publicity accorded his victory in the race so embarrassed the circumspect Mr. Fanning he hurriedly disclaimed any intention of being a partner in the incident. He had planned only to show the horse; the decision to race him had been that of the jockey and trainer, he tried to explain. But stockbreeding continued to share with religious concerns the primary place in his life, and on the morning of the fatal accident he had gone to the barn to placate a fractious bull. The bull turned on him, goring him so severely he succumbed to the wounds within a few days. He was sixty-four years old, in the full vigor of manhood, active to the last in attempting to stem the tide of innovations in the Movement. His leadership among the conservative segment was unquestioned, and his mantle fell on David Lipscomb, by now a mature, forceful personality in his own right and already occupying the editor's chair at the *Gospel Advocate*. He could not have chosen a more capable, or tenacious, heir.

"The church is God's only appointed institution for teaching and converting the world," David Lipscomb shouted again and again in the pages of his paper as innovations continued to fasten themselves on the church with what the editor felt to be an alarming grip. He deplored located preachers, Sunday schools, lesson leaflets, Bible colleges, missionary societies, instrumental music. Like David of old, the stocky, defiant, fearless David Lipscomb rolled up his sleeves and reached for his pen to do battle with them all. He questioned even such things as standing erect when offering prayers. "We do not say prayers made standing are not acceptable, but we say it is not the position approved in the Bible," he said.

Such literal interpretations were embraced by many devout people, but even Mr. Lipscomb must have foreseen to what embarrassing lengths the practice could go when he replied to a brother asking for the exact date on which the Sixth Seal of the Book of Revelations was broken. "We say to this brother, and to all," he said with obvious impatience, "we have not a single idea as to when the first, second, third or sixth seal was opened. . . . I know enough to know that I know nothing about them. Brethren, let us study and learn and practice and teach the portions of the Bible that teach our practical duties, and not be wasting our time on vain speculation."

The patience, likewise, of a few other people was exhausted. Isaac Errett, in his office at the *Christian Standard* in Cincinnati, and James Harvey Garrison, occupying what he wistfully termed "the editor's easy chair" in St. Louis at the *Christian*, were both open-minded on most of the innovations Mr. Lipscomb deplored. Mr. Errett disliked the use of the organ in worship, but did not object to others using it if they saw differently. Mr. Garrison, on the other hand, welcomed its use. He was twenty years younger than Mr. Errett, a product of the Ozark hills of Missouri, and had inherited from his Baptist parents, James and Diana Kyle Garrison, a rational view of religion as well as a profound sense of its spiritual realities. Service in the Union army as a captain had implanted in the youthful James Garrison political ambitions, but upon graduation later from Abingdon College in Illinois, now Eureka College, a Disciple institution, he had decided on the ministry as his lifework, won by the broad appeal of the Campbell Movement for the unity of all Christian people. A flair for vivid expression, however, directed his course into the Movement's journalistic paths, and he had reshaped the *Gospel Echo*, which he had first edited at McComb, Illinois, into a merger with another paper, the *Christian*, and assumed the new title for his journal, moving it eventually to St. Louis and organizing the Christian Publishing Company. This was later to become the well-known Christian Board of Publication and presented as a gift to the brotherhood by a Kansas City philanthropist, Robert A. Long.

Despite the difference in their ages, James H. Garrison and Isaac Errett were warm personal friends, intimate and trusted co-laborers, their journals standing for the same great principles. Both refused, although their views toward the organ question differed, to promote its agitation in their columns. Each followed a policy of centering attention on larger issues. And each paper had adopted an attitude of patience, born of something akin to amused tolerance, at the vociferous objections of the conservative papers, especially David Lipscomb's *Gospel Advocate*, to innovations. But when Mr. Lipscomb, probably aggravated by their attitude, seemed bent on driving a wedge between them, their patience was exhausted.

The two publishing houses which the two friendly editors represented—the Standard Publishing Company in Cincinnati, and the Christian Publishing Company in St. Louis—both happened to issue in 1882 new hymnbooks for the use of the churches. As the two editors announced their publications, and urged their purchase, David Lipscomb saw in the situation a chance to point the finger of outraged conscience at them. They were using the work of the church to advance their private gain and personal welfare. At first the charge was ignored, but as it became evident that suspicion had been aroused among the brethren, Isaac Errett became incensed. His previous exchanges with David Lipscomb had been carefully couched in restrained language, but now he spared no words. "We are done with David Lipscomb," he said in bold, unrelieved headlines.

The words gave indication of what many thoughtful people already were aware, that a cleavage which could not be bridged was rapidly developing. "The day for dilly-dallying has passed," John Rowe wrote in his *American Christian Review*, his ire aroused at the public slap at Mr. Lipscomb. "Let our men of faith and integrity be in frequent consultation."

Isaac Errett, his own ire further aroused at the rebuke, issued a warning of his own. A conspiracy was abroad, he announced, a secret organizing of effort to capture as many of the churches as possible with a view to separation.

Contributing to the increased tension was a new apprehension not only on the part of the opponents of innovations but of those who had at first welcomed such things as the organized missionary societies. The very success of the societies, they feared, would spawn a succession of other organizations, bent on doing other needed work, until the brotherhood would become machinery-ridden.

Their forebodings soon seemed justified. In 1888 two additional national boards took form. The Board of Church Extension came into existence as an innocent arm of the languishing American Society, its purpose to assist struggling congregations with their building financing. Within a few years it became a separate and powerful agency, its ability to grant construction loans giving it the power of life and death over many struggling churches. The same year the cry of the orphans was heard by a group of women in St. Louis, and their answer resulted in the formation of another society, the brotherhood's first national agency in the field of human welfare, the National Benevolent Association. Not long after, the plight of older preachers was brought to the attention of the churches when Ira J. Chase, a former governor of Indiana, who had forsaken the lure of public life to return to his first calling, the ministry, died while preaching before a startled congregation in Lubec, Maine. His name was widely known because of the public office he had held, and news of his death directed attention to the plight of his destitute family. The brethren had always been responsive to human distress, and now the need of some form of organized assistance to ministers unable to lay by for old age was evident. A Board of Ministerial Relief was formed within a few years which for two generations succored many aged preachers, and later became a firmly based Pension Fund.

The formation of these two new national boards did more than reveal the tendency within the Movement to depart from literal scriptural adherence; it ushered the brethren all unwittingly into the arena of social welfare.

If they had so far seemed to neglect this field, it was not because the local churches were without a social conscience. Church records of the times reflect ready responses to human need; acts of benevolence were constant. But the conversion of sinners was still their paramount job and, conditioned to shunning involvement in public or political life, they were content to render their help in the form of relieving the distress of the needy and forego the advocacy of social reform. It is significant that these first two pieces of organized work on a national scale undertaken to alleviate human distress were still in the form of relief only; they held no suggestion of reforming the conditions which caused the distress. Even the temperance movement was supported by most of the churches through local church discipline more than by participation in temperance legislation.

When Alexander Campbell had been besieged to state his views on the social evil of slavery, he countered by saying, "I am determined to simply work for the greatest of all reforms—Christianity." When Walter Scott in the early days supported factory women in Pittsburg in their fight for a ten-hour working day, going so far as to advocate that "right and safe rules" be urged upon employers, even he, probably the most socially minded of the early leaders, felt it necessary to justify his action by scriptural authority. It was the statement of Jesus, "Go, and compel them to come in." Later Benjamin Franklin questioned this authority. "Jesus and his apostles never attempted to correct the political institutions of the country," he said, "no matter how corrupt."

The occasion of Mr. Franklin's statement was the endorsement of the preservation of the Union, and the abolition of slavery by the convention during the Civil War, an occasion which proved to be the closest the brotherhood ever came until the dawn of the ecumenical era, to making a firm pronouncement on a public issue. If this course casts reflection today in the minds of many on the brotherhood's early conception of itself as a socially responsible body, it also had its better points. In view of the demonstrated ability of the brethren to wage warfare over doctrinal disputes, it could be interpreted as merciful that divergent viewpoints on social issues were not at that time forced into collision.

This reluctance to come to grips with social problems was especially apparent when, with the abolition of slavery, the welfare and status of the bewildered Negro freedmen forced itself on the conscience of the churches. Before the Civil War Negro members of the Movement were expected to attend worship services in white churches. They sat in segregated sections, but they were there, joining with their "white folks" in songs of praise, in prayers and supplication; sharing in the comfort and consolation to be found in the old, old story. Their names were included on the church rolls.

But after the war, things changed. The racial consciousness born of the struggle affected the general climate of friendly rapport to such an extent that, as freedmen, the Negroes drew apart, forming their own Christian churches. The pattern became so embedded in the brotherhood thinking that, as time passed, the presence of a Negro worshiper in a white congregation of the Disciples of Christ became the subject of comment and, in the South, of alarm. The Negro churches were recognized, however, as part of the brotherhood, but somewhat as a branch, in but not of its life. As they were poor not only in money but in leadership, a variety of forms of paternal assistance was rendered them.

In 1872 the state society of North Carolina voted to allow two colored delegates to sit in the house "for the purpose of learning how to conduct their own annual meetings." In Mississippi a colored preacher, William Ramy, was presented during the annual state meeting with a gift of seventy-eight dollars "to enable him to extend his labors among his brethren." In 1870 the General Convention voted "to look toward educating children of slaves."

But it was five years before the brethren looked hard enough to establish the first school, and then it was largely the result of the concern of one man and his wife, Mr. and Mrs. Randall Faurot, who founded Southern Christian Institute in Edwards, Mississippi, a remarkably well-conceived school. This paternalistic attitude persisted for fifty years with no serious thought of integrating the Negro into the mainstream of the church. Along with most of the Protestant world, such a thing as a racially inclusive local congregation in the Movement was at that time never contemplated.

When the first graduates of the Southern Christian Institute gave proof of the ability of the Negro to respond to education, the American Christian Missionary Society began sponsoring other such schools in Kentucky, Virginia and North Carolina. By 1900 this program, supplemented by evangelistic work among the Negroes, had grown to such proportions it was relinquished to the women who conducted and enlarged it through their Christian Woman's Board of Missions. But the education offered by most of the schools was minimal, all of it emphasizing vocational training rather than work in the liberal arts, and none of it giving adequate attention to the training of Negro ministers. The American Society eventually employed a national Negro evangelist, Preston Taylor, to work in Negro communities, but the early Negro churches had little dynamic.

In 1917 the Negroes in Disciple churches attempted to lift themselves by their own bootstraps by organizing at Nashville, Tennessee, their own National Christian Missionary Convention. The venture was encouraged by the brotherhood's white leadership, but as the years passed and the Civil Rights movement took form, the existence of a separate convention served to increase rather than diminish the consciousness of the "branch" concept of the Negro churches. Tension developed, relieved in recent years only by plans for realignment, and an acknowledgment on the part of both Negro and white Christians that their brotherhood was an inclusive fellowship, all congregations and all members equal.

But as the nineteenth century advanced, the brotherhood seemed unaware of the far-reaching implications of the Negro's needs and rights. Other problems, more immediate and more expressive of the peculiar temper of the times, dominated the scene. Indeed, winds of hurricane proportions were beginning to pound at the brotherhood's foundations. In scores of churches, already beset by friction over the organ and the missionary society, the steady accretion of agencies was now undeniable proof that the brotherhood was departing from its original course. It was being led by the "progressive" wing down the dreaded pathway toward denominationalism. Resentment of such a course became open; breaks were threatened, and in some cases occurred. In others they were heroically resisted. But a general unease existed. The timber was dry, awaiting only a spark to ignite it.

In 1889 the spark was provided.

CHAPTER XVI

The Great Divide

Curiously, the division in the ranks of the brotherhood approached a climax just at the period of its greatest evangelistic activity. As the country pushed westward, and frontier territories laid claim to statehood, the plea of the Movement that all God's children get together held a strong appeal for hosts of settlers confused by and weary of competing denominational claims. A score of mighty evangelists endowed with a passion for saving souls, and with a ready tongue, as well as the conviction they were working for the unity of Christendom, invaded the western area, planting what became strong churches of the Movement.

A preacher of this type was J. M. Monroe, who went to the Oklahoma Territory when the Cheyenne and Arapahoe sections were readying for settlers in 1892. He roamed among the families in their covered wagons converged at the dividing line, waiting the day of entry, and explained the Campbell doctrine of unifying the Christian world by restoring the simple plan of the New Testament church. He followed the wagons into the country when the signal was given, organizing his converts into churches wherever a group of them staked their claims. When the Cherokee Strip was to be opened the following year, 1893, he made over five hundred converts while the families waited. Then, realizing he could not be everywhere at once, he persuaded a preacher, E. F. Boggess, who had come to the area to pastor the church Mr. Monroe had started at Guthrie, then the state capital, to mount his horse and be ready to charge with the others when the gun sounded. Mr. Boggess was one of the first to dash across the line and staked out a claim for a church lot in what he had learned was to be the capital of the Strip, the town of Perry.

Such activity resulted in churches of the Movement in every settlement of a thousand people, even before statehood for Oklahoma was declared.

The evangelistic urge which led some preachers to the West, led others in the more settled communities to forsake a located ministry and become "professional evangelists." They regularly visited established churches, sensing the need of every Christian for a periodic revival of his spiritual life. The majority of these men were colorful characters, spectacular in their preaching, employing devices in their revival meetings that attracted and delighted the townspeople, and converted hundreds of them.

Knowles Shaw, a lanky, rawboned, red-haired preacher from southern Indiana, set forth after the Civil War on a career of such meetings, impelled by the need to replace the hatreds engendered by the war with an awareness of the meaning of Christian love. He was about twenty-five years old, and possessed a remarkable musical talent, and a variety of eccentricities. For almost twenty years he traveled among the churches, baptizing during his sojourns over eleven thousand people. Of his manner of preaching one contemporary wrote:

"During his discourse you may see him pacing the platform singing some thrilling song of Zion, or seated by the organ playing some touching sentimental ballad. You may behold him on bended knee before some cruel king, in tender tones imploring mercy, or perched upon the end of a bench off in the 'Amen corner,' stiff as a poker, cold as a midnight spook, burlesquing the lukewarm Christian. You may behold the audience baptized in tears, or convulsed with laughter."

In addition to his preaching, Mr. Shaw made the personal acquaintance of every person he encountered on the streets when visiting a town. He called on every known sick person, and worked so assiduously in the temperance cause he persuaded two thousand people in one town to sign the pledge. His ability as a musician was demonstrated not only in his vocal solos which interspersed his sermons at odd moments, and violin and piano playing, but in the scores of Gospel songs he wrote, many of which still ring out in churches across the land, especially the happy strains of "Bringing in the Sheaves." The death of Knowles Shaw in 1878 was in keeping with the dramatic character of his

life. He was killed in a train wreck in Texas while en route to a
revival meeting, the only casualty of the unfortunate occurrence.

The emphasis on evangelism bore its numerical mark on the
brotherhood. The followers of Alexander Campbell appeared in
1880 to be a vital, aggressive church of over one thousand congregations and more than 500,000 adherents. In 1900 they were
to pass the one-million mark, a religious body of recognized national importance, and one which was to become a bulwark of
righteousness in the nation. Yet divisions in both the new and the
more settled churches also were multiplying, almost in direct ratio
to the brotherhood's growth. For a fire that no man could put out
had been set ablaze by a relatively obscure man in Illinois named
Daniel Sommer.

Mr. Sommer was a tall, kindly, bewhiskered individual, utterly
convinced of the rightness of the gloomy predictions he held concerning the way things were going, and to which he gave frequent
utterance in his paper the *Octographic Review*. The paper was the
successor to the *American Christian Review*, founded by Benjamin Franklin, and it had inherited his fighting spirit.

In the heat of an August day in 1889, Mr. Sommer attended
the yearly meeting of the churches in the community of Sand
Creek, in Shelby County, Illinois, as one of its speakers. He was
not a gifted orator, but what he lacked in eloquence he made up
in conviction, and as he addressed the assembled brethren on the
spreading evil of innovations, he inspired a perspiring group of
them to compose a "Declaration" against the men who com-
mended "the objectionable and unauthorized things taught and
practiced in many of the congregations, to the great grief and
mortification of some of the members."

Similar objections to the inroads of the innovations had been
made before by other groups, but they had been in the form of
rebukes, carrying the hope that the "progressive" brethren would
turn from the error of their ways. This declaration, however, went
further; it called for a general repudiation of the progressive group.
"We are impelled from a sense of duty to say," the statement
continued, "that unless, and until, they turn from such abomi-
nations we cannot and will not regard them as brethren."

It had happened at last. A public call for division had been made. For a time the brotherhood tried to ignore it; then a mood of anxious second thought prevailed. Even David Lipscomb, champing in impatience in Tennessee at the spreading innovations, considered the Sand Greek Declaration had gone too far. The call for an open break within the ranks was too precipitous; he was not ready for it;—not yet.

"The Sand Creek manifesto is manifest folly," ran a statement in the *Gospel Advocate*, "and the *Advocate* emphatically denies any sympathy with Sommerism, whatever that is, Sand Creekism, sand-lotism, Standardism, or any other partyism in religion. The *Advocate* is for Christ and his church, and is in ardent sympathy with all those who are drawing their life from Him who is the true vine."

But the Sand Creek spirit had been set loose; the harm had been done. Thoughtful, watching men in both segments of the dispute grew alarmed. The unity of the brotherhood was dear to their hearts, yet all about them they observed local churches dividing, and groups of former friends regrouping themselves as separate congregations, eying each other in silent, and sometimes vocal hostility. Should they urge the dissident groups to remain together in endless confusion? Or should they agree they should separate and have peace?

Among the concerned was John W. McGarvey in Lexington, Kentucky. Moses Lard had died in 1880, and with his passing his close friend, the irascible but beloved "Brother" McGarvey, as he was affectionately called by practically everybody, somewhat lessened his attacks on the use of the organ. Now he made tentative gestures, as did scores of other preachers, toward reconciling the two factions. Whether he would have succeeded will never be known as, a few months after the second Sand Creek Declaration was published, this time calling upon every church to insert in its property deed a clause stating no instrumental music or other innovation should ever be used on the premises, a darker and more ominous cloud appeared which was to divert Brother Mc-Garvey from his role of pacifier and turn him again into a warrior.

Isaac Errett, also, would doubtless have tried to heal the gaping wound despite the increasing and open disdain with which he had been viewing the dissenting brethren. But Isaac Errett was dead. Only the year before, in 1888, a year before the first

Sand Creek Declaration was issued, he had succumbed to the effects of an injury received while traveling in Europe a few months previously. His death had depleted the editorial ranks of those seeking forbearance. For his son, Russell Errett, was now in charge of the editorial policy of the influential *Christian Standard*, and while the young Errett condemned the Sand Creek Declaration he did it with little enthusiasm. Soon it was evident that he was more inclined than his father had been to take a militant look at the growing tendency to liberalize the thinking of the Movement.

In this attitude Russell Errett was given unexpected support by the same development which diverted Brother McGarvey from attempting to heal the breach, and which set in motion a new wave of dissention.

One of the popular preachers in the brotherhood was Robert L. Cave, whose resonant voice rang from the pulpit of the Central Christian Church in St. Louis. He was a gracious man, whose ability as a student of the Scriptures had been highly regarded by Brother McGarvey during the four years the two had worked together in editing, with others, the *Apostolic Times*. During that period he had come to know Brother McGarvey's mind apparently better than Brother McGarvey had come to know his, for he left that position to cast his lot with a group under circumstances which should have given a clue to his thinking.

The Central Christian Church to which he was called had been formed by a dozen or so "progressives" who had broken away from the First Christian Church in St. Louis because of the refusal of the rest of the members to use an organ they had installed. Ironically, when they left, they left behind the organ where it gathered dust, unused, while they, the organ lovers, were forced to rely on a tuning fork in their new location. The situation was absurd, and when Mr. Cave mounted the pulpit he let it be known he so considered it. He announced, in fact, his rejection of all such literal adherence to the silences of the Scriptures. Neither was he long in making no secret of the fact he likewise viewed some of the speech of the Bible as not altogether valid. On the Sunday before Christmas in 1889, he arose in his pulpit and attacked the validity of the Virgin Birth, the Bodily Resurrection and other basic tenets of the Christian faith.

This was apostasy, pure and plain, and the brotherhood united in shocked disbelief.

James Harvey Garrison had merged his paper with a journal called the *Evangelist* in 1882, and through the editorial columns of that journal, now renamed the *Christian-Evangelist*, his voice sounded loud and clear, steadying the reeling brotherhood. He was himself a "progressive," and an Elder in Mr. Cave's church, an advocate of a less rigid interpretation of the Scriptures, and certainly the use of the organ. But apostasy had no place in the thinking of even the "progressives." He denounced Mr. Cave's views in such vigorous and unqualified terms Mr. Cave resigned from his position as pastor of the church, and the brotherhood's confidence in the orthodoxy of its leaders was to an extent restored. The incident marked James Harvey Garrison as a trusted spokesman for the "progressives," and established for him a following which eventually allowed the *Christian Evangelist* to rally the forces of the organizational life of the brotherhood when the *Christian Standard* swung into more militant, hostile questioning of the plans and purposes of all the agencies.

But Brother McGarvey did not recover from the shock of Mr. Cave's apostasy. It diverted his attention from his self-appointed task of healing the wounds over innovations, to the more serious task of combating the threat of apostasy. Soon thereafter he began vigorously writing a column in the *Christian Standard* dealing with biblical criticism, which was to continue for twenty years as the most widely read feature of the paper.

Mr. Cave's apostasy may also have contributed to David Lipscomb's abandonment of his tone of lofty detachment, and encouraged his announcement that he was siding once and for all with the spirit of the outspoken Sand Creek Declaration. At any rate, he professed that Mr. Cave's announcement did not surprise him. To him it was indicative of where the brotherhood was headed, and he wanted no part of it. It was not in the direction he was going. "If we depart from the order of God in one point," he wrote in his paper, "we could with no consistency maintain it on the others."

If Robert Cave's apostasy did not surprise Mr. Lipscomb, neither did Mr. Lipscomb's attitude surprise the brotherhood. The independent cast of his mind was by this time well known. In 1880, when the elevation to the high office of President of the United States of one of the brotherhood's preachers, James A. Garfield, met with pride and enthusiastic acclaim from the rest of the brethren, David Lipscomb took occasion to scoff, reaffirming his conviction that a Christian should have nothing to do with civil government. "I firmly believe," he wrote during the campaign, "that his [Garfield's] election would be a source of great corruption and injury to the church of Jesus Christ. I would be glad not only on political, but purely religious grounds, to see him and every other member of a church of Christ who aspires to office, defeated, so badly defeated, too, that it will crush all hope that any one of them can ever be elected."

This reaction, typical of many he displayed, gave David Lipscomb an unflattering and in a way a false posture before much of the brotherhood, even his own segment of it. He was in many ways a sour and gruff man, rough in manner and certainly opinionated. But he was not ignorant or lacking in a native, shrewd wisdom. In the minds of many of the "progressives," however, his uncouth ways personified his followers, increasingly called the "anti" group because they seemed to be "against" more things than they were "for," and the impression gained wide currency that intellectual vigor was lacking in that group of the church. This was a fallacy which the scholastic attainments of the men and women who followed in his train have disproved, and a close scrutiny of even Mr. Lipscomb's behavior itself refutes it. He not only ably edited one of the most influential journals in the brotherhood, the *Gospel Advocate*, but enlarged it by repeated mergers with other papers, and around it established a printing and publishing company from which flowed a diversity of printed material. He assisted the widow of his old friend Tolbert Fanning in reshaping Franklin College, which burned in 1865, into Hope Institute and then into an institution for helping needy children, Fanning Orphan School. Despite poor health he traveled incessantly, preaching, teaching, spreading the truth as he saw it, yet found time to manage his farm so well that his land holdings substantially increased, and not until his late years did he ever incur a debt. As a rebuke to the human agencies of the church which he opposed with unrelenting vigor, and as a demonstration of what he considered a more scriptural method, he led a group of Nashville churches to send their own missionary in the person of an Armenian, Azarish Paul, who had been a student at the College of the Bible in Lexington, back to his native land as a Gospel preacher, thus initiating a totally new plan of independent missionary work. The flourishing David Lipscomb College in Nashville, Tennessee, which he started in 1891 as Nashville Bible College, stands today as testimony to the leadership he gave to the cause of restoring the New Testament church in all its practices.

But at the time David Lipscomb's increasing lack of toleration toward those who disagreed with him confirmed what many had already accepted as inevitable—that the absence of a central body of belief in the Movement had given birth to two widely different approaches to its primary purpose of restoring the early church. For Mr. Lipscomb's group the way was plainly marked; the New Testament provided a fixed pattern for all time. For others the mission of the Movement was to be fulfilled by restoring the spirit of the early church, a spirit of freedom in adjusting to conditions as they arose. To these men the stand of Mr. Lipscomb and his followers seemed so rigid it resembled a creedal statement. To Mr. Lipscomb's group, the freedom desired by the others implied a lack of conviction, and lack of conviction would never produce a church which could conquer the world for Christ.

In most of the local churches where divisions were occurring, the initiative was taken by the "anti" brethren. The "progressives," while deploring the restrictions the dissenting members tried to place upon the congregation, were nevertheless more inclined to tolerate the "antis" than the "antis" were inclined to tolerate them. So, generally, it was the "antis" who left, or who made the others so uncomfortable they left, their common assets being distributed with little fanfare. A few separations, however, were accompanied by court action which the world delighted to watch.

One such spectacle was created by the church at Newbern, in Dyer County, Tennessee, in 1902. The charge brought by the "antis" against the pro-organ group was that "they have corrupted the faith, principles and practices of said church and diverted it from the purposes for which it was founded by the introduction of innovations' which are unscriptural, sacrilegious and objectionable." The trial dragged on for over three years, with David Lipscomb on the witness stand more or less regularly for eighteen months. The deposition which exists today covers more than two thousand pages of tedious testimony. The decision of the Court in April, 1905, was in favor of the "organ people," based on the judgment that the things complained of were "not of sufficient importance to justify the intervention of the Court."

The same urge which provided the "antis" with the initiative to separate in their local churches now impelled them to seek a means of making public the news that they were severing relationship generally with the rest of their brethren. Since the only visible framework of the brotherhood, aside from the local churches, was the collection of hated agencies which they had never recognized, the "anti" brethren were for a time in a dilemma as to how to establish the fact that they were going their own way. Ironically, it was the United States government, with which David Lipscomb had often said he would have nothing to do, which came to their rescue. The government was setting about collecting data in 1906 for its census.

Writing of this later, David Lipscomb said: "I had never done or thought of doing anything to make this [division] manifest, nor had it ever occurred to me that the civil authorities were taking note of this growing division until I received a letter from the Census Bureau saying they had noted it in the paper, and asking to know the facts in the matter. I gave, as impartially and as truthfully as I could, the real state of the case. They then asked for the statistics of the churches walking in the old paths. While I have never cared for statistics or numberings, I did not see how such a request could be well refused, and referred them to Brother J. W. Shepherd as a man having a talent for statistics, and the Government employed him to gather them for its use."

Brother Shepherd evidently lost no time in attempting to assemble the statistics, although in view of the resulting confusion their accuracy could be questioned. "I have sent out hundreds of blanks but not many have been returned," he wrote in the *Gospel Advocate*. "One difficulty has been caused by the fact Mr. G. W.

Hoffman has been sending similar requests to report to him. But he is gathering statistics for the 'digressives.' Those who have been misinformed and sent blanks to him, should cancel them and send them to me."

However inaccurate the lists as finally compiled, they constituted a public acknowledgment that a division had taken place. The chagrin this undoubtedly caused among leaders on both sides may have been mitigated by another situation revealed in the advance sheets of the Census, especially for those who still considered the primary function of the Movement to be the demolition of the denominations. The followers of Alexander Campbell had increased during the previous sixteen years by 78 percent, while the Baptists had gained by only 53 percent, and the Methodists by but 25 percent.

CHAPTER XVII

Running Up the Flag

Although both segments of the Campbell Movement deplored the division in the ranks, the break had long seemed inevitable and the bickering that had preceded it had distressed many people. Now that it was a publicly acknowledged fact, most of the members drew a breath of relief. Perhaps a period of peace would now envelop them all.

For a time this hope was realized in the "anti" group. Its churches began at once emphasizing their now unquestioned autonomy, recognizing their kinship with each other by their common strict adherence to the Bible and their renunciation of all human innovations, but refusing to qualify their independence of each other by even labeling themselves as a collective body. Today they are still known, not as the Church of Christ but as Churches of Christ. But their mood was such that they entered into a period of remarkable growth, reveling in their freedom from contamination with the heresies of their former brethren. Indeed, annoyed that they continued to be associated in the eyes of the world with the remaining wing, they drew their skirts even more firmly about them, affirming their dissociation by carefully displaying nothing in common with their former comrades except shared memories of happier days. As the twentieth century advanced, communication between these two branches of the followers of Alexander Campbell practically ceased, and hopes for reconciliation became a mound of forgotten dreams.

Those remaining in the mainstream, meanwhile, were equally happy to feel free now to explore unrestrained the path of intellectual inquiry, claiming a willingness to follow wherever it might lead. But when it soon led, as it did, to biblical criticism, hopes for peace faded within their ranks, and seeds were sown for another disruption in the brotherhood's forces.

Even before Robert Cave's heretical pronouncements had shocked the churches, a fear had been spreading among the leaders that the mood of inquiry which they cherished would inevitably lead to trouble. Biblical criticism was already washing the shores of the rest of the religious world. Rumors of it were vague and remote; few laymen, and not all the preachers, had a clear notion of what was involved in the term.

One of the preachers who knew all too well was Brother John W. McGarvey. He was also aware that precisely because of their innocence, his brethren were vulnerable to its attacks, and he felt called upon to alert them.

Mr. McGarvey was teaching a course called Sacred History at the College of the Bible in Lexington at the time of Mr. Cave's outburst. In this course of lectures he felt free to teach textual criticism of the Bible, since he believed careful scrutiny of its passages would throw light on the original text. But he stood firmly against teaching any other kind of criticism, especially "historical criticism," the method in which the principle of growth and development of faith is recognized. For him, God's manner of revealing himself to the world was not a continuous process; religious truth was a matter of revelation and not development. He believed, as did the "anti" brethren in whose camp he had one foot, that the Bible not only contained the word of God—it *was* the word of God, final and complete.

Alarmed at the biblical criticism to which Mr. Cave had given voice, he negotiated with the *Christian Standard* to conduct what became a famous column dealing with the subject. If slanting the facts had been a phrase in current usage at the time, it can be said he used such tactics brilliantly. He employed a peculiar method of reducing complex theological reasoning to the level which lay people could grasp, or thought they could. In the process many of the fine points and essential elements of the principles involved seemed to many to be distorted, but the people were alerted to the dangers inherent in biblical criticism, and that was what mattered.

The alarm Mr. McGarvey sounded had foundation in real fact. The theory of evolution that burst on a stunned world in 1850 had loosed a flood of questions. Archeological discoveries going on at the time, and the unearthing of new manuscripts, were forcing many Bible scholars to question the literal facts of Bible stories. The brotherhood's colleges, by now occupying a high standing in the academic world, began including courses in "historical criticism," attempting to bring traditional thinking into line with new scientific discoveries in biology and astronomy, admitting the subject matter discussed had little if anything to do with the study of the Bible as history. Fresh winds were rising, soon to blow through musty corridors; new light was being shed on old truths; and stained-glass windows in the brotherhood's city churches, and their plain-glass counterparts in rural meetinghouses, were being pushed wide open to let the new light in.

The light came streaming in, but it was so sudden and so strong it threatened for a time to blind rather than illuminate. Many good people drew back in alarm. While they were beginning to suspect Brother McGarvey leaned too far to the fundamentalist view of things, the new school of thought was leaning too far in the other direction. In granting to science the final word as to the nature of the universe; in discarding the notion of revelation as a process of obtaining religious truth; in abandoning the doctrine of original sin, the scholars were acting prematurely, and giving rise to shallow conclusions. Many thoughtful people saw danger in accepting only that truth which could be scientifically determined; danger in sacrificing the terrible beauty and profound meaning of worship; danger in diluting religion with philosophy.

The colleges were the first of the brotherhood's institutions to be engulfed in the heat of the controversy. Most of the people considered the colleges the handmaidens of the church. They had established them to promote the Christian faith, and not to question it. One of the first schools to be scorched was the great Butler College in Indianapolis, an institution that had become the pride of the brotherhood. Here the training of young ministers was the task of a man with an original mind, Hugh C. Garvin, whose credentials as a scholar were unquestioned. He had become professor of biblical literature and modern languages in 1889, and his insistence on excellence and high standards in his courses, standards which some of the young men fresh from rural areas with scanty academic preparation could not meet, caused an undercurrent of dissatisfaction. In probing for charges which could be leveled against Dr. Garvin, his detractors unearthed some liberal views on his part. These they equated with his emphasis on scholarship.

"What is demanded today in the pulpit is great preachers, not great scholars," the Indiana state paper cried. "The great scholar will never save the world."

This attitude did not accurately reflect that of the host of church members who had respect for education. They sought to offset the reflection it cast on the intellectual reputation of the Movement by supporting the school's refusal to dismiss the scholarly, controversial teacher. But suspicion of the school's liberal leanings were planted, and in 1896 Professor Garvin voluntarily resigned, and the great Butler College abandoned for a time its ministerial courses.

But the departure of the professor did not quiet the school's critics. Suspicions of its liberal tendencies continued, sharpened by a loose affiliation the college maintained with the University of Chicago.

The University of Chicago was generally considered a hotbed of liberalism, reflecting the liberal tendencies of its president, William R. Harper, and of its chief benefactor, John D. Rockefeller. The school's liberal leanings had first been impressed upon the brotherhood by the discovery that there had been organized in connection with it something called the Disciples' Divinity House. The only visible form of this structure was a circle of Disciple students who gathered informally but regularly to critically scrutinize Disciple doctrine. In this they were encouraged and abetted by the nearby Hyde Park Christian Church which most of them attended, and which was shot through with liberal thinking itself and thus bore, along with the University, the mark of Cain. Although the affiliation the University maintained with Butler College amounted to little more than an arrangement whereby graduates of Butler were given special credit from the Chicago-based institution, leading to further degrees, that was enough to arouse suspicion of Butler's purity.

The spreading uneasiness over biblical criticism was not long in reaching and beclouding the missionary work of the church, but it came in a circuitous route.

Scores of the Movement's missionaries were blazing trails for the Christian faith in nearly a dozen foreign lands and in needy areas of America, supported by the women through their well-organized Christian Woman's Board of Missions, by the American Society and by the Foreign Christian Missionary Society under the inspired and inspiring leadership of Archibald McLean. The brotherhood rejoiced in the task, and as the "anti" brethren folded their tents and departed in 1906, a new spurt of concern seemed to develop that the far-flung work of the missionary societies, whose dust the "antis" had shaken from their feet, be not retarded. As a consequence every available dollar was coveted for its furtherance.

Among the coveted dollars were some sizable numbers which had come in recent years from the Rockefeller Foundation. The money had been given with "no strings attached," as Archibald McLean made haste to emphatically explain when, following the uproar over Butler College's suspected contamination, attention was focused on the source of the annual contributions. This satisfied many people, and it is probable the matter would have been dropped if agitation had not developed from an unexpected source.

The fortune of the financially liberal but theologically conservative Phillips family of Pennsylvania had been founded on oil holdings. Mr. Rockefeller's Standard Oil Company was not only a competitor of the T. W. Phillips Gas and Oil Company, but had forced the Phillips company into bankruptcy at one time. Only skillful management enabled it to survive, and understandably the injury was never forgotten. Now Mr. T. W. Phillips, genuinely troubled lest there be a connection between Mr. Rockefeller's gifts and his liberal theological views, took occasion to point out in a series of plainly worded articles in the *Christian Standard*, that the Rockefeller Company was not possessed of Christian ethics. He based his charges on disclosures of some shady company practices being revealed in a national magazine at that very moment in history. Gifts from its profits he branded as "tainted money." He insisted all its contributions be returned.

Nobody was quite sure what "tainted money" was, but everybody was suddenly concerned that the missionary cause not be contaminated by it. Yet nobody relished the idea of giving back the sizable sums with which the Rockefeller Foundation had enriched the yawning missionary treasury of the brotherhood, and nobody offered to replace the amount. The upshot of the matter was a compromise. An agreement was reached to allow the Foreign Society, the chief beneficiary of the Rockefeller gifts, to keep the money but to refrain from accepting more from the same source.

The linking of Mr. Rockefeller's name with the missionary work had, however, a more serious effect than that of suspicion of the purity of his money. It directed attention toward the young ministers coming from his arch-liberal University of Chicago. One of them in particular. He was a brilliant man named Guy Sarvis, who had received his undergraduate degree at sober Drake University in Des Moines, Iowa, a brotherhood college founded in 1881 through gifts from the esteemed Disciple F. M. Drake, Governor of Iowa. Young Sarvis had gone on for graduate work at the University of Chicago, where, it was charged, he was ruined by imbibing heretical ideas. One evidence of this was his zeal, as an assistant pastor of the liberal Hyde Park Christian Church, in advocating "open membership."

The practice of "open membership" was (and still is) to many a violation of a fixed procedure in the Apostolic church. It provides for the acceptance into church membership of the "pious unimmersed," by which is meant Christians who have been administered, and are content with, other forms of baptism. But a few people were beginning to wonder, however, as Barton Stone had done at the inception of the Movement, if the church had not created a creedal bar to membership by insisting upon immersion as the only acceptable form of baptism. To them it seemed arrogant to question the validity of the Christian commitment of those baptized by other forms. But only a few preachers braved the traditional concept to take a public stand against the exclusive practice. The Cedar Avenue Christian Church in Cleveland adopted an "open membership" stand for a short time, and the South Side Church in Indianapolis in 1896 opened its rolls to Christian believers coming with other forms of baptism. Other churches attempted a compromise by a variety of means. The most widespread was that of accepting the unimmersed into the "congregation" but not into the "church." When this proved to be a distinction without any noticeable difference, the plan fell into disuse.

But these churches, and others sanctioning "open membership" in any way bore a stigma, and Mr. Russell Errett, flexing his muscles in his editorial office at the *Christian Standard*, insisted that even the missionary offerings from such congregations be rejected. The support of a missionary by an "open membership" church suggested to his mind that the missionary himself was tarred with the same brush and would not hesitate to follow the practice on the distant foreign field, where the observing eyes of the faithful could not observe him. Rigid doctrinal tests were proposed to gauge a missionary's fitness.

If the method of baptizing converts on the foreign field could not be readily observed, not so the working contacts the missionaries established with the denominational friends serving beside them. So when Mr. Guy Sarvis, already an advocate of "open membership," was sent as a missionary to China and soon thereafter became a member of the faculty of the University of Nanking, a cooperative union institution, he was charged with "consorting with the denominations," a practice which Mr. Russell Errett and others felt could only lead to the preaching of a more liberal doctrine than the church at home realized.

Russell Errett had been a warm friend of Archibald McLean when Mr. McLean first assumed leadership of the Foreign Society. Both were young men at the time, and unmarried. But personal rivalry, it was rumored, over the affections of a young lady, caused a rift in their friendship, which now widened into official and open hostility as their positions on this aspect of the missonary work veered into different paths. Archibald McLean made no secret of his opinion that penetration of foreign fields called for a close relationship among Christian bodies laboring in those lands. Indeed, he had been partially responsible for the existence of the cooperative enterprise now causing the trouble, the University of Nanking. He had persuaded the Foreign Society to back the efforts of another missionary in China, F. E. Meigs, in not only "consorting with the denominations," but in aggressively courting the Methodists and Presbyterians in Nanking to join the Disciples in abandoning the boys' schools each was struggling to maintain, and consolidate their efforts. The resulting University of Nanking, one of the first monuments to united effort on the foreign field, was therefore a logical place in his mind for Mr. Sarvis to invest his scholarly talents.

But to Russell Errett the appointment confirmed his charge the doctrine of the Movement was being diluted. He sought to bolster his charge by calling into question comity agreements the Foreign Society and the Woman's Board had entered into in other mission fields which exhibited bits of evidence, both real and imagined, that departures from established procedures were taking place in the lands beyond the seas. Soon he broadened his attacks to include the agencies themselves. He was detecting an increasingly dictatorial attitude on their part which boded no good. The agencies, just recovering from bruising attacks leveled by the "anti" group, now girded again for battle as the peace the churches had anticipated enjoying with the departure of the "anti" brethren was rent asunder.

The first to come to the defense of the organized work was the *Christian-Evangelist*. Its editor, James H. Garrison, was a remarkably gracious spirit, by nature given to Christian tolerance and respect for every man's opinion. He was not an advocate of "open membership," but neither did he advocate sitting in judgment on those churches indulging in the practice. Nor did he countenance the questioning of missionaries suspected of sanctioning it through their fraternal contacts on the faraway fields. At first he attempted to pour oil on the troubled waters, hoping the controversy would run its course and disappear. But he had not reckoned with the tremendous impact of the swelling biblical criticism on the whole missionary enterprise. With the best intentions in the world he sponsored a series of congresses in 1899, hoping to counteract the confusion over biblical criticism. In these meetings many moot points were clarified, and many fears quieted, but the series of meetings also tended to draw an even sharper line between the liberals and the conservatives, whose editorial spokesman was now Russell Errett. And the line threatened to become a cleavage when, in 1907, the General Convention aligned itself with the newly created Federal Council of Churches of Christ in America. To many this action was nothing more than recognizing an expression of "the visible unity of the Christian churches." But to others it was proof that the Movement had indeed been infiltrated, and would in time be dissipated, by liberalism.

In such a mood the brotherhood approached the celebration of its hundredth anniversity in 1909.

CHAPTER XVIII

"He Drew a Circle"

The selection of the city of Pittsburgh as host to this remarkable convention in 1909 reflected a common bond of pride that, despite their differences, the church leaders shared in the Movement's heritage. Here, in the mountains of western Pennsylvania, the Movement was born. Here Thomas Campbell had migrated when he first came to America in 1807, and it was here, in an attic room in the home of Nathan Welch in the village of Washington, Pennsylvania, that he had written his famed "Declaration and Address." To that village he had brought his wife and children when they followed him to the new country in 1809, and it was from their two-story home on Strawberry Lane that the son Alexander had ridden horseback across the state line into what was then Virginia, now West Virginia, to put down his roots and to organize on the banks of Brush Run Creek a congregation of twenty persons, the first church of the new Movement to unite Christian men by restoring the original New Testament church.

The idea of celebrating the one hundredth anniversary of that historic occasion amid these surroundings had been circulating for some time before it crystallized in action in 1901, with the appointment of Thomas W. Phillips as chairman of a steering committee. Neither Mr. Phillips's unhappy experience as one of the founders of the *Christian Standard*, nor his alarm at the creeping liberalism, had lessened his interest in the ongoing of the brotherhood or his support of its projects. He not only had continued to give liberally of his great wealth to most of the brotherhood's educational institutions, including Oklahoma Christian University, founded by E. V. Zollars and later to bear his name as Phillips University at Enid, but there had recently come from the presses of Funk and Wagnalls a remarkable little book authored simply "By a Layman," entitled *The Church of Christ*. Mr. Phillips had written the treatise as his contribution toward clarifying in language the man in the pew could grasp the story of what the Movement was about. It was to sell almost a million copies. The confused brotherhood was grateful, and his appointment to lead in marking the significant milestone in its life was a deserved honor. It was also a strategic choice, for the goals Mr. Phillips set for the brotherhood to reach in the intervening years before the actual celebration in 1909 captured everybody's imagination: Every church debt was to be paid by the time of the celebration; every church member was to be a tither, a Bible class student and a participant in weekly prayer meetings; one thousand young men were to enter the ministry; ten thousand adult Bible classes were to be organized.

Nobody actually expected the goals would be attained, but the vision they provided dimmed for a time the current controversies, and a semblance of harmony in working toward them pervaded the brotherhood. When the convention assembled in Pittsburgh on October 11, 1909, the stimulation of the effort was gloriously evident.

Over thirty thousand people came, journeying from every state in the Union, some by chartered trains, some in wagons, a number on horseback. They taxed the hotel capacity of the city and of the great auditorium in Carnegie Hall, and the thousands who could not squeeze into the general sessions were directed to simultaneous and hastily arranged meetings in the city's churches, its warehouses and its parks. At the closing session which featured the celebration of the Lord's Supper, the meeting was moved to Forbes Field, where over twenty thousand people filled to overflowing the three-tiered grandstand.

But greater than the enthusiasm engendered by the crowds was that greeting the reports of the brotherhood's progress in its various endeavors. Nearly 75,000 women were actively at work in the ranks of the beloved Christian Woman's Board of Missions, supporting 244 workers in America and 256 missionaries in eight foreign lands. The women also reported they had braved unchartered seas by establishing a College of Missions in Indianapolis for the training of missionaries, the only institution of its kind in

America at the time, and, as if in unspoken answer to the rise in biblical criticism and the controversies raging around it, which they chose to ignore, they had begun endowing "Bible Chairs" in connection with state universities for the teaching of the Bible.

Jubilant Archibald McLean, transcending the criticism which had flooded his beloved missionary work, his unruly hair now a cap of white, let his voice rise to its shrill height as he reported the Foreign Christian Missionary Society had 167 missionaries at work in thirteen countries, assisted by more than five hundred native helpers as they ministered through seventeen hospitals, thirty-four schools and one hundred and seventeen churches to the more than ten thousand converts to the Christian faith they had made, as well as to uncounted heathen. The heart of Africa, the "dark continent," was the latest foreign field to been entered. Here missionaries had only recently penetrated its interior, establishing a station where the Congo River crossed the Equator. Dramatizing that fact, Mr. McLean led six thousand convention delegates to a shipyard one afternoon to witness the unique service of dedicating a steamer to ply the Congo River. He broke over the bow of the steamer a bottle of pure water, christening it *The Oregon* in honor of its donors, the churches of Oregon, and sent it on its destiny of chugging up and down the great African river carrying the Gospel message for the next forty years.

The timid start made twenty years before by a group of St. Louis women in caring for orphan children had resulted in the establishment of twelve homes for destitute children and the needy aged under the aegis of the National Benevolent Association. Scores of aged preachers and their families had received help in time of need through the Board of Ministerial Relief.

The Pittsburgh Centennial Convention was a mass meeting in every sense. Intermittent efforts had been made during the years to transform the annual assembly of the brethren from mass meetings into delegate conventions, but the people had resisted the change. The independent cast of the brotherhood mind was reflected in the claim of every man to the right to have his say, and few people warmed to the idea of a few chosen delegates speaking for them. Certainly it is doubtful if the contagious enthusiasm evident at Pittsburgh, the spirited sense of belonging, the high sense of common achievement, the identification of every participant with the whole body of believers, could have been produced by an orderly assembly limited in its voting power to chosen delegates, solemnly conscious of their responsibility. For the lack of solemnity contributed to the occasion. Everybody was happy. While a few listening ears were tuned to catch any over-tones of "higher criticism" in the flow of oratory, and a few watching eyes were kept on the liberal-leaning Chicago-related men who were allowed to mount the platform only after careful scrutiny, and some of them actually barred, most of the people were intent only on marching to Zion. Not a ripple of discord appeared in public, and if anyone suspected the celebration marked a calm before another storm, nobody voiced the horrendous thought.

The aura of peace hung over the brotherhood for a whole year following the Pittsburgh convention. Ironically, it was the gentle voice of a man destined to become known as an "Apostle of Good-will and Unity" who broke the spell. The next summer, 1910, the convention again assembled, this time in Topeka, Kansas. Its president was Peter Ainslee.

As a young man Peter Ainslee had sat at the feet of John W. McGarvey at the College of the Bible, and his mind had seemed to take on the same legalistic cast. He was a scion of a preaching family in Virginia, rich in aristocratic heritage and intellectual vigor. His grandfather, Peter Ainslee the first, had been a force in advancing the Campbell doctrine of free churches among the landed Virginia gentry. He was the bright hope David Burnet had encountered upon his trip to the state in 1833. His son, Peter the second, had imbibed his father's enthusiasm for the Movement and become a lay preacher although he lived the life of a country squire, directing his twenty slaves in the cultivation of considera-ble land holding near Dunnsville, Virginia. Seven children came into his home but only three survived—an older boy, Charles; a girl, Etta; and the youngest, Peter the third. Charles tried preach-ing for a while but later went into business. Etta remained un-married, her health frail, and as her younger brother Peter grew to manhood and fulfilled the promise of becoming a preacher, she became his housekeeper and hostess, joined in that happy role after a few years by their widowed mother.

Young Peter was baptized in Essex Lake by the Dunnsville village mill when he was ten years old. He was frail as a youth, able to take little more than a nominal part in outdoor activities, and frequent bouts of illness, which confined him to the house, developed in him close ties with his mother and sister Etta. He read widely and constantly, especially historical works. War heroes fascinated him, probably because of his own frailty; but the story of Napoleon convinced him the use of the sword seldom settled differences, a discovery that sowed the seeds for his later widely publicized rejection of the institution of war as a national policy.

The wave of biblical criticism was just beginning to lap at the doors of the brotherhood's colleges when Peter Ainslee studied with Mr. McGarvey at the College of the Bible in Lexington. Mr. McGarvey was aware of its threat and, in an effort to forestall its impact on his students, concentrated on inculcating in them a passion for the peculiar tenets of the Disciple doctrine, and a dedication to the task of saving people from the sects by adding them to the rolls of the brotherhood's churches. The focus of his teaching was the plan of salvation as enunciated by Walter Scott, the plan alone that offered salvation.

Later, writing of his experience in college, Peter Ainslee said: "It was a college of a denomination, and a denominational atmosphere was inevitable. At first I resented this, but I had sense enough to know that a fellow in his teens should suppress his mental fermentations; besides, everything was so pleasant it looked unappreciative to be protesting. Unconsciously, however, I yielded little by little until by my third year I was a thorough denominationalist. I did not recover for the next fifteen years."

When he left college in 1891 to assume the pastorate of what he considered the most promising, and also the most difficult church he could obtain, the Calhoun Christian Church in Baltimore, Maryland, he was thoroughly inoculated with Disciple doctrine and imbued with a zeal for its dissemination.

The Calhoun Church was in the throes of a family dispute. Its quarrels were frequent and bitter, and a divisive spirit had prompted increasing numbers of its members to depart, some in sullen silence, others in open temper. Peter Ainslee made little effort to restrain the tide of the departing ones. Instead, he gave some of them a gentle push and began a campaign for new converts who gave more visible evidence of Christian love. The result within a short time was a virtually complete new roll of church members, individuals who were to become devoted to him. He remained their pastor for the next thirty-five years, and also their autocrat.

The hold Peter Ainslee developed over this Baltimore congregation has no parallel in the brotherhood's records, and bespeaks the strength of his unique personality. He was born with a natural courtliness of manner, which developed as he reached manhood into a charm few could resist. He remained unmarried until he was fifty-six years old, a target of romantic interest in all groups. His marriage at that age to Miss Mary Weisel was a love match, but Mr. Ainslee was frank in stating to his intimate friends that it was also the result of the sudden void in his life created by the death of his housekeeper sister, Etta.

But beneath the courtliness was a quality of iron. His will for the church became the church's will. He "persuaded" the women in the Ladies' Aid Society to adopt his ideas in the conduct of their work by getting himself elected their president. He "persuaded" the church's official board to condone actions he had taken on its behalf by the astonishing device of requesting the resignation of those who opposed him. Under this remarkable type of leadership the church grew to such size a new building was required and, against the judgment of a few skeptical members, he mortgaged all tangible assets to secure property on a more prominent corner in the city, and began the construction of an edifice he envisioned as a Christian Temple, which name it later bore. The structure was eighteen years in the building, its imaginative minister determining from time to time as he saw fit on additional units and a reshaping of its features. Through it all, the rank and file of his members remained loyal. They were possessed by his mind and his heart.

The change in Peter Ainslee's vision of the purpose of his ministry came gradually, evolving with the slow rising of the walls of his Temple. In his early preaching he had concentrated on a sectarian message, urging as the only way to unite the Christian world, the Movement's plan to restore the early church. In effect it embodied the idea that Christian unity would be achieved only when "everybody came over and joined us."

But as he matured he came to terms with reality. He no

longer expected, nor did he find it necessary, for all others "to join us." His sermons began sounding a new note. Let Christians simply unite with one another.

The change was influenced by his embroilment in Baltimore's teeming social problems. Shattering contacts with these problems in a working girls' home he established, in a Seminary House he founded, in noonday worship services he conducted for the down-and-outers, led to a strong sense of the sin of extending the ranks of one segment of God's church at the expense of extending his love. The crying need of the world was for Christian love. Hampering divisions among those seeking to express it became to him a scandal, a blight on the Gospel which could be eradicated only by forming a bond of brotherhood.

By the time Peter Ainslee was ready to mount the platform at the General Convention of the Christian Churches in 1910 at Topeka, Kansas, to deliver his president's address, an occasion which traditionally set the tone of each year's assembly, a totally new concept of the mission of the Movement had formed in his mind. The mission had to do with opening the doors of the brotherhood's churches as wide as those of the Kingdom of God.

Mr. Ainslee well knew the nature of the battle he was starting. Conformity to certain practices, such as baptism only by immersion, had taken deep root; habitual thinking was embedded; sheer inertia had overtaken much of the brotherhood. But these were among the things which had set the prow of the Movement's ship toward sectarian harbors, and he rejected all insistence on the Movement's peculiar tenets as partisan, destructive and sinful. "Unless we turn our course in conformity to Thomas Campbell's clarion call for unity, we are destined to become one of the most sectarian bodies," he bluntly stated, as he challenged the assembled brethren to a fresh appraisal of their task, shaming them for their quarrels.

Few occasions in the brotherhood's life evoked the public display of emotion that followed Mr. Ainslee's rebuke to his brethren. His address was scheduled for eleven o'clock on Friday morning, October 14, the fourth day of the convention. Long, arduous sessions, involving lengthy reports of the various agencies had preceded him, and the people were tired; they were anxious to get on with the business at hand, proud of their accomplishments and in no mood to be rebuked. That is perhaps the most charitable explanation of the unseemly manifestations that took place as he proceeded to recount the shortcomings of the brotherhood in respect to its primary function, the creation of a climate in the religious community conducive to the unity of God's people. A few irascible brethren did not wait for him to conclude before calling out in angry rebuttal. Their protests seemed a signal, and as Mr. Ainslee concluded his address a splattering of polite applause was punctuated by voices from all parts of the house, some challenging not so much the truth of Mr. Ainslee's words as his temerity in so frankly expressing himself; others commending his courage. Mr. Ainslee stood at the center of the storm for some minutes before he turned to leave the platform. "Are these my people?" he is reported to have said sadly to a man he passed in the hallway.

Peter Ainslee continued to voice the conviction that his own brethren had been sidetracked into giving priority to the Movement's form rather than its purpose. Enough of his brethren agreed with him to enable him to form a "Commission on Unity," which later took organizational shape as the Association for the Promotion of Christian Unity. He envisioned the agency as a bridge across which others who felt as its founders did would travel in an open-armed embrace of the rest of the Christian world. But the framework was heavy; those of like mind who had joined with him became preoccupied with other things, and eventually the organization all but collapsed before it was restructured with the advent of the ecumenical era.

Meanwhile Mr. Ainslee watched with hopeful eyes as several overtures toward actual union were made to the Disciples by the Baptists and the Congregationalists. But each such encounter was terminated with the reluctant conclusion that the time for union had not yet come. He also applauded the brotherhood's cautious ventures into cooperative endeavors, on the mission fields and at home. The Christian Endeavor Movement delighted him. It planted an awareness in the minds of young people at an impressionable age that there were Christians in all denominations. He rejoiced when the brotherhood became a part of cooperative Sunday school work. Every Bible student in every denomination, studying the same topic every Sunday through the International Uniform Lessons, gave promise of another cementing bond between Christians.

Yet cooperation was not union, and no substitute for it, and as time passed he became resigned to the stark truth that his church brethren could not be counted upon as an instrument to correct the disunity of the Christian world.

Discouraged, he turned to other ecclesiastical bodies. There he encountered largely the same lack of rapport. Denominational pride and vested interest had taken their toll. At an interdenominational conference at Lausanne, Switzerland, when he proposed the leaders representing the different churches sit down together and partake of the Lord's Supper, the instant rejection of the proposal brought home to him another dismaying truth—that the proud leaders were not yet willing to acknowledge the equality of all professing Christians before God. This belief Mr. Ainslee held as a basic essential in any platform for unity. Thereafter, with incisive realism, he admitted that reconciliation among the Protestant church hierarchy, including his own body, was useless. The warped emotions and allegiance of the "men at the top" were too strongly centered in their own doctrinal positions. Henceforth, he would depend on individuals; he would strive for a unity at the grass roots which would be beyond the control of boards and vested interests.

He returned from his experience in Lausanne to write what became a historic document in the annals of the ecumenical movement. The "Pact of Reconciliation" he issued, and which was signed by literally thousands of men and women in all denominations, said in part:

"We acknowledge the equality of all Christians before God, and propose to follow this principle as far as possible in all our spiritual fellowship. We will strive to bring the laws and practices of our several communions into conformity with this principle so that no Christian shall be denied membership in any of our churches, nor the privilege of participation in the observance of the Lord's Supper. . . . We affirm that a divided Christendom is opposed to the spirit of Christ and the needs of the world, and we are convinced that the Christianizing of the world is greatly hindered by divisive and rivaling churches. . . . Irrespective of denominational barriers, we pledge to be brethren one to another in the name of Jesus Christ."

In transcending conformity to the commonly held interpretation of the "Plea" of the Disciples of Christ, that which urged unity on the basis of the brotherhood's proscribed terms, Peter Ainslee incurred a degree of disfavor on the part of the rank and file of the Movement which amounted for years practically to ostracism. His activities in other fields did little to help the situation. His bold pacifist stand during World War I embarrassed the majority of his brethren, and his crusades against social injustice and racial barriers came before the conscience of the church was sufficiently aroused to take them in stride. Almost visibly the brotherhood drew together to form a circle which shut him out; heretic, rebel, a thing to flout. But Peter Ainslee steadily refused to break his connection with his brethren. He remembered he was not only a Disciple of Christ but a disciple of the lowly, forgiving Jesus, and he drew a circle which took them in.

CHAPTER XIX

The Church with Three Faces Emerges

As they entered the second century of existence as a religious group, the followers of Alexander Campbell, representing a Movement which for all its sound and fury was essentially a simple doctrine, presented an untidy appearance to the world. Lines crisscrossed as its members collided regarding biblical criticism but moved in harmony on organizational lines; others refused to countenance agencies in the conduct of their work but accepted liberal interpretations of the Scriptures. Only one sharp line, clear and distinct, ran across its mosaic pattern. There was no mistaking the separate identity in the Movement of the Churches of Christ.

Soon after their emergence as a separate body in 1906, the Churches of Christ began putting into practice the passion they inherited from the early leaders in the Movement for spreading the Gospel. One of their ablest leaders to emerge at this time was Nicholas Brodie Hardeman of Hendersonville, Tennessee, whose evangelistic drive was typical of that of scores of others among them. Over a period of years Mr. Hardeman held five successive series of "Tabernacle Meetings" in the largest auditorium in Nashville which attracted over fifty thousand people and resulted in planting hundreds of churches. The meetings were significant, however, not so much for their numbers as for the emphasis placed on the things that came first with the Churches of Christ, preaching of the Gospel and saving souls. No offerings were taken at any of the meetings. They were financed by faith, and the faith was justified; adequate private support was always forthcoming. This continues to be the custom generally followed in local Churches of Christ in the sense that no pledges of financial support are ever solicited. The custom is followed not only as a demonstration of faith but as an effort to allow nothing to divert attention from the main purpose of presenting the Gospel. The Hardeman meetings demonstrated also the depth of the group's conviction regarding the use of any innovation, especially instrumental music, in worship. The scripturally correct position the Churches of Christ felt they occupied on this matter so permeated Mr. Hardeman's preaching that, at the close of one of the meetings, a debate on the subject was arranged between him and one of the "mainstream" preachers, Ira Boswell, of Kentucky. The debate lasted for five sessions of two to three hours each, and drew approximately seven thousand people at every session.

It was at a Hardeman meeting that one of the first instances of interracial accord was displayed among churches of any branch of the Movement. A beloved preacher of the Negro race, Marshall Keeble, was asked to come to the platform and offer a prayer. Negroes had freely attended the series of meetings which, in itself, was a bit unusual as few Negroes ever entered a white church service following the Civil War. To invite one of them to participate in the service was more than unusual. But Mr. Keeble was an unusual man.

He was born of slave parents in 1878 in Middle Tennessee, and reared in a poverty which put a stop to his schooling at the seventh grade. But the education of his heart was in no way abated, and he developed a bubbling, warmhearted personality and an incredible alertness to things of the spirit. He made his living as a huckster, driving a vegetable wagon on the streets of Nashville, preaching often from the wagon-bed and occasionally in Negro churches. Eventually his record of changing the lives of those to whom he told the Gospel story caught the eye and ear of the wealthy A. M. Burton of Nashville, founder of the Life and Casualty Insurance Company. Thereafter, for the next sixty-five years, with Mr. Burton "paying the fare," Mr. Keeble roamed the length and breadth of the land and journeyed around the world, preaching and teaching. He baptized more than fifty thousand people and established literally hundreds of Negro Churches of Christ.

In those days a Negro who presumed to change the lives of white people was tolerated as a curiosity, and sometimes viewed as a menace. But Marshall Keeble had no desire to be either. He started his itinerant preaching in Mississippi, where he gave evidence of such power to sway his hearers he found a note from the Ku Klux Klan tucked into his Bible one evening when he started to speak. "We will visit you at some late hour of night," the note said. No visit was ever made, and Mr. Keeble traveled on to Alabama where he was pushed off the sidewalk so brutally one night on his way to his meeting he lay sprawled in a ditch for dead. He disconcerted his frightened tormentors, however, as they conferred on means of disposing of his body, by scrambling to his feet and tipping his hat. "Good evening, gentlemen," was his only comment. Frequently his revival tent was cut down, but scores of helping hands always restored it before the meeting hour arrived. By the time he invaded Georgia public attitude toward him had changed to such an extent the Georgia Power and Light Company in Atlanta silenced the motors of its streetcars so they could coast by his revival tent without disturbing the service. He was named the first Negro colonel on the Tennessee Governor's staff; Harding College in Arkansas honored him and itself by conferring on him a Doctor of Laws degree; and when he visited Africa the Nigerian government named him a chieftain of one of its African tribes.

Under such evangelistic leadership, typical of that displayed by scores of other preachers, it is no wonder the influence and numbers of the Churches of Christ expanded with noticeable rapidity. The religious community took note of this vigorous newcomer, and viewed its rapidly sprouting congregations as comprising a single entity, united in purpose and in body. But the image of a single entity was more apparent than real. For the insistence of the Churches of Christ on maintaining to the fullest degree their local autonomy in matters of biblical interpretation as well as church government, soon forced them to make room under the family umbrella for more than twenty-five distinct types of congregations, each holding, and expressing its own peculiar view regarding the validity of some of the "silences" of the Scriptures. "One cup" groups and "cups" groups exist today, depending on the congregation's view of the number of cups used at the original Last Supper. Sunday schools function in some churches and are rejected in others as unscriptural. The premillennialists and the postmillennialists view the second coming of the Lord from separate vistas of time, and the stand-up-to-pray group believes it occupies a more scripturally correct position than the sit-down group. But their basic tenet of "standing on the Bible" rests on a more solid rock than any outward procedure, and it has enabled them to accept their differences without public display of rancor, and to move forward as a mighty army, all of them equally confident they have restored the church born at Pentecost.

Today the army has encampments around the world. Churches of Christ have been established in seventy nations, with an estimated membership approaching three million. Their intrepid evangelists, not content with penetrating heathen strongholds, have planted their banner in even more hostile territory—that behind the Iron Curtain and under the shadow of the Vatican in Rome. Although the message of individual redemption through the saving power of Jesus Christ is paramount in their preaching, they have not neglected the welfare of men here on earth. Hospitals, orphanages, welfare centers abound around the world under the aegis of voluntary groups of their churches; and scores of their day schools, high schools and colleges in this country are their answer to the lack of spiritual values they sense in the nation's public educational system.

While the Churches of Christ were consolidating their position, the same could not be said of the rest of the Movement. The crisscrossing of lines which contributed to its untidy appearance reflected an untidy reality. A number of factors lent aid and comfort to this condition, resulting in a gradual pulling apart of factions within the remaining mainstream. One of them was the cherished spirit of inquiry.

The spirit of inquiry was leading an increasing number of men step by somewhat painful step toward a denial of bits and pieces of the Movement's traditional concepts. One such concept had to do with that of restoring the Ancient Order of Things. Many brethren had long suspected that the early order of things which the founders of the Movement had started out to restore had no justification in fact. No uniform pattern to be followed existed. But they had resisted giving more than a hint in public of their thinking. It was not until the turn of the century that the notion was put into clear and unmistakable words by an able scholar in the liberal wing of the Movement, Dr. Herbert L. Willitt, dean of the Disciples' Divinity House in Chicago.

"Restoration of the conditions prevailing in the apostolic churches is both impossible and undesirable," he said. "Moreover the movement of the church is forward, not backward. The real cry of the church should be, 'Forward to Christ,' not 'Back to Christ,' for our leader is ever before us!"

This acknowledgment that one of the basic tenets of the Movement was actually untenable convinced many conservatives still in the mainstream, led by the alarmed and alarming *Christian Standard*, that the Movement's original purpose was, as the "anti" group suspected, about to be abandoned. They drew back in righteous wrath.

Another factor contributing to further disunity within the mainstream was the approach of the ecumenical era. The term "ecumenical" was not yet current among the Disciples of Christ when Mr. Ainslee issued his famous "Manifesto of Reconciliation," which serves, according to many, as a blueprint for the whole present-day ecumenical emphasis. As it grew in use, to most Disciples the term meant simply an awareness of the kinship of all believers, a kinship that transcended organizational patterns and doctrinal views. As such it was a thrust toward unity, and unity was to them a hope long deferred, and still desperately sought. But others saw it in a subtle pressure to surrender cherished positions. They had developed a loyalty to the Movement, and their vested interest would allow them to give up no part of it.

Caught in the crossfire of the ensuing disputes were the cooperative endeavors with the denominations. Cooperation, as Peter Ainslee had pointed out, was not unity, but it was a step in that direction, and as the surging ecumenical waters engulfed the religious world, Disciple leaders in the liberal wing of the "mainstream" made a joyful display of entering into interdenominational councils, hastening to Stockholm, Oxford, Edinburg, Jerusalem, Madras, or wherever such councils assembled. It was as if they were suddenly aware the train for the ecumenical era had started and they had better climb aboard. The Episcopalians seemed to be in charge with an actively functioning Commission on Christian Union, and the Congregationalists and the Presbyterians were occupying the front seats. When, in 1907 the General

Convention of the mainstream churches, meeting in Norfolk, Virginia, had joined the Federal Council of Churches, a year after its founding and three years before Peter Ainslee spoke at Topeka, the action was taken cautiously. It was, in actual fact, the action of an *ad hoc* mass meeting. But as there seemed little distinction between that meeting and the convention itself, which was an undelegated mass meeting, it was considered by most people as the action of the convention itself. Now caution was gone, and the dream to which the Federal Council was committed became the dream of the liberals, strengthened when one of their own preachers, the polished Edgar DeWitt Jones of Detroit's great Central-Woodward Christian Church, was elected president of the Federal Council in 1936. Dr. Jones was not only polished in his appearance but in his speech, a master of words, his sermons lyrical poems, and the brotherhood to a man was proud of him. But even before he assumed leadership of the Federal Council, interchurch cooperation at every level appeared to the liberal wing of the Disciples as the appropriate means to reclaim their rightful position among the leaders in the unity surge.

As it turned out it was also the means of furthering disharmony within the brotherhood's ranks. The watchful *Christian Standard*, already deploring the habit of "consorting with the denominations" on the mission fields, viewed the increasing tendency to cooperate with the same denominations at the home base as an equally insidious, creeping denial of the Movement's nonsectarian character. And the tocsin of alarm was sounded with renewed force in the churches.

But it was not alone cooperation with the denominations that alarmed the *Christian Standard*; it sensed a danger in a suggested consolidation of the agency forces within the brotherhood.

Following World War I, Christian men everywhere felt the need to counteract the wave of secularism that swept the country by standing more firmly shoulder to shoulder with each other. The situation gave rise to an awareness of the brotherhood's need to strengthen its own work by consolidating its scrambled forces.

Six strong agencies had by this time come into existence. Each had a worthy purpose, but in the confusion of the brotherhood's expansion some of their work overlapped, and their appeals for support had become increasingly competitive. Various solutions were offered whereby their functions could be clarified, their overhead expense lessened, their competitive approach eliminated and their work strengthened. The best idea seemed to be for them to merge.

When plans toward that end began taking shape, The *Christian Standard* let it be known at once it was not of a mind to throw its hat in the air over the creation of a single giant organization. If the questioning eye of Russell Errett had detected signs of too much power in the separate agencies, he was not about to overlook the potential power inherent in an inclusive structure.

The merger took place, however, in 1919, and the resulting United Christian Missionary Society reared its proud and hopeful head in St. Louis, determined to surmount the hostility of the group the *Christian Standard* had agitated into vocal protest, and prove its worth.

The consolidation had not been accomplished without great soul-searching on the part of each of the agencies involved. No other religious body in America at that time had ventured to similarly risk upsetting the balance of pride and vested interest with which organized agencies notoriously become encrusted, by submerging their agency identities in a single body. As a pioneer in the united effort the new giant organization realized it was picking its ways in the full glare of watchful denominational eyes, as well as in stares of glaring resentment from some of its own household of faith. Indications that it exercised caution are seen in the care with which it rearranged its component parts.

The logical choice, for instance, of a president was, everybody agreed, the personable Archibald McLean. He had been the embodiment of the brotherhood's missionary zeal for thirty years, an acceptable and proven leader. But he was not given the post. His close ties with the foreign work, it was felt, would give undue emphasis to that phase of the total task. Mr. Frederick W. Burnham, at that time the president of the American Christian Missionary Society, the oldest agency in the brotherhood, was named president and Mr. McLean accepted the spot of vice-president, while Mrs. Anna R. Atwater, the president of the Christian Woman's Board of Missions, became second vice-president.

The women Mrs. Atwater represented had not yielded to the

arguments in favor of such a union with alacrity. They were not convinced men and women could work together as full equals, and for the first few years of the partnership they kept out a wary eye lest male dominance engulf them. Their cautious stance was reflected in varying degrees, and for different reasons, by the other boards—the National Benevolent Association, the Board of Church Extension, the Board of Ministerial Relief, the American Christian Missionary Society, and the Foreign Society—each committed to the united effort but each guarding his own.

The choice of St. Louis as a headquarters city also was made with cautious care. The selection was narrowed to the central region where the strength of the brotherhood existed, but one by one its other convenient cities were eliminated. Indianapolis was associated in the minds of the people too strongly with the women's work (although the United Society later moved to that city). Kansas City centered attention on the Board of Church Extension, and Cincinnati was too closely identified with the American Society and the Foreign Society.

The boards closed their separate offices and moved to St. Louis in the spring of 1919, bringing their files and their furnishings, surrendering their identities to the common cause, and offering, most reluctantly of all, their cherished periodicals. Submerging this beloved bit of each board's life called for genuine sacrifice. No other feature so embodied the peculiar personality with which each agency identified itself. But the journals were relinquished, and the resulting monthly magazine, bearing the significant name *World Call*, assumed the tremendous task of speaking for the six former separate agencies.

For the first few years of its corporate life the United Christian Missionary Society carefully felt its way, legally, heroically, hopefully a single entity. Everybody realized time would be required to merge the waters of its various streams and allow them to flow together to become one in truth as well as in name. But the process was hastened and its component parts forced to close ranks almost immediately because of the threat of a common foe.

Virulent, relentless attacks began showering upon the consolidated agency, led by the *Christian Standard*. Whereas heresy and dictatorship had been detected before primarily in the agencies engaged in foreign missionary work, now, the paper claimed, the germs had infected every agency consorting with these boards under the new family tent. A hierarchy had been born among the ecclesiastical-shunning, independent-minded, liberty-loving followers of Alexander Campbell.

For seven years the attacks continued. The battle came to a head in 1926, when the General Convention, now called the International Convention of the Christian Churches of North America in recognition of its Canadian adherents, met in Memphis, Tennessee.

The charges of dictatorship had not much support, but evidence of heresy seemed to many of the Society's critics to be obvious. Two years before the Memphis convention the charges had become so severe an investigating commission had been sent to the Orient mission fields to observe what was going on. Its findings were laid before the Memphis convention. While the facts revealed were subject to differing interpretations, they confirmed in many minds the charge that some of the missionaries supported by the United Society in the lands visited were indeed practicing "open membership," still the unmistakable badge of departure from the Movement's basic doctrine. Officials of the Society were subjected during the convention sessions to such hostile questioning a few gentle spirits became alarmed. At one point prayer was called for.

"No!" a strong voice rang out in protest. "This is the time to speak! Then we can pray."

The voice belonged to a preacher named Pearl H. Welshimer, pastor of the largest church in the brotherhood. It was the First Christian Church in Canton, Ohio, its membership rolls exceeding three thousand, and its influence for good extending throughout the state and far beyond. The voice of the man who had brought a church of the Movement to that high eminence was not to be ignored in any assembly.

Mr. Welshimer was another very tall man. He had brooding, intense, gray eyes, and a commanding presence. He had graduated in 1897, from Hiram College, once known as Western Electic Institute, so filled with conviction that Alexander Campbell had restored the original New Testament church that, during his first pastorate at Millersburg, Ohio, while he was only twenty-four years old, he wrote a remarkably logical tract called "Facts Concerning the New Testament Church," which circulated for years and eventually sold almost two million copies, influencing untold thousands to accept the doctrine.

When he accepted the pastorate of the church at Canton, in 1901, he was actuated by the single ambition to transform the halfhearted congregation he saw before him in its inadequate building on a side street, into a church worthy of proclaiming itself the successor of the New Testament body. Within months he started achieving his ambition.

Mr. Welshimer possessed a fighting spirit. He believed the spirit of competition had produced America's wealth, and he believed it likewise could bring in a harvest of souls to the Kingdom. He organized an adult Bible class with three members, and within a short time transformed it into a thriving group. At one time the Bible school reached an attendance of seven thousand. His method was that of holding a constant series of stimulating contests. He reorganized the women's missionary society, breathing into it such liveliness that it became the largest such group in the state. His competitive spirit led him twice to debate the unbeliever, Clarence Darrow, on the claims of Christianity, debates arranged by the Redpath Chautauqua Company. At the second debate, held in Akron, Ohio, it was estimated the audience numbered fourteen thousand people. For forty-six years he wrote a weekly Bible school lesson in a nationally circulated Sunday-school paper, the *Lookout*, by which he influenced thousands of young minds in the brotherhood's Sunday schools, indoctrinating them with the solid assurance that they had embraced the one true plan of salvation.

It is not surprising that such a man, devoted beyond measure to the Movement which had for its initial purpose the restoration of the Apostolic Church, was distressed by the repeated charges that the purpose was being diluted for foreign consumption. P. H. Welshimer believed in prayer, but he also believed in action. And the time for action was now.

Convinced by the reports of the investigating commission that the United Christian Missionary Society had indeed allowed, even if it had not encouraged, its missionaries to violate a cardinal

plank in the Movement's platform by receiving unimmersed converts into full fellowship, he encouraged a group of like-minded
distressed people to march out of the convention hall and across
the street to a nearby theater, there to form themselves into
what became a rival convention, the North American Christian
Convention. Although no formal statement was issued, the action
symbolized and made manifest another break in the ranks of the
Movement.

Mr. Welshimer was not the sole, or even the chief, leader in this
move. But his persuasive powers and his high standing among
his brethren, as the pastor of their largest church, carried weight.
He had already withdrawn the support of his great Canton Church
from the United Society. He was a firm believer in the missionary
enterprise but he believed even more firmly it could be carried on
better by a church which adhered to the early New Testament
pattern than one which veered toward sectarian cooperation. Later
he was to say, "While unity is desirable, restoration of the church
of the New Testament is more desirable. In place of spending
so much time talking about unity we had better be about the
business of having in every community the restored church of
the New Testament. When we have that we will have unity, and
we will never have it without it."

His example in refusing to support the United Society was now
followed by other churches and scores of leading preachers, who
declared their allegiance to the missionary cause, but declared
also their determination to henceforth conduct such work independent of the United Christian Missionary Society.

The newly severed branch of the Movement thereby gained
the name of "Independents." And, although some of the agencies
which originally formed the United Society eventually assumed
again their separate identities, resentment of the agency method
of conducting the church's work proved so strongly implanted that
the followers of Alexander Campbell in his pursuit of unity became
a church which now pursued the goal along another diverging
path.

CHAPTER XX

"Onward, Christian Soldiers"

When the Churches of Christ departed from the rest of the family twenty years before, they availed themselves of the opportunity to announce the separation by listing their group as a distinct body in the 1906 United States Census. But no such opportunity was available to the Independents in 1926. No means of a public announcement were at hand, and for a time the break seemed nothing more than a bad dream. Many on both sides of the severed body attempted to ignore it. They continued to fraternize in the International Convention as if ashamed of the absurdity of making support of any agency a test of Christian fellowship. P. H. Welshimer himself joined in this effort, even serving as a representative of the brotherhood to the Convention of British Churches in 1938. In a statement of his position about this time he voiced an attitude which many hoped could heal the break and preserve the church's solidarity. "The fact of organization is not objectionable," he said. "It is the way the organization is run. Everything depends on the personnel and the policy. A brotherhood of churches does not owe its existence to missionary work whether it be organized or unorganized. Missionary methods and plans and organizations are not the bonds that hold a brotherhood together any more than the type of architecture of a house of worship, or the order and time of services. These are expediencies, and there need not be agreement upon them to be a brotherhood. The unity of a brotherhood is not dependent upon methods of work, but upon the essential doctrines of the New Testament and the spirit that pervades the hearts of the people."

But while Mr. Welshimer fraternized in genuine Christian forbearance with his brethren in the International Convention, he also fraternized with those in the rival body of the conservative, or Independent, brethren, the North American Christian Convention. As if in rebuke to the business-laden sessions of the parent convention, the new group emphasized its devotion to the restoration of the New Testament church by making the preaching of the Gospel the primary aspect of its sessions. Soon it became known as a "preaching convention" and attracted hundreds of Gospel-hungry people both within and without the ranks of the critics of the United Society. Few business matters were allowed to interfere with this primary activity. Since the work of its undergirding churches relied for the most part on direct support from local churches which went through no agency treasury, little more than a skeleton of connectional framework was necessary. This direct-support program reflected, the group felt, the methods of the Apostolic church in its evangelistic emphasis. But that did not mean they were laggards in conducting their own good works.

As the years passed the Independents increased with greater rapidity in numbers and in work than the remaining mainstream, and soon the dissident brethren were supporting totally separate institutions than those maintained by the rest of the brotherhood through the United Society. They today have separate hymnals, Sunday-school curricula, colleges, journals, youth work, summer camps and missionary work. At the time of the pulling apart in 1926, five of the brotherhood's colleges swung into line behind them. Soon the need was felt for additional schools to enable the group to discharge its responsibility of preparing preachers who could perpetuate the original purpose of the Movement. Today more than two dozen Independent educational institutions are in full operation, inculcating around five thousand students every year with the passion for uniting the Christian world by restoring the Apostolic church, differing in their emphasis from their estranged sisters, the Churches of Christ, only on a less rigid insistence on a literal interpretation of certain passages in the Scriptures.

Two years before Peter Ainslee's plain-spoken admonition to the Disciples at Topeka to be up and doing in unifying the Christian world, an event occurred which received little attention at the time but which eventually contributed to the climate of thinking in which the break between the Independents and the churches aligned with the United Society became even firmer.

In 1884 a weekly journal had been started in Iowa among the Disciple brethren called the *Christian Oracle*. It weathered a succession of financial and theological storms, moving to Chicago in 1888 to enjoy a climate more agreeable to its liberal bent. But its financial difficulties continued, and in 1908 it was purchased at a sheriff's sale for fifteen hundred dollars by an idealistic but shrewd young preacher in Illinois. His name was Charles Clayton Morrison.

As the *Christian Oracle*, the paper had felt obliged to largely limit itself to news of the Movement's churches, and to stifle its liberal leanings by walking a circumspect path in doctrinal matters. But now it had moved to Chicago, and changed its name to the *Christian Century*. To its new editor and owner, this entitled it to widen the focus of its interests and become the spokesman for the point of view he held, and which he felt a "vigorous minority" of liberals in the Disciples' fold shared. He soon found, however, that of the vigorous minority, fewer than six hundred were willing to part with the price of a subscription. Besides, the nebulous term "Disciple liberal" described, he discovered, stragglers who dotted the theological landscape at every one of the brotherhood's doctrinal turns, and the great majority of them, heretical as they appeared to the readers of the *Christian Standard*, and the brethren in the Churches of Christ, were still of a mind to enjoy the status quo.

He was not long in coming to grips with reality. He would have to interest others, in addition to the Disciples, if the journal was to survive.

Charles Clayton Morrison was pastor of the Monroe Street Christian Church in Chicago in 1908 when he launched his journalistic career. He was thirty-four years old. Forty years later, at the age of seventy-four, he was described by *Time* magazine as "a slender, decorous man with old-world manners, wearing gold-rimmed glasses that do not quite hide the fire in his eyes. Even in his youth he never lacked for words."

While still a youth of seventeen years his remarkable mastery of words was apparent in a full-time pastorate he held at that age of the Christian Church at Clarinda, Iowa. Even then he had been preaching intermittently for two years for rural Iowa churches. He further developed his striking speaking style when he attended

Drake University in Des Moines. Several pastorates were held during his student days, and in 1898, following his graduation, he was called to the Monroe Street Church in Chicago. In the liberal atmosphere of that city his affinity for pioneering in social and theological fields was recognized by the University of Chicago, which granted him a fellowship in philosophy. For four impressionable years he drank deeply at the liberal fountain, sifting and examining all the new notions then floating about, preaching meanwhile for the Christian Church in nearby Springfield, Illinois, until, in 1907, he resumed the oversight of the Monroe Street Church in Chicago. By this time he not only understood the nature of the forces at work in the religious world, but, anticipating the arrival of the ecumenical era, he determined to become a spokesman for it. The sheriff's sale of the *Christian Century* gave him that opportunity.

Soon after he took over the editor's chair of what was still a mildly liberal Disciple paper, his uninhibited way of stating things startled his Disciple subscribers. When many of them refused to renew he realized the time had come to widen the paper's appeal. He included news and comments on everything pertaining to contemporary religious thought, editing the material with keen insight and rare literary verve. The fact that he was dependent on no denominational hierarchy for permission to express himself lent a certain pungency to the paper, and a flood of new and more enthusiastically liberal subscribers, their religious affiliations cutting across all denominational lines, followed.

In 1919, ten years after acquiring the paper, Dr. Morrison proclaimed it "An Undenominational Journal of Religion," and the circulation tripled. For almost half a century he guided the paper as it explored matters ranging from the outlawry of war as an instrument of national policy to an examination in depth of God's existence and the nature of his deity. Its influence penetrated every nook of the religious world, including his own household of faith. The brotherhood was proud to claim him but most of the brethren were bewildered by him, even those who loyally attempted to follow his forays into obscure theological waters. In turn he attempted to help them find again the pathway to unity by taking under his guidance the journal of the brotherhood's wavering Commission on Christian Unity, called the *Christian Unity*

Quarterly. Later he edited the journal *Christendom,* transferring it to the World Council of Churches after the formation of that body in 1958 where it is published today as the *Ecumenical Review.*

Throughout his lifetime Charles Clayton Morrison remained a member of the Disciples of Christ brotherhood, remaining in the fold despite its questioning view of him, as Peter Ainslee had done, believing implicitly it had a witness to bear in ushering in the unity of the Christian world.

The two severed branches of the brotherhood, the Churches of Christ and the Independents, considered they were already properly bearing that witness. But as the twentieth century advanced, those remaining in the mainstream were not so sure of their own purpose. They began feeling the tide of searching scrutiny which was starting to swirl over the established order of religious as well as secular society following World War II. Their gradual realization that they were called to a greater destiny than they were fulfilling gave rise to a mood of healthy self-criticism. The Movement had been founded on the doctrine that "the Church of Christ upon earth is intentionally, essentially and constitutionally one." Yet it had not produced that reality. Why? What was the church? What was its nature and its mission?

As the questioning mood spread it produced a new collective courage. If roadblocks existed which hindered the achievement of the Movement's purpose, they must be removed. If deadwood in the machinery had accumulated, it must be cleared away. If cobwebs clouded thinking, they must be swept clean. If old positions were no longer valid, fresh ones must be taken. The brethren refused to continue as mindless captives of tradition. The church in the twentieth century was called upon to function in a new world. The peaceful, rural background enjoyed by the early leaders was gone. The Movement was called upon now to wrestle with secular forces in a materialistic society embedded in a blurred and complicated social system. Yet its early design persisted; it was still a loose-knit aggregation of congregations and agencies, still officially nameless and still unable to speak with one voice or act as one body.

By 1960 when the International Convention assembled in

Louisville, Kentucky, the brethren were ready to take action. They formally adopted as the name for their segment of the severed brotherhood, the Christian Church (Disciples of Christ), and they created a Commission on Brotherhood Restructure.

In subjecting to scrutiny what had become the entrenched structure of the Movement's life and practice, the Commission knew it was taking a calculated risk. Its efforts could create another controversy; its findings might even lead to another division. But as surgeons digging at the root of an infection, its members began an honest examination and evaluation of the polity which had allowed not only the purpose of the Movement to become obscured but had created fragmentations within the body.

It centered its findings on the concept of a church that could and should be manifest at many levels. The church, it said, does not exist only in the local congregation; it embodies several ministries of concern for the advancement of the Kingdom of God. Each should be recognized as being on a par with the others. Education, social action, publishing, benevolence, each are ministries which should witness along with the local congregation, yet each "joined and knit together." To make realistic this concept, and to create a framework in which all parts of the church would be responsible to and for one another under Christ, the Commission recommended basic changes in the brotherhood's structure.

This new concept of the church was admitted by many to be valid. But to others it was so alien to the original idea on which the Movement had embarked—that of the all-sufficiency of each local church to witness and bring in the Kingdom in its own way and by its own efforts—it seemed another repudiation of the Movement's original tenet and a break with its life. That the church could exist apart from the local congregation was news to a great host of the faithful. So nobody was surprised when, as the work of the Commission progressed, and the machinery of the newer structure became visible in a "provisional plan," strong and increasingly vocal schools of thought developed among the brethren. Some saw in the plan a complete surrender of the Movement to the status of a denomination; some felt it was an attempt to create the machinery by which the brotherhood could merge into the ecumenical processes and lose its identity in an organic union with the denominations; some detected in it a scheme to make more vocal the "social gospel."

But others were more hopeful. The "provisional plan" called for a church governed by representative bodies at three levels— local, regional and general, unifying the various phases of work under the general body, "joined and knit together." The realignment of the work into administrative units of the church would thus transfer the witness and service from single, independent groups to the church as a whole, strengthening the fabric of the brotherhood. And if in the process, many were frank to say, the social concerns of the church received added emphasis, such concerns they considered as more relevant in the turmoil of the times than restoring the Ancient Order of Things. Or if the plan would, indeed, create the machinery by which the brotherhood could move with greater ease in the labyrinth of the religious community, that was an end devoutly to be desired.

The "provisional plan" was studied for eight years with more or less thoroughness by the six thousand churches comprising the mainstream of the brotherhood. By 1967 everybody who had an opinion seemed to have been heard, and the plan was presented to the International Convention when it met that fall in St. Louis. The tide was overwhelmingly in its favor. Final action on its adoption was deferred for another year, and in October, 1968, when the brethren assembled ten thousand strong in Kansas City, its adoption was enthusiastically confirmed.

The Churches of Christ had appeared as unconcerned spectators at this latest development within the Movement which had given them birth. They conceived of themselves, not as a body whose basic tenets were threatened by the radical plan but as a replica of the church founded at Pentecost which no man or plan of restructuring could touch. The Independents, although they had more recent intimacy with the mainstream, also largely ignored the whole business. As their numbers and work had grown, their concerns had centered on their own affairs, and their attacks on the liberal wing had lessened. As the plan for restructuring the brotherhood gave evidence it was headed toward the status of a denomination, occasional warnings came from the *Christian Standard* and evoked replies from the chief defender of the plan, the *Christian-Evangelist,* but on the whole each seemed to have abandoned hope of convincing the other of the error of its ways.

Only a few months before the ten thousand mainstream brethren assembled in October, 1968, in Kansas City to take final action in adopting their plan of restructure, the Independents met in Cincinnati for their North American Christian Convention. The fact the Cincinnati conclave attracted three times the number of people attending the Kansas City meeting was significant. Increasing hundreds of the Movement's adherents had found the restructure plan unpalatable. Confirming evidence of this was the action by two thousand churches which had attempted to keep a foot in each camp by listing themselves in the brotherhood's only official directory, the *Year Book,* published by the International Convention, in now asking that their names be dropped. By this means they made manifest the severance of their relationship with the restructured mainstream. A few months later another overt action occurred when a number of concerned leaders among the Independents released a statement to the press identifying their group as an "undenominational fellowship." This was followed by overtures toward listing it as such in the *Year Book of American Churches,* issued by the National Council of Churches. This public acknowledgment that a break had been made indicated that the point of no return had been reached.

Today the unity of all Christians continues to be the goal of all three segments. Each avows its willingness to "sink into the body of Christ at large," as Barton W. Stone graphically stated in his "Last Will and Testament of the Springfield Presbytery." But that process is to be undertaken, say the Independents and the Churches of Christ, by restoring the Apostolic church in its beliefs and practices. They are not willing to lose their identity in a merger with other groups to form just a bigger denomination. The mainstream segment, on the other hand, will seek through ecumenical discussion to advance (their way now smoothed by their restructured state) toward their goal, a united church which allows for diversity in structure and in doctrine, and which considers no Christian as alien to its communion.

AFTERWORD

So, here we leave the story, confident that in the final reckoning the Restoration Movement will be a blessing to all believers. As with any history, the Movement's progress has been scrambled, personalities as much as doctrine deciding its course. In untangling its threads, in separating the important from the unimportant, we have of necessity limited the events related to those essential to the weaving of an orderly sequence. Likewise, only the more significant protagonists have been portrayed, selected from the thousands of dedicated men and women who contributed to the Movement's onward march.

There is, of course, no way to write "Finis" to a history of such a continuing body. There is also no adequate way to encompass the wide spectrum of information which threw light for us on the unfolding drama of the story to date.

We brought to this writing an empathy for the early leaders and a sense of identification with the events recorded which reflect the months and years of research spent in preparing to write "The Fool of God" and "Raccoon John Smith." All of the libraries we haunted, the people interviewed, the documents perused, the localities invaded, the help rendered by individuals too numerous to again mention, but whom we call blessed—all of this has overflowed into this work, and contributed as much as, and perhaps more than the sources more recently consulted.

But as every proper "history" must give evidence of more tangible authority than the authors' accumulated knowledge and inner awareness, we list under "Basic Sources" the books, periodicals and other documents we found of special value in writing this volume. Many of them are in our private library, but for access to others we are indebted chiefly to two rich mines of the Movement's lore, both located in Nashville: The Disciples of Christ Historical Library, where we were rendered every possible assistance by its gracious president, Dr. Willis Jones, its knowledgeable former Curator, Dr. Claude E. Spencer, and its capable librarian, Marvin Williams; and the Gospel Advocate Company, whose great-souled leader, Dr. B. C. Goodpasture, also thoughtfully called to our attention and made available to us much rare and significant material.

Louis Cochran
Bess White Cochran

Nashville, 1969

NOTE TO THE UNINITIATED

As a help to those confused by the positions of the three religious bodies existing today which developed from the Restoration Movement initiated by Thomas and Alexander Campbell, the following chart is provided to clarify at a glance some of the major differences and similarities. It is not designed as an definitive statement of their positions; in view of the winds of change blowing through the whole religious community, the notations should be considered as simply indicating their present general positions.

	Christian Church (Disciples of Christ)	*Christian Church (Independent)*	*Churches of Christ*
Church Gov't.	Self-governing congregations aligned with policies of a national General Board	Local autonomy, not subject to any higher body.	Full local autonomy; no connectional framework among churches, or with any general body.
Baptism	By immersion only, but congregations free to accept members baptized by other forms.	By immersion only; no other forms recognized as valid	By immersion only; no other forms recognized as valid.
Assemblies	Delegated General Assembly for business as well as fellowship and inspiration.	Mass undelegated assembly for fellowship and preaching only.	No conventions; Lectureships encouraged.
Conduct of Work	Through organized boards	By direct congregational support; few organized boards.	No organized general boards; direct congregational support.
Bible	Considered as containing divine Revelation of God's will; its spirit rather than its letter stressed.	Considered as all-sufficient Revelation of God's will.	Considered as all-sufficient Revelation of God's will, its silences as well as its speech to be observed.
Worship	Liturgical forms often followed; weekly Communion open to all believers.	Liturgical forms shunned; weekly Communion open to all believers.	Simplicity stressed; no instrumental music; weekly Communion to which unimmersed believers are neither invited nor excluded.
Purpose	Unity of Christian world paramount; to be sought by any means other than exclusively through restoration of early church.	Restoration of early church primary as far as consistent with current conditions.	Restoration of early church in all its practices and forms, as only means of uniting Christian world.
Ecumenical	Full cooperation with denominations seeking ecumenical ideals.	Occasional cooperation with denominations on local level; largely reject higher alignments.	No formal cooperation with other religious bodies.

BASIC SOURCES

Richardson, Robert: "Memoirs of Alexander Campbell" (2 vols), J. B. Lippincott, Philadelphia, 1868.

Moore, W. T.: "Comprehensive History of Disciples of Christ," Fleming H. Revell Co., New York, 1909.

Campbell, Alexander: "Popular Lectures and Address," James Challen and Son, Philadelphia, 1866.

"The Christian Baptist," Buffaloe, Virginia, 1823–1830.

"The Millennial Harbinger," Buffaloe and Bethany, Virginia, 1830–1864.

Garrison, James Harvey: "Reformation of the Nineteenth Century," Christian Publishing Co., St. Louis, 1901.

"Story of a Century," Christian Publishing Co., St. Louis, 1909.

"Memories and Experiences," Christian Publishing Co., St. Louis, 1926.

Garrison, W. E.: "Religion Follows the Frontier," Harper and Bro., New York, 1931.

"Christian Unity and Disciples of Christ," Bethany Press, St. Louis, 1955.

"Disciples of Christ, a History" (with A. T. DeGroot), Bethany Press, St. Louis, 1948.

DeGroot, Alfred T.: "The Restoration Principle," Bethany Press, St. Louis, 1960.

"Disciples of Christ, a History" (with W. E. Garrison), Bethany Press, St. Louis, 1948.

West, Earl I.: "Search for the Ancient Order" (2 vols), Gospel Advocate Publishing Co., Nashville, 1949.

Murch, James DeForest: "Christians Only," Standard Publishing Co., Cincinnati, 1962.

Harrell, David Edwin: "Quest for a Christian America," Disciples of Christ Historical Society, Nashville, 1966.
Panel of Scholars: "Renewal of the Church" (3 vols), Bethany Press, St. Louis, 1963.

SPECIFIC SOURCES

From which much of the material found in each chapter, or quoted statements therein, were obtained:

CHAPTER I *In the Beginning*
  "Reformation of the Nineteenth Century," by Garrison.
  "Memoirs of Alexander Campbell," by Richardson, Vol. I.
  "Thomas Campbell, Man of the Book," by Lester G. McAllister; Bethany Press, St. Louis, 1854.
  "The Restoration Principle" by DeGroot. pp. 134–142.
  "Christians Only," by Murch. pp. 35–52.

CHAPTER II *Dawn of Seventeen Uneasy Years*
  "Memoirs of Alexander Campbell," by Richardson. Vol. 1, pp. 472–501. Vol. 2, pp. 70–172.
  Millennial Harbinger, 1846, p. 493 (full text of sermon on "The Law").
  "Walter Scott, Voice of the Golden Oracle," by Dwight E. Stevenson; Christian Board of Publication, St. Louis, 1946.
  "Life of Walter Scott," by William Baxter; Bosworth, Chase and Hall, Cincinnati, 1874.
  "Debates that Made History" by J. J. Haley; Christian Board of Publication, St. Louis, 1920.

CHAPTER III *Following the Finger of God*
  "Barton Warren Stone" by Charles C. Ware, Bethany Press, St. Louis, 1932.
  "Barton Warren Stone" by William G. West, Disciples of Christ Historical Society, Nashville, 1954. pp. 76–79.
  "Alexander Campbell as a Preacher" by Archibald McLean, Fleming H. Revell Co., New York, 1908.

"Memoirs of Alexander Campbell," by Richardson, Vol. 2, pp. 88 and 134.
"Christians Only" by Murch. pp. 83–95.

CHAPTER IV *Come Out of Babylon*
"The Western Reserve" by Harlan Hatcher, Bobbs Merrill Co., Indianapolis, 1949. pp. 28–79–87.
"History of Disciples on the Western Reserve" by A. S. Hayden, Chase and Hall, Cincinnati, 1875. pp. 117–120.
"Hoosier Disciples" by Henry K. Shaw, Christian Board of Publication, St. Louis, 1952. pp. 48–54.
"Historical Collections of Ohio," Vol. 2, by Henry Howe, Laning Printing Co. for State of Ohio, Norwalk, Ohio, 1888.
"Voice of the Golden Oracle," by Dwight E. Stevenson, Christian Board of Publication, St. Louis, 1946. p. 87.
Millennial Harbinger, 1833, p. 227, as quoted from "The Presbyterian," Philadelphia, April 10, 1833.

CHAPTER V *Without Tarrying For Any*
"Buckeye Disciples" by Henry K. Shaw, Christian Board of Publication, St. Louis, 1952. p. 56.
"Disciples of Christ, a History" by Garrison and DeGroot, Bethany Press, St. Louis, 1948. p. 210.
Christian Baptist, 1826, Vol. III, p. 373.
"Search for the Ancient Order," by Earl West, Vol. 1, Gospel Advocate Co., 1949, Nashville.
"Biography of Elder J. T. Johnson," by John Rogers, privately printed, Cincinnati, 1861.
"Memoirs of Alexander Campbell" by Robert Richardson, Vol. II, p. 241.
"Debates that Made History" by J. J. Haley, Christian Board of Publication, St. Louis, 1920.
"Life of Elder John Smith," by John Augustus Williams, Standard Publishing Co., Cincinnati, 1870.

CHAPTER VI *Good-bye to the Baptists*
"Early History of Disciples on the Western Reserve" by A. S. Hayden. pp. 128. 133. 183. 197. 329. 296. 368. 456.
"Buckeye Disciples" by Shaw. p. 35.

"Quest for a Christian America," by David Harrell. pp. 46. 63. 82.
Christian Baptist, Vol. I, p. 12.

CHAPTER VII *To Your Tents, O Israel*
Millennial Harbinger. 1832, p. 5010. 1837, p. 411. 1839, p. 353. 1839, p. 270. 1841, p. 533.
"Memoirs of Alexander Campbell" by Richardson, Vol. II, p. 389.
"The Living Pulpit of the Christian Church," by W. T. Moore, R. W. Carroll Co., Cincinnati, 1868. p. 35.
"Underserved Obscurity," by Noel Keith, Bethany Press, St. Louis, 1954.
"Hoosier Disciples," by Henry K. Shaw.

CHAPTER VIII *Captives of the Word of God*
"Restoration Principles" by DeGroot. pp. 143–146.
Millennial Harbinger. June, 1836, p. 282. Dec. 1837, p. 340. 1842, p. 523. 1844, p. 41.
"Religion Follows the Frontier" by Garrison. pp. 168–169.
"Home to Bethphage" by Cloyd Goodnight and W. E. Stevenson, Christian Board of Publication, St. Louis, 1949.
"Voice of the Golden Oracle," by Stevenson. pp. 150–153.
The Evangelist, Vol. III, 1834, p. 81.
"Franklin College and its Influence," by James E. Scobey, Gospel Advocate Co., Nashville, 1954. pp. 11–12. 124.
"Memoirs of Alexander Campbell" by Richardson, Vol. II, p. 400.
"Life and Times of David Lipscomb" by Earl West, Religious Book Service, Henderson, Tenn., 1954. pp. 41–44.
"Debates that Made History," by J. J. Haley.

CHAPTER IX *The Starting Flag is Down!*
Millennial Harbinger, 1845, p. 272. 453. 1848, p. 646. pp. 599–600. 1849, p. 269.
"Memoirs of Alexander Campbell," by Richardson, Vol. 2, p. 319.

The Christian Messenger, edited by Barton W. Stone, George-town, Ky., 1826–37; Jacksonville, Ill., 1839–43. Aug. 1843, p. 49.

"Voice of the Golden Oracle" by Stevenson, pp. 194–195.

"Debates that Made History," by Haley, p. 229.

Papers of David Patrick Henderson, Disciples of Christ Historical Society, Nashville, Nov. 16, 1843.

"Biography of Elder J. T. Johnson," by Rogers, p. 206.

"Religion Follows the Frontier," by Garrison, p. 185.

"Disciples of Christ, a History," by Garrison and DeGroot, p. 243.

"Buckeye Disciples," by Shaw, p. 147.

"Undeserved Obscurity, the Story of David S. Burnet" by Noel Keith, Bethany Press, St. Louis. p. 80.

CHAPTER X *The City of Confusion.*

Unpublished M.A. Thesis of James R. Welburn, Abiline Christian College, Abiline, Texas. 1961: "The Life and Times of Tolbert Fanning"

"Life and Times of Benjamin Franklin," by Joseph Franklin, John Burns Pub. Co., St. Louis, 1879. p. 210.

"Search for the Ancient Order," by West, Vol. I, pp. 215–216.

"Early History of Disciples on Western Reserve" by Hayden, pp. 398–400.

"Reformation of Nineteenth Century," by Garrison, pp. 138–150.

Lard's Quarterly, edited by Moses Lard, Lexington, Ky., 1862–1866. Vol. 3, April, 1866, p. 334.

For running account of Campbell-Ferguson dispute, see each issue *Millennial Harbinger*, 1852–1853.

The Christian Review, edited by Tolbert Fanning, Nashville, 1844–1847. Oct. 1845. Dec. 1844.

The Christian Magazine, edited by Jesse Ferguson, Nashville, 1848–1853.

Millennial Harbinger, May, 1849.

"Recollections of Men of Faith," by W. C. Rogers, privately printed, 1889; re-issued by Old Paths Book Club, Rosemead, Calif., 1961.

CHAPTER XI *War of Words and Guns*

Millennial Harbinger. 1854, March, p. 109. 1845, Jan. p. 51; 1846, April, p. 84. 1856, April, p. 227. 1850, June, p. 331. 1851, Jan. pp. 27–35; pp. 52–54.

"Memoirs of Isaac Errett," by J. S. Lamar, Standard Pub. Co., Cincinnati, 1893.

North-Western Christian Magazine, Cincinnati, 1854–58. Jan. 1856, p. 213. Aug. 1857, p. 302.

"Quest for a Christian America," Harrell. pp. 115–123.

"Life of Benjamin Franklin," by Joseph Franklin, p. 305.

"Pea Ridge and Prairie Grove" by William Baxter; Poe and Hitchcock, Cincinnati, 1864.

CHAPTER XII *The Long, Dark Tunnel*

"Memoirs of Alexander Campbell," by Richardson. Vol. 2, pp. 581–606.

Millennial Harbinger, 1834, Jan. p. 8. 1850, Aug. p. 79.

"Life of Benjamin Franklin," by Joseph Franklin, p. 197. p. 287.

"Biographical Sketches of Gospel Preachers," by H. Leo Boles, Gospel Advocate Co., Nashville, 1932.

"Biographies and Sermons of Pioneer Preachers," edited by B. C. Goodpasture and W. T. Moore, privately printed, 1954; first published as "The Living Pulpit of the Christian Church," 1860.

CHAPTER XIII *The Saints Their Watch Were Keeping*

Lard's Quarterly, edited by Moses Lard. 1864, March, p. 332. 1865, April, p. 22. 1865, Oct. p. 93. 1866, April, p. 316.

American Christian Review, edited by Benjamin Franklin, Cincinnati, 1856–1887. 1859, April, p. 105. Each issue, 1866–67–68.

The Gospel Advocate, edited by Tolbert Fanning, Nashville, 1855–1861; edited by David Lipscomb, 1866–1905. 1866, Feb. pp. 83–84.

"Search for the Ancient Order," by West. Vol. 2, p. 18. pp. 41–92. Vol. I. pp. 289–306.

"Religion Follows the Frontier," by Garrison, p. 232. p. 266.

"Disciples of Christ, a History," by Garrison and DeGroot, pp. 345–349.

"Life of David Lipscomb" by West. p. 258.

"Brother McGarvey," by W. C. Morro, Bethany Press, St. Louis, 1940.

CHAPTER XIV *Into All the World*

"Forty Years of Service" by Ida W. Harrison, privately printed, 1909, Lexington, Ky.

"Historical Sketch of Christian Woman's Board of Missions," compiled by Elmira Dickinson, 1897.

"Reformation of the Nineteenth Century," by Garrison. pp. 313–322.

"Life and Labors of Archibald McLean," by Wm. R. Warren, Bethany Press, 1923.

"Pioneering in Tibet," by Albert Shelton, Fleming H. Revell Co., New York, 1921.

"With the Tibetans in Tent and Temple" by Susie Rijnhart, Foreign Christian Missionary Society, Cincinnati, 1901.

"Shelton of Tibet," by Flora Beal Shelton. George H. Doran Co., New York, 1923.

"Hoosier Disciples" by Shaw. p. 212.

Original Record Book, Hopkinsville, Ky. Church of Christ; Disciples of Christ Historical Society, Nashville.

CHAPTER XV *Approaching the Eye of the Hurricane*

Millennial Harbinger. 1836, June, pp. 282–283. 1835, Dec. p. 587.

"Religion Follows the Frontier," by Garrison, p. 266.

"Disciples of Christ, a History," by Garrison and DeGroot, p. 405.

"Memories and Experiences" by J. H. Garrison, Christian Board of Publication, St. Louis, 1926.

"Design for Renewal and Growth," compiled by Emmett J. Dickson and William K. Fox for the National Christian Missionary Convention, 1966. Mimeographed, Indianapolis.

"Two Races in One Fellowship" by Robert Jordan, United Christian Church, Detroit, 1944.

"Life of David Lipscomb," by West. pp. 159–162.

"Quest for a Christian America" by Harrell, p. 58.

CHAPTER XVI *The Great Divide*

"The Singing Evangelist" by William Baxter, Central Book Concern, Cincinnati, 1879. p. 152.

"Christians Only" by James DeForest Murch, p. 216–217. p. 316. p. 193.

"Memories and Experiences" by James H. Garrison, pp. 87–90.

The Gospel Advocate. 1908, April 25, p. 265. 1909, Oct. 28.

"Disciples of Christ, a History," by Garrison and DeGroot, p. 387.

"Life of David Lipscomb" by West. p. 258.

CHAPTER XVII *Running Up the Flag*

"Hoosier Disciples" by Shaw. p. 271. p. 301. p. 267.

"Brother McGarvey," by W. C. Morro.

"Ely Vaughn Zollars," by Ronald Osborn, Christian Board of Publication, St. Louis, 1947.

"Religion Follows the Frontier," by Garrison. p. 269.

The Indiana Christian, published by Association of Christian Churches in Indiana, 1887–. June 15, 1896.

"Christians Only," by Murch. pp. 238–245.

"Fifty Years of Attack and Controversy," by Stephen J. Corey, published by the Committee on the Publication of the Corey Manuscript, St. Louis, 1953.

"Disciples of Christ, a History," by Garrison and DeGroot, pp. 432–434.

CHAPTER XVIII *He Drew a Circle*

"Christians Only" by Murch. pp. 208–214.

"Peter Ainslee, Ambassador of Goodwill" by Finis S. Idleman; Willett, Clark and Colby, Chicago, 1941.

"Fifty Years of Attack and Controversy" by Corey. pp. 32–33.

"Disciples of Christ, a History," by Garrison and DeGroot, pp. 420–421.

Peter Ainslee Centennial Issue of *Discipliana,* Disciples of Christ Historical Society, Nashville, July, 1967.

"The Message of the Disciples for the Union of the Church," by Peter Ainslee; Fleming H. Revell Co., New York, 1913.

CHAPTER XIX *The Church with Three Faces Emerges*

"N.B.H., Biography of Nicholas Brodie Hardeman," by James Powell and Mary Powers; Gospel Advocate Co., Nashville, 1964.

"Roll Jordan Roll," by J. E. Choate; Gospel Advocate Co., Nashville, 1968.

"Our Plea for Union and the Present Crisis" by Herbert Willett; Christian Century Co., Chicago, 1901.

"Reformation of Tradition," edited by Ronald Osborn for Panel of Scholars, Bethany Press, St. Louis, 1963. Vol. I. p. 283.

Christian Standard, Cincinnati, July 17, 1943. p. 629.

"Fifty Years of Attack and Controversy" by Corey. pp. 60–101.

"Christians Only," by Murch.

"P.H., the Welshimer Story," by Francis M. Arant, Standard Publishing Company, Cincinnati, 1948.

CHAPTER XX *Onward, Christian Soldiers*

"A Fork in the Road," by W. E. Garrison; Address delivered at Oreon E. Scott Ministers' Breakfast, Detroit, Mich., Oct. 7, 1964. Published in pamphlet form by Pension Fund, Indianapolis, 1964.

"Freedom or Restructure," Pamphlet published by Committee for Preservation of the Brotherhood, Indianapolis, 1965.

"Provisional Design for the Christian Church," edited by Granville Walker for Commission on Brotherhood Restructure, 1967.

International Convention Reports and Proceedings, 1959–1968.

Unpublished B. D. Thesis, "Charles Clayton Morrison, the Voice of the Century," by James W. Carty, Jr., 1948, University of Chicago.

"The Tradition of Christ," by Dean E. Walker, Milligan College Press, undated.

Index

Abingdon College, 197
Abolitionism, 106, 107, 139
Achison, Thomas, 7
Ainslee, Charles, 224
Ainslee, Etta, 224, 226
Ainslee, Peter, 79
Ainslee, Peter, I, 224
Ainslee, Peter, II, 224
Ainslee, Peter, III, 224–30, 235, 236, 247
  background of, 224–25
  baptized, 225
  education of, 225
  Topeka Convention address, 227–28, 244
  World War I pacifism, 230
Ainslee, Mrs. Peter, III, 226
Alliance College, 174
Altars, Abraham, 6
Amend, William, 93
American and Foreign Anti-Slavery Society, 131
American Christian Bible Society, 123, 143
  founding of, 110–12
  merger of, 143
  opposition to, 111–12
  proposal for, 100, 110–11
American Christian Missionary Society, 135–36, 137, 139–42, 146–47, 164, 237–38
  formation of, 123, 125
  Franklin's opposition to, 164–65, 169
  Negro education program, 201
  slaveholding members of, 139–40
American Christian Review (magazine), 142, 158, 162, 165, 195, 198, 205

Apostolic Times (journal), 175, 207
Arapahoe Indians, 203
Arny, F. T., 114
Associate Seceder Synod of North America, 4
Atwater, Anna R., 237–38

Bacon, Francis, 90
Bacon College, 89–90, 96–97, 98, 137
  founding of, 96
Badger, Joseph, 36
Baker, Edward D., 105
Baptism
  Campbell (Alexander) on, 19–20, 27
  Campbell (Thomas) on, 11–12
  religious positions on, 254
Baptist Church, 131, 212
  Campbell Movement and, 12–71, 228–29
    association with, 12–13
    end of association with, 61–71
    reunification overtures (1864), 67–68
  Mahoning Association, 21, 23, 25, 27–50, 61–66, 70, 75, 94
    Austintown Convention, 63–66, 68, 71
    formation of, 20
    Scott's evangelism and, 32–33, 35–47
  Miami Association, 78
  Philadelphia Confession of Faith, 5, 17, 28, 43, 45, 46
  separations from Orthodox groups, 70
  Redstone Association, 13, 15–21, 23, 24, 25

Barclay, Dr. James T., 123–26, 127, 139, 143, 154
  background of, 132–24
  slaves of, 135–36
Barclay, Mrs. James T., 123–24, 154
Barclay, Judson, 124
Barclay, Robert, 124
Barclay, Thomas Jefferson, 124
Barton, Henry, 85
Baugh, John, 115
Bear's Creek Church, 162
Beardslee, James O., 127, 139–40
Beaver Association, 49
Beecher, Dr. Lyman, 98
Bell, Dr. Theodore, 28
Ben-Hur (Wallace), 85
Bentley, Adamson, 20–21, 68
Bethany College, 100, 112, 121, 144, 165, 166, 185
  enrollment (1840), 99
  founding of, 98
  slavery controversy at, 132
Bible Society. *See* American Christian Bible Society
Biblical criticism movement, 213–16, 225
Bishop, R. M., 144
Blue River Baptist Church, 43–44
Board of Church Extension, 198–99, 238
Board of Ministerial Relief, 199, 238
Boggess, E. F., 203
Boggs, John, 131–32, 139
Box, John, 115
"Bringing in the Sheaves" (Shaw), 204
Brown, John, 12
Brush Run Church, x, 11–13, 15–21, 23, 24–25, 221
Brutus (vessel), 4
Burgess, Mrs. Otis A., 179, 180
Burnet, David, 66–67, 77–81, 87, 89, 96, 110–14, 122, 125, 141, 144, 185, 224
  background of, 77–78
  Bacon College presidency, 90–91, 137
  Bible Society proposal, 100, 110–111
  death of, 154

differences with Campbell, 111–14
  pastoral system of, 118, 119
Burnet, Glenn, 98
Burnet, Isaac, 77
Burnet, Jacob, 77
Burnet, Peter, 98
Burnet family, 77
Burnham, Frederick W., 237
Burton, A. M., 232
Butler, Ovid, 140, 180
Butler, Pardee, 139–41, 143
Butler College, 180, 215–16, 217

Calhoun Christian Church, 225–26
Calvin, John, 155–56
Calvinism, 3, 4, 42
  Presbyterian form of, 5–6
Campbell, Alexander
  arrested, 113
  Austintown Convention (1830), 63–66
  background of, 3–4
  on baptism, 19–20, 27
  baptized, 12, 27
  birth of, 3
  British Isles visit (1847), 111–12
  on being a Christian, 82
  death of, 154, 173
  differences with
    Burnet, 111–14
    Scott, 93–96, 107, 130
    slavery and, 95–96, 107, 130
    Stone, 53–56
  education of, 8–9
  first American sermon, 10
  Kentucky debate, 27–28
  "Law" sermon, 17–19
  licensed to preach, 11
  Mahoning Association and, 20, 21, 23, 25, 27–33
  Negro emancipation plan, 129
  oratorical abilities, 28, 29
  ordained, 11
  Owen debate, 57–59, 68
  Purcell debate, 97–98
  reaction to Fugitive Slave Law, 131, 132, 134
  rebukes Ferguson, 119–21
  Redstone Association and, 15–21, 23, 24–25

Rice debate, 108–10
slavery views of, 131, 132, 134, 199
slaves of, 130
Virginia Convention (1829), 59, 95, 129
Walker debate, 19–20
wealth of, 151–53
Western Reserve visit, 60
Campbell, Mrs. Alexander (Margaret), 12, 28
Campbell, Mrs. Alexander (Selina), 28–29, 129
Campbell, Archibald, 3
Campbell, Enos, 126–27
Campbell, Thomas, x, 3–7, 9, 10–12, 19, 23, 66, 82, 129, 155, 221
  background of, 3, 4–6
  on baptism, 11–12
  baptized, 12
  birth of, 3
  censured, 4–5
  consecrated Elder, 11
  death of, 153–54
  deposed, 5
  trial of, 4
  Western Reserve visit, 50–51
Campbell, Mrs. Thomas, 3, 12
Campbell, Wickliffe, 113
Campbell Movement
  Baptist Church and, 12–71, 228–29
    association with, 12–13
    end of association, 61–71
    reunification overtures (1864), 167–68
  basis of doctrine, 100
  church periodicals and, 83
  Cincinnati Convention, 146
  Congregationalists and, 228–29
  Convention of 1849, 121–23
  cooperative assemblies, 83–84, 85, 115
  Declaration and Address, 5–6, 9–10, 16, 23, 66, 221
  division in, 203–12
  emergence of separate identity, 231–41
  intellectual inquiry, 213–20
    biblical, 213–16
    missionary work and, 216, 217–20

Louisville Convention, 178
membership, 109, 205
merger with Stone's followers, 75–76, 84, 96
missionary activities, 123, 125–27, 137, 139, 146–47, 164, 179–93, 194, 195, 217–20, 223, 237–38
open membership practice, 218–20, 239
organ controversy, 156–58, 161, 167–69, 196–97, 206, 207, 210–11
Scott's evangelism, 32–33, 35–47
slavery controversy, 91, 107, 108, 127, 129–47
  at Bethany College, 132
  Campbell (Alexander) and, 131, 132, 134, 199
  Errett's views on, 132, 134–35, 136, 143–44
  first public stand on, 135
  Kansas, 139, 140–41
  Millennial Harbinger on, 129, 130
  Shannon's views on, 137–38
  statewide assemblies, 86
  westward migration and, 115–16
  Wooster Convention, 135
  See also Christian Church (Disciples of Christ); Christian Church (Independent); Churches of Christ
Carroll, R. W., 174
Cave, Robert L., 207–9, 214
Cedar Avenue Christian Church of Cleveland, 218
Census of 1906, 211–12, 243
Central Christian Church of St. Louis, 207
Central Christian Church of Indianapolis, 85
Central-Woodward Christian Church, 236
Chase, Ira J., 198–99
Cheyenne Indians, 203
Christendom (journal), 237
Christian (journal), 90, 196
Christian (magazine), 119
Christian Age (newspaper), 141
Christian Association of Washington, 6–7, 11, 16
  constituted a church, 11

"Declaration and Address," 5–6, 9–10, 16, 23, 66, 221
Christian Baptist (journal), 28, 29, 42, 45, 53, 56, 62, 78, 79, 81, 83–84
discontinued, 59–60
first issue of, 24, 129
reaction to, 27, 51
Christian Board of Publication, 123, 143, 197
Christian Casket (journal), 83, 84
Christian Century (journal), 245, 246
Christian Church (Disciples of Christ)
membership, 113
religious position of, 254
Christian Church (Independent), x, 244–50
emergence of, 241
official directory of, 250
religious position of, 254
Christian Church of Clarinda, Iowa, 245
Christian Church of Springfield, Illinois, 246
Christian Endeavor Movement, 228
Christian-Evangelist (journal), 175, 208, 220, 249
Christian Intelligencer (newspaper), 158
Christian Messenger (newspaper), 76, 106
Christian Missionary Convention, 139
Christian Oracle (journal), 245
Christian Preacher (journal), 81, 89, 90, 99–100
Christian Psalmist (hymnbook), 156
Christian Psaltery (hymnbook), 156
Christian Publishing Association, 171, 179, 197
Christian Review (magazine), 117
Christian Standard (journal), 142, 171–74, 175, 179, 184, 196, 207, 208, 214, 219, 221, 235, 236, 237, 238–39, 249
first issue of, 173
"Christian System, The" (Campbell), 81, 93

Christian Unity Quarterly, 246–47
Christian Woman's Board of Missions, 179–83, 201, 217, 220, 222–23, 237
founding of, 179–81
St. Louis Convention (1884), 183
Church of Christ, The (Phillips), 222
Church of England, 5
Church of Scotland, 3, 4, 5
Churches of Christ, x, 243, 244, 247, 249
emergence of, 231–34
membership, 234
Negro, 232–33
religious position of, 254
Cincinnati Christian Church, 78–79, 121
Cincinnati College of Teachers, 97
City of the Great King, The (Barclay), 126
Civil rights movement, 201
Civil War, 129, 144–47, 154, 200
begininng of, 144
Clay, Henry, 95, 109
Cleaveland, Moses, 35
Coleman, R. L., 124–25
College of the Bible, 210, 214, 224, 225
founding of, 169–70
College of Missions, 222–23
Commission on Brotherhood Restructure, 248–49
Commission on Christian Unity, 235, 246
Congregationalist Church, 228–29, 235
Connecticut Missionary Society, 36
Convention of British Churches, 243
Crawford, David, 185
Crihfield, Arthur, 83
Cross, Alexander, 126, 127
Cross, Thomas, 127

Dale, Robert, 57
Darrow, Clarence, 240
David Lipscomb College, 210
Dawson, John, 11
"Declaration and Address," 5–6, 9–10, 16, 23, 66, 221

Design of Civil Government and the Extent of Its Authority, The (Errett), 107, 132

Dickinson, Elmira, 179

Disciples of Christ Historical Library, 251–52

Disciples' Divinity House (Chicago), 235

"Discourse on the Holy Spirit, A" (Scott), 67

Domestic Manners of the Americans, The (Trollope), 58

Drake, F. M., 218

Drake University, 218, 246

Dunlavy, John, 30

Ecumenical Review, 247

Ecumenicism, 235–36, 254

Embargo Proclamation, 124

Episcopal Church, 235

Erie Canal, 37

Errett, Henry, 23, 132

Errett, Isaac, 132–37, 142, 146, 179, 186, 196, 197–98
  anti-slavery views of, 132, 134–36, 143–44
  background of, 132
  Christian Standard editorship, 171–74, 175
  death of, 206–7
  Foreign Society presidency, 184

Errett, Mrs. Isaac, 133, 134

Errett, Russell, 207, 219–20, 237

Essay on Toleration (Locke), 4

Eureka College, 197

Evangelist (journal), 67, 92, 95, 208
  discontinued, 107

Evangelizing Society of Rush County, 84

Evolution, theory of, 214–15

Ewing, Greville, 8

"Facts Concerning the New Testament Church" (Welshimer), 240

Fall, Phillip Slater, 102

Fanning, Tolbert, 100–3, 117–19, 139, 142, 161–64, 209
  arrested, 162
  background of, 100–1

Convention of 1849, 122
  death of, 195
  on pastoral system, 118–19
  stockbreeding activity, 118, 195–96

Fanning, Mrs. Tolbert (Charlotte), 102–3, 117

Fanning, Mrs. Tolbert (Sarah), 102

Fanning Orphan School, 209

Faurot, Randall, 201

Faurot, Mrs. Randall, 201

Federation of American Baptists, 46

Federal Council of Churches of Christ in America, 220, 236

Ferguson, Jesse, 118–21, 142

Ferguson, William Neil, 187

Field, Nathaniel, 95–96

Fillmore, Augustus Damron, 156

First Baptist Church of Nashville, 101

First Christian Church of Canton, 239

First Christian Church of St. Louis, 207

Foreign Christian Missionary Society, 182, 183–94, 217, 219, 220, 238
  founding of, 183–84
  number of missionaries, 223
  Tibetan work, 187–93

Forrester, George, 22

Fort Meigs, 36, 52

Fort Sumter, bombardment of, 144

42nd Regiment, 144

Foster, James, 11

Franklin, Benjamin (preacher), 141–43, 158–62, 170, 172, 199–200, 205
  death of, 195
  opposition to Missionary Society, 164–65, 169

Franklin College, 117, 144, 161–62, 209

Fugitive Slave Law of 1851, 131, 132, 134

Garfield, James A., 144, 209

Garrison, James Harvey, 180, 196, 197, 208, 220

Garrison, Mrs. James Harvey, 197

Garvin, Hugh C., 215–16
General Christian Missionary Convention, 178–82
Georgia Power and Light Company, 233
Gilchrist, William, 11
Glas, John, 4, 8
Goodpasture, B. C., 252
Goodwin, Mrs. J. M. B., 181–82
Gospel Advocate (journal), 142, 144, 161, 164, 175, 196, 206, 209, 211
Gospel Advocate Company, 252
Gospel Echo (journal), 175, 179, 197
Gospel Restored, The (Scott), 93, 166
Great Revival of 1803, 52
Greenville, Treaty of, 35

Haldane, James Alexander, 4, 8, 23
Haldane, Robert, 4, 8
Hall, Alexander, 114, 120
Hall, B. F., 145
Hardeman, Nicholas B., 155, 231–32
Harding College, 233
Hardy, Dr. William, 191
Harper, William R., 216
Harp of Zion (hymnbook), 156
Harris, Captain John, 124
Harrison, William Henry, 52
Hawley, Dr. Zerah, 37
Hayden, A. S., 63
Hayden, Daniel, 39, 63
Hayden, William, 39–40, 61, 63, 64
Henry, John, 64, 65
Henry, Mrs. John, 64
Heretic Detector (journal), 83
Hibernia (vessel), 8
Hiram College, 239
Hoffman, G. W., 211–12
Holley, John, 35–36
Hope Baptist Church, 54
Hope Institute, 209
Hopson, W. H., 144
Humphrey, Dr. Herman, 152–53
Hyde Park Christian Church, 216, 218

Hymnbooks, 156, 197

Indians, 35, 36, 115, 203
International Convention of the Christian Churches of North America, 239, 243, 247–48, 249
Iowa Territory, 115–16
Israelite (journal), 83

Jackson, Andrew, 53, 80
Jameson, Mrs. Maria, 179, 180
Jefferson, Thomas, 124
Jews, 126, 137
Johnson, Andrew, 162, 163
Johnson, John T., 56, 76–77, 89, 90, 96, 110, 125
   background of, 52–53
   Convention of 1849, 122–23
   death of, 154
Johnson, Mrs. John T., 52
Johnson, Richard Mentor, 52
Johnson, Robert, 52
Johnson, T. F., 89–90
Jones, Edgar DeWitt, 236
Jones, Dr. Willis, 252

Kansas, slavery and, 139, 140–41
Kansas-Nebraska Bill, 140
Keeble, Marshall, 232–33
King, Joseph, 182
King, Mrs. Joseph, 179
Kirk, John, 135
Knox, John, 5
Ku Klux Klan, 233

Ladies' Aid Society, 226
Lane Theological Seminary, 98
Lard, Moses, 165–69, 170, 172, 174
   background of, 165–66
   death of, 206
   education of, 166
Lard's Quarterly (journal), 167, 172, 174
Latonia (vessel), 9
Levy, Mr., 124
Liberia, Missionary work in, 126, 127
Life and Casualty Insurance Company, 232
Lincoln, Abraham, 105

Lipscomb, David, 161–65, 169, 170, 172, 196–98, 206, 208–10, 211
  background of, 161–62
  on Garfield's election, 209
Lipscomb, Mrs. David, 163
Lipscomb, Granville, 161
Lipscomb, Mrs. Granville (Jane), 161
Lipscomb, Mrs. Granville (Nancy), 161
Lipscomb, William, 142, 161–63, 164
  background of, 161–62
Littell, Absolem, 45
Littell, John, 45
Locke, John, 4, 23, 93
Loftis, Dr. Zenas, 191
Long, Robert A., 197
Lookout (Sunday-school paper), 240
Louisiana State College, 137
Louisville Plan, 178
Luce, Matthius, 12
Luther, Martin, ix, 155

McCalla, W. L., 27, 145
McCullock, General, 145
McGarvey, John, 168, 169–70, 175, 206, 207, 214–15, 224, 225
  background of, 165, 166
McLean, Archibald, 184–87, 188, 190, 191, 217, 219, 223, 237
  background of, 184–85
McLean, Malcolm, 184
McLean, Mrs. Malcolm, 184
McNemar, Richard, 30
Madison, James, 59
Mahoning Association, 21, 23, 25, 27–50, 61–66, 70, 75, 94
  Austintown Convention, 63–66, 68, 71
  formation of, 20
  Scott's evangelism and, 32–33, 35–47
Main Street Christian Church of Lexington, 109–10, 166
Marshall, Robert, 30
Masonic Order, 113
Meigs, F. E., 219
Memphis Convention (1926), 239
Methodist Church, 13, 37, 50, 212
  slavery and, 131

Miami Baptist Association, 78
Michigan Territory, 115
Millennial Herald (newspaper), 29
Millennial Harbinger (newspaper), 70, 75, 80
  first issue of, 60
  on slavery, 129, 130
Millennial Journal, 90–94, 96, 99, 100, 110–14, 116, 121, 168, 171, 174
Miller, William, 69
Missionaries
  number of, 222, 223
  training of, 222
  See also names of missionaries
Missionary Tidings (journal), 183
Missouri State University, 138
Monroe, J. M., 203
Monroe Street Christian Church of Chicago, 245, 246
Moore, W. T., 77–78, 184
Morrison, Charles Clayton, 245–47
Morrisonians (religious sect), 113
Moyes, John, 190
Moyes, Mrs. John, 187–89, 190, 193
Munnell, Thomas, 177, 178
Musical instruments, use of, 156–58

Nashville Bible College, 210
Nashville Church, 118–21
National Benevolent Association, 198–99, 223, 238
National Christian Missionary Convention, 201
National City Christian Church, 125
National Council of Churches, 250
National Presbyterian Synod, 3–5, 10–11
Negroes, 126, 127, 129, 200–2, 232–33
Nashville Convention (1917), 201
Newcomb, Obadiah, 70–71
New Harmony, Indiana, 57, 68
Norfolk Convention (1907), 235–36
North America Christian Convention, 241, 244, 250
Northwestern Christian College, 180
Northwestern Christian Magazine, 131, 139
Northwestern Christian University, 132, 138, 140

Octographic Review (journal), 205
Ogden, James, 190–91
Ogden, Mrs. James, 190
O'Kane, John, 83, 84–85, 110, 122
O'Kelley, James, 84
O'Kelly, James, 54
Oklahoma Christian University, 221
Oklahoma Territory, 203–4
Open membership, practice of, 218–20, 239
Oregon, The (steamer), 223
Organ controversy, 156–58, 161, 167–69, 196–97, 206, 207, 210–11
Owen, Robert, 57–59, 68

Pacifism, 230
"Pact of Reconciliation" (Ainslee), 229–30, 235
Panic of 1837, 91
Panic of 1873, 175, 195
Parrish, John G., 158
Paul, Azarish, 210
Pea Ridge, Battle of, 145
Pearre, Mrs. Caroline Neville, 179–81
Pendleton, William K., 121, 122, 130–31, 168–69
Phillips, Charles, 170–71
Phillips, John T., 170–71
Phillips, Isaac, 170–71
Phillips, Thomas W., 170–71, 221–22
Phillips family, 217
Phillips Gas and Oil Company, 217
Phillips University, 221
Pinkerton, L. L., 110, 156–57
Pittsburgh Centennial Convention, 220, 221–24
Poole, Charlie, 130
Poole, Jim, 130
Presbyterian Church, x, 3–6, 108–9, 124, 185, 235
  Calvinism and, 5–6
  Seceder branch, 3–5, 9, 19
Psalms and Hymns (Watts), 37
Purcell, Bishop John B., 97–98

Rabim, 188, 189
Raines, Aylett, 111
Ramy, William, 200

Reconstruction period, 151
Red Jacket, Chief, 36
Redpath Chatauqua Company, 240
Redstone Baptist Association, 13, 15–21, 23, 24–25
Reformed Baptists, 43–47
  opposition to, 47
Rice, Dr. Nathan L., 108
Richardson, Nathaniel, 22
Richardson, Robert, 19, 22, 92–93, 100
Richmond Street Christian Church, 178
Rigdon, Sidney, 20–21, 68–69
Rijnhart, Charles Carson, 188, 189
Rijnhart, Petrus, 187–89
Rijnhart, Mrs. Petrus. *See* Moyes, Mrs. John
Robinson, Dr. J. P., 146
Rockefeller, John D., 216, 218
Rockefeller Foundation, 217–18
Rogers, John, 76–77
Rogers, Mrs. J. K., 179
Roman Catholic Church, 97–98
Rowe, John, 195, 198

Saltonstall, Gürdon, 166
Sand Creek Declaration, 205–6, 207, 208
Sandeman, Robert, 4, 8, 23
Sanders, Dr. John, 85
Sarvis, Guy, 218, 219
Schaeffer, John, 70
Scott, Emily, 39
Scott, John, 39
Scott, Sarah Jane, 39, 67, 122
Scott, Walter, 21–24, 27, 71, 77, 82, 90–96, 107–8, 133, 166, 199, 225
  background of, 21–22
  Convention of 1849, 122
  death of, 154
  differences with Campbell, 93–96
  slavery and, 95–96, 107, 130
  marital discord, 122
  Miller prophecy and, 69
  Western Reserve evangelism, 35–47, 50–51, 56, 61–66
  appointment to, 32–33
Scott, Mrs. Walter, 23, 29, 39, 67
Scott, William, 39

Seminary House (Baltimore), 227
Shannon, James, 91, 110, 137–39
  death of, 138
  pro-slavery views of, 137–38
Sharp, George, 11
Shaw, Knowles, 204–5
Shelton, Dr. Albert L., 190–93
Shelton, Mrs. Albert L., 190, 192
Shepherd, J. W., 211
Siddon (ship), 112
Silver Creek Baptist Church, 45
Slavery controversy, 91, 107, 108,
  127, 129–47, 158
  at Bethany College, 132
  Campbell (Alexander) and, 131,
    132, 134, 199
  Errett's views on, 132, 134–35,
    136, 143–44
  first public stand on, 135
  Kansas and, 139, 140–41
  Millennial Harbinger on, 129, 130
  Shannon's views on, 137–38
Sloan, Mrs. R. R., 179
Smith, Elias, 54, 69
Smith, John "Raccoon," 51–53, 56,
  76, 110, 251
  background of, 51–52
Smithfield Street Christian Church
  of Pittsburg, 133
Sommer, Daniel, 205–206
Southern Christian Institute, 201
South Side Church of Indianapolis,
  218
Spencer, Dr. Claude E., 252
Springfield Presbytery, 30–31
Standard Oil Company, 217
Stone, Barton Warren, 30–32, 43,
  75–76, 84, 106–8, 134, 145, 218
  background of, 30
  death of, 106, 154
  differences with Cambell, 53–56
Stone, Barton, Jr., 145
Stoneites, 30, 31, 75–76, 84, 96
Sunday School and Tract Society,
  111
Sycamore Street Baptist Church of
  Cincinnati, 78, 97
Synod of Kentucky, 30

Taylor, Preston, 201

Texas Rangers, 145
Theological Baptist Institution, 137
Thomas, Joseph, 84
Thompson, John, 30
Tibet, missionary work in, 187–93
Time (magazine), 245
Topeka Convention of 1910, 224,
  227–28, 244
Trollope, Frances, 58

United Christian Missionary Society,
  237–41, 244
U. S. Bureau of the Census, 211,
  243
University of Chicago, 216, 218
University of Georgia, 137
University of Nanking, 219

Van Buren, Martin, 52
Virginia Constitutional Convention
  of 1829, 59, 95, 129

Walker, John, 19
Wallace, David, 85, 179
Wallace, Mrs. David, 85, 179
Wallace, Lewis, 85
War of 1812, 52
Washington, George, 124
Watts, Mr., 37
Wayne, Anthony, 35
Welshimer, Pearl H., 239–41, 243–
  44
  background of, 239–30
Western Reserve Electric Institute,
  144, 239
Western Reserve Territory, 32–33,
  35–47, 50–51, 56, 61–66
  first missionary in, 36
  settlement of, 35–36
Westminster Confession of Faith, 5,
  11
Whig Party, 105
Williams, Marvin, 252
Williams, W. J., 183
Williams, Mrs. W. J., 183
Willitt, Dr. Herbert L., 235
Wilson, William, 4
Wisconsin Territory, 115
Wolfe, James, 3
Woman's rights movement, 177–78

World Call (magazine), 238
World Council of Churches, 247
World War I, 230
Wright, Amos, 42
Wright, Amos, Jr., 42, 43
Wright, John, 42, 43
Wright, Joshua, 42
Wright, Levi, 42
Wright, Peter, 42, 43

Yang (bandit), 192
Year Book (Independent), 250
Year Book of American Churches
        (National Council of Churches),
        250

Zellner family, 163, 164
Zollars, E. V., 221